THE MASTERS OF

IMPACT NEGOTIATING

Insight Publishing
Sevierville, Tennessee

THE MASTERS OF

IMPACT NEGOTIATING

Disclaimer: This book is a compilation of ideas from numerous experts who have each contributed a chapter. As such, the views expressed in each chapter are of those who were interviewed and not necessarily of the interviewer or Insight Publishing.

Published by Insight Publishing Company
P.O. Box 4189
Sevierville, Tennessee 37864

10 9 8 7 6 5 4 3 2

Printed in The United States of America

ISBN: 1-60013-038-0

Table of Contents

A Message from the Publisher

Negotiation. You don't have to like it but you do have to use it. Getting along with others means negotiating, and negotiating should be more collaboration than confrontation.

I really learned a lot when I interviewed the people in this book. You will too. If you have ever wondered how to get the best deal at a car lot or anywhere else, you need the information we have compiled between the covers of this publication. I was amazed to learn about the power questions every good negotiator asks. Jim Hennig told me about some common errors made by even experienced negotiators and then he told me the secret weapon used by truly great negotiators.

In any group of professionals there are several who stand out, who are really getting the job done and raising the bar. When these people speak, others listen. They are relevant, experienced, and trusted. This is a good definition of the people I was privileged to interview for this project. These people have insights to share that you will definitely appreciate. *The Masters of Impact Negotiating* is the resource you need to do your homework so that you can make informed decisions when you negotiate—for anything.

It is our hope that you will read and re-read this book—that you will share its contents with your friends, colleagues, and family. You will be glad you did. So will they. I assure you.

Interviews conducted by:
David E. Wright
President, International Speakers Network

Chapter 1

DR. JIM HENNIG

THE INTERVIEW

David Wright (Wright)

We are speaking today with Dr. Jim Hennig, past President of the 3500 member National Speakers Association and holder of its two highest speaking awards, including being inducted into the coveted Council of Peers Award for Excellence Speaker Hall of Fame.

His experience is diverse: As a businessman he was president of four corporations, in four divergent fields. His innovative approach to the topic of Negotiation has brought him acclaim from major associations and fortune 500 companies worldwide. As a salesperson he led all salespeople in a top international sales company. As an educator he received his doctorate and taught at Purdue University. As an author he has written and published many articles, books and audio/video programs that have been translated into twenty-three languages and marketed in fifty-two countries. As an athlete he was a member of the University of Wisconsin Big Ten Championship Football Team. As a pilot he's flown the equivalent of forty times around the world . . . and crashed only once! He is the proud father of ten children and stepchildren, which he claims is his greatest qualification for the topic of negotiation.

Jim, a general question first: Is there anything that jumps out at you as being a characteristic found in most top negotiators?

Jim Hennig (Hennig)

Yes, definitely, several of them. When I ask my audiences that same question, the first response is usually, "*a good listener.*" I agree wholeheartedly! Pay attention in your next negotiation. Who does most of the talking? Who does most of the listening? Nine times out of ten, the person who speaks less and listens more is the better negotiator. Diogenes said:

"We have two ears and one tongue
That we may hear more and speak less."

I'm sure this is no surprise to our readers. Another common characteristic of great negotiators—and interestingly enough it is *rarely* identified as such by my audiences—a great negotiator *asks questions. Ask the right questions and then listen carefully to the answers.* Find needs. That just might be the most important advice I can give to any negotiator. Voltaire said,

"Judge a man by his questions
Rather than by his answers."

No place is that statement more true than in judging the ability of a negotiator.

Wright

Will you give us some examples of good negotiating questions—perhaps questions that can be used in most any negotiation situation?

Hennig

Yes. I strongly suggest that every negotiator build his or her list of power questions. Here's a start:

"What else can you tell me?"—Just assuming there is more information to be shared, normally gets more information. Information is power.

"Yes . . . Really . . . Uh-huh . . . Oh, that's interesting."—Most people can be led to share more information by simple verbal prompting.

After they have answered use silence as though you are expecting more—"To every thing there is a season . . . a time to keep silence, a time to speak" (Ecclesiastes 3:1, 7).

"What have we not discussed that I really should know in this matter?"—Put yourself in the position of the party who has been asked that question—what are you thinking? Ask yourself what is

this person going to find out later (that I should have shared when they asked that question)?

Where is there room for compromise?—Fishing for mutual gain.

"Would you explain that? I'm not sure I understand."—Very often the offer will be modified in some way when you asked to have it explained. And virtually always it is in a favorable direction for you.

"What is your thinking or rational behind that proposal (or offer, or position)?"—Find the needs! Positions are always harder to satisfy than needs.

"If I could do this . . . for you, what could you do for me?"—A great question at an impasse, this *conditional concession* alternative provides the opportunity for a win-win trade of concessions.

"Are there others involved or do you make the final decision?"—This question effectively eliminates the later use of *"agent of limited authority"* by the other party.

"Would you repeat that offer?"—I remember my son, Ryan, placing an ad in the paper to buy a shotgun the year he turned old enough to hunt. He talked with someone by phone who offered to bring over a gun that he wanted to sell. Ryan had done his homework and was prepared to pay $75 to $100 for the right gun. When the seller showed him the gun, it was just what he wanted.

"Fifty dollars," the seller said.

"Fifty dollars!" Ryan exclaimed, shocked that the price was that low.

"Well, okay. I'll take $40 cash for it right now."

It didn't take Ryan long to produce $40. And, he learned a valuable lesson—always ask to have the offer repeated.

Wright

Are there any strategies or tactics that you are often asked about or that you see used effectively?

Hennig

With over thirty to choose from that's a difficult question. The key is timing. Any one of those thirty is the right strategy, at the right time, in the right situation. In other words, know them all and selectively use them at the right time. Before giving you a couple of examples, let me list a number of them:

- Surprise
- Agent of Limited Authority

- A Piece of the Pie (Salami)
- Take It or Leave It
- Forbearance
- Doomsday
- Funny Money
- Standard Practice
- The Nibble
- Act and take the Consequences
- Walkout
- Apparent Walkout
- Good Guy/Bad Guy
- Lowballing/Highballing
- Feinting
- Cost Breakdowns
- Invoking the Competition
- Add Something
- Bracketing
- Changing Levels
- Association
- Feel, Felt, Found
- Flinching
- Budget constraints
- Reluctant Seller/Buyer
- Puppy Dog
- Crunch
- Humble and Helpless
- Playing Dumb

Now let's look at two specific examples:

First, *The Nibble*: Great negotiators know that you can practically always get a small item thrown in by asking for it at the time you offer to close the deal. Both timing and the size of the concession are critical here.

For example, a few years ago, I was replacing my aircraft and had just about concluded a deal. The owner clearly wanted to sell. His price was a bit high but I was in love with the airplane. He had mentioned two minor problems that he would have fixed prior to the sale.

After negotiating the price, I decided to use The Nibble. I mentioned the two items and indicated that I would pay the negotiated price minus the $500 it would take to get the two items fixed. (It was a true nibble—it might only have cost $100 to $200 to get them fixed.)

What did he say? "It's a deal!" Compared to the price of the airplane, $500 wasn't much—but it was $500 extra in my pocket just for the asking!

I shared that example not to say I was a great negotiator, but rather to ask you what you would have done as the seller—what is the counter to the nibble?

Here's the important question: What would I have done if the seller had said, "No"? You guessed it! I would have bought the aircraft anyway and he would have the extra $500 in *his* pocket.

Remember, whenever you recognize that The Nibble is being used on you, the deal does not usually hinge on the other person receiving The Nibble. Give it away only when you feel comfortable doing so.

Or better yet, reduce The Nibble. If he had said, "That's a good idea, but it will only cost me $100 to get both items fixed, so I'll knock $100 off the price, okay?" To which I would probably have said, "Okay."

The nibble is a buyer's strategy. Let's look a seller's strategy, *The Puppy Dog*. Definition: Allowing the other party to "try" without a commitment to "buy" (or agree).

Purpose: To get the other party emotionally involved—they will like it so much they can't say "No."

This strategy is effectively used only when you know the other party will have a great experience with the "try." It's used all the time at car dealerships, stores selling chairs that deliver a massage, etc.—in essence, anywhere that positive emotions will be experienced.

Perhaps the best example is the great salesman just mentioned who sold me an aircraft. The first thing he said was, "Jim, jump in the pilot seat and let's take it up." What pilot can resist that invitation?

"Have you ever had an aircraft with color radar?"

"No."

"Then you'll love this, Jim!" he said as he turned it on and explained how safe it would be with my family aboard.

"Ever have a plane with a Storm Scope?"

"No."

"Then you'll love this!"

Next he got my wife on the flight phone so I could tell her how I was enjoying the airplane! Was I getting excited or what?

Finally, on the approach to landing, he turned on the Radar Altimeter. "Ever make an instrument approach where you got down to minimums, couldn't see the runway, and had to execute a missed approach?"

"Yes, many times."

"This Radar Altimeter tells you exactly how high you are when you are making that low instrument approach—with all the kids in the back seats!"

Did I pay more than I should have for that airplane? I sure did!

But I learned two important lessons:

1. The Puppy Dog strategy works! So what did I use when I sold the plane? That's right, the Puppy Dog. And I made a good profit on it, too!

2. Don't forget the counter to The Puppy Dog: Negotiate before you try. Imagine what would have happened at the beginning if I had said, "Before we give it a test flight, we've got to talk price. I just looked at a similar plane priced at $10,000 less, and I've got another one priced at $15,000 less that I want to look at before making my final decision—today."

Would I have been in a much better negotiating position? Unquestionably!

Wright

Concessions play a big part in negotiating, both getting and giving them. Any suggestions here?

Hennig

A couple of examples come to my mind. First, when you make concessions, make them in a manner that implies you are close to your bottom line, that is:

Make small concessions
Make them slowly
Make them progressively smaller!

For example, let's assume a seller is negotiating a product or service for which he or she is asking $10,000. Examine two different scenarios:

Scenario Number One: after a brief negotiation, a quick concession is made to $9,500, then to $9,000, then to $8,500.

Scenario Number Two: after a long negotiation, a reluctant concession is made to $9,800, then to $9,700, then to $9,650.

In each case, three concessions were made. But in scenario number two, they were smaller concessions, made much more slowly, and each was made progressively smaller than the previous one.

Don't you just get the feeling that in scenario number two that the negotiator is close to their bottom line? They may not be, but one might perceive that they are on the basis of the timing and amount of their concessions. In negotiation, perception often becomes reality. Use this fact to your advantage.

A second example: There is a great negotiating strategy called "A Piece of the Pie" (sometimes called "Salami") where the negotiator asks for very small concessions, one at a time, and ends up with the "whole pie."

This is why a good negotiator always tries to *determine all requests before granting any concessions.*

Here is the ideal question you should ask when confronted with any request for a concession (no matter how small): "In addition to that, is there anything else you need before we close the deal?" (Or sign the agreement, complete the paperwork, etc.?)

That question actually accomplishes two purposes:

1. It forces the other party to reveal their entire agenda before you make any concessions.
2. It effectively eliminates the further use of "A Piece of the Pie." The other party soon learns that when they ask for something, you will ask for something in return.

Wright

I've often had people begin a negotiation with a completely unreasonable offer. What do you suggest here?

Hennig

Most often my advice would be *don't make a counter-offer to an unrealistic offer.*

Most experienced negotiators simply refuse to negotiate until the negotiating range falls within a reasonable level. Why negotiate when there is not a reasonable chance of reaching an agreement? Refusal to move forward with the negotiation in this way is risky, but often very powerful. It saves time. Either the other party concedes, moving the negotiation forward, or it is terminated.

For example, I was living in Wisconsin and planning an eventual move to Arizona. A neighbor of mine approached me with some interest in buying my house. He asked what I wanted for it.

"Gee, I don't know," I said, "I haven't really thought about it."

He quickly made me a lowball offer.

"Oh, no," I said, "I know that is considerably below what I could consider."

He relatively quickly came back to me with a significantly higher offer. My response was the same.

To make a long story short, he came back to me several times, each time with a higher offer. When he got within a reasonable price range, we began serious negotiations. I was in a much stronger position because I had simply, but kindly, backed away from the unrealistic offers.

Wright

How tough should we be in making concessions?

Hennig

That varies greatly with the situation. You practically always want to *make people work for their concessions.*

For example, here's a hypothetical situation: You want to buy my boat. You ask, "What do you want for the boat, Jim?"

"Seventy-five thousand dollars."

After a quick inspection and brief test run on the lake, you say,

"Okay. I'll have a cashier's check here at noon. You get the title ready and we'll complete the deal then. I want to spend the evening on the boat with my family."

I just got exactly what I asked for the boat in less than an hour from the very first person who approached me to buy it. Put yourself in my position. I'm happy, right?

Wright

Wrong!

Hennig

Why?

Wright

You're probably thinking, "I could have gotten more! I asked too little! I should have asked for $85,000! I left money on the table!"

Hennig

That's exactly what I'm saying. Why do I feel that way? Because I didn't *make you work* for any concessions.

Go back to the beginning of the transaction. You look at my boat. You find a few problems with it. (Every boat has got some problems!) We negotiate for some time. You end up paying $71,000 for my boat. But guess what? I'm happy!

It's human nature. What happens when your kids ask you for something? If they get it quickly without a discussion or argument, what happens the next time? They ask for a whole lot more!

Remember: *Make people work for their concessions* (if you want them to be happy, that is).

Wright

Power is important in a negotiation. What factors determine who has the power in a negotiation and how can you gain more power?

Hennig

The first one that comes to my mind is *"alternative power."* Nothing increases your power in a negotiation more than having good, viable alternatives. Never enter a negotiation without having at least one strong alternative. In other words, what are you going to do if you don't get satisfaction with this party?

For example, assume you are buying a new car. The dealership near your home has the exact vehicle you want—color, style, and all the accessories, right down to the GPS map. They have the best service department in the area—an important point for you. Your spouse is ecstatic about the car. Perfect negotiation scenario, right?

Wrong!

No alternatives, plus your need is too great puts you in the worst possible negotiation situation. Here are some practical alternatives:

1. Call the next closest dealership and explain your situation—you were planning to buy the vehicle at the local dealership but you heard that they often cut some amazing deals. You wanted to check them (and another dealership) out before making a final decision. Wouldn't a very small profit look good to this second dealership that now has this immediate potential sale coming out of the blue? They are likely to give you a very good deal, considering the circumstances.
2. Approach a local dealership of a make that is most competitive with the vehicle you really want. Use the same procedure as above.

3. Go online and search for the vehicle that is exactly (or almost) what you want. Get a price quote.

Armed with the above three options (and perhaps more options you may come up with), you are prepared to approach the original dealership with some realistic options. You are not at their mercy. You don't absolutely need the vehicle they have available.

Alternatives create power!

Wright

Jim, what part does risk play in gaining power in a negotiation?

Hennig

The greater amount of risk you can afford to take (or are willing to take) greatly increases your power in a negotiation. I enjoy demonstrating the concept this way:

I give each audience member ten to one odds in their favor, on a fifty/fifty coin flip. Here is how it goes: If they call the coin flip correctly, I give them $1,000,000 cash. If they call it incorrectly, they owe me $100,000. (I do hasten to point out that this is a *hypothetical* situation!). But if the bet was real, and I had the cash ready to deliver, I would ask, "How many of you would take me up on the deal?" Less than 10 percent of my audience members take me up on the deal!

Why?

Wright

Well, it's certainly not because they don't want $1.000,000. Nor is it that the odds are not good.

Hennig

That's right! It is simply because they can't afford to take the *risk!* Imagine having to get the spouse on the phone and explain how they had to come up with $100,000! It wouldn't much matter to the spouse that it was ten to one odds on a fifty/fifty flip.

Then I just change the situation slightly. I say, "Let's change only the dollar amounts—$10 to you if you call it correctly, $1 to me if you call it incorrectly."

I always get 100 percent of the group taking me up on that deal! The difference? They could *afford* to take the *risk*!

I often have two people come up to me at the break and say, "We've changed our minds and we are both going to take you up on the coin flip—he is heads and I am tails!" What did they do? Very simply, they figured out a way to reduce their risk (in this case down to zero). If it weren't hypothetical, they would have $900,000 to split between them.

The same is true in any negotiation—the person who is able to take the most risk has the most power in that negotiation.

Many experienced negotiators have shared with me that this was the most important concept they learned. They say, "I used to close eight out of ten deals. Now I close only seven out of ten; but my profitability on the seven is so much better than on the eight. I am much more profitable taking more risk even though I close less deals."

Wright

So you're suggesting we always take more risks in our negotiations to increase our power?

Hennig

Well, I will agree you have more power taking more risk; but that doesn't mean you *always* want to take more risk.

Here's another example: A young friend approached me wanting my help in negotiating his first house. He mentioned the seller was asking $150,000 for the house. I asked him how he felt about the price. He said, "That's fantastic, it's really a bargain." He pointed out his family had been looking for a house like this for years and hadn't found one. He said they were considering building a house and didn't think they could build one they liked any more than this one.

I asked him what it would cost to build. He said, $200,000, maybe $250,000. I asked him what would happen if someone else bought the house this afternoon. He said, "That would be a disaster!"

My advice to him? Buy the house! It was not worth the risk of losing it.

You must decide on the risk you are willing to take, but remember this: *The more risk you can (or are willing to) take in a negotiation, the more power you have.*

Wright

Before we leave power factors, Jim, are there any others that are really important?

Hennig

In reality one power factor supersedes all others. We call it "perception power." The reason is simple: it's not necessarily *who* has the power but who is *perceived* to have the power that really matters.

Take "alternative power" for example: the person who has alternatives has power. But suppose you and I are negotiating. Let's assume I have alternatives—many powerful alternatives. But let's assume also that you *don't know* that I have alternatives—it is your *perception* that I don't have alternatives.

How much power do I have in this situation? I may think I've got a lot of power but you are not going to respond as if I do until you *know* (i.e., *perceive*) that I have those alternatives. As a good negotiator I must recognize this fact and, in some appropriate way, make sure you know what power I have. If not, it does me little good.

Take "risk power" for example: We know that generally speaking the negotiator who can (or who is willing) to take the most risk increases his or her power. Again, suppose you and I are negotiating. Let's assume I absolutely can't afford to take a risk. But let's also assume that it is your *perception* that I can and am willing to take great risk. As far as this negotiation is concerned *I have the power*—at least until you figure out (perceive) that I can't afford to take a risk.

One final thought: Some may be thinking, "If I can just deceive the other party into believing I have power, I'll have it!" You're right! You will! But what happens when they find out later that you have deceived them? Is it worth the risk? Is that your style to begin with? It's not mine.

Wright

Jim, what are some common errors made by even experienced negotiators that our readers should know and avoid?

Hennig

Several errors come quickly to mind:

Underestimating your own power. It's a natural tendency. You know all your limitations, but not necessarily those of the other side. Studies consistently indicate, and my observations confirm, that most negotiators consistently underestimate their strength. *Don't!* If you do, you will probably take less risk—thus further reducing your power.

Offering to split the difference. If you do, the experienced negotiator will capitalize on your offer. "I'm here [their original position] and you're here [your offer to split the difference position]. Now let's see what we can work out." Rather than offering to split the difference, try to draw that offer out of the other party. "I just want to work out a fair solution. There has to be a way. Got any ideas?"

***Not* recognizing that "feelings are facts."** My wife often feels a certain way. I feel another. If she only knew the truth, she wouldn't feel that way! Right? Wrong! I must begin by accepting the *fact* that she does feel that way—whether she *should or should not* doesn't matter. Recognizing and acknowledging her feelings is the first step in changing them and in reaching agreement.

For example: Your four-year-old son falls and skins his knee. He comes to you crying in pain. You say, "Look son, you didn't even break the skin. There is no blood. That can't hurt that much. Stop crying." Does he stop crying? No! You forgot to accept that feelings are facts.

Contrast that response with this one: "Oh, son, that must really hurt. I'm so sorry you fell. Tell me how it feels—" Listen! How long does it take him to stop crying? It will take much less time than when you listened. In negotiations, as with kids, *feelings are facts.*

Wright

Do you have some final thoughts for our readers?

Hennig

Several come to mind:

Make your negotiation skills a habit. It's one thing to *know* all the techniques we've talked about. It's quite another thing to *apply* them in the heat of the negotiation. An adage I've coined about this is, *"Successful negotiators have formed the habit of doing those things unsuccessful negotiators dislike doing and will not do!"*

Application comes through habit. Habit comes through repetition and practice. Repetition and practice take time and effort. Plan for it. "There ain't no free lunch."

But remember also what my good friend and fellow speaker, Roger Dawson, said, *"You'll never make more money than when you are negotiating."*

Og Mandino, Author of *The Greatest Salesman in the World,* said, *"In truth the only difference between those who have failed and those who have succeeded lies in the difference of their habits. Good habits are the key to all success. Bad habits are the unlocked door to failure."*

Go with your gut. Negotiation is an "art" not a "science." Once you've acquired the *knowledge* and the *habits,* let your gut be your guide. In negotiation, there is usually more than one "right" answer. Your "right" answer may not be another's "right" answer, and yet both of you may be "right."

The French philosopher, Emile Chartier said, *"Nothing is more dangerous than an idea when it's the only one you have."*

Use the secret weapon. I figured out early in my career that there is a secret weapon used by many (but certainly not all!) great negotiators. This technique alone may be more important than any other technique I've shared in this entire discussion. Are you ready for it?

Wright

I am, Jim. I've got a feeling it's going to surprise me and probably will surprise some of our readers.

Hennig

Really care about the other party! It's an intangible. It's hard to explain. It doesn't necessarily work for everybody. Some may not know how to use it. Some may be incapable of using it. But I will tell you this: *For those who know how to use it, it works wonders.* It's like sincerity—it's tough to fake. But when you really care about the other party, it shines through everything else. *People make better deals and more deals with people they like and people they trust.*

I challenge you to find this secret weapon. I challenge you to use it. It just may transform your negotiating experiences.

The other thing I would conclude with, David, are some great quotes on negotiation. They contain some real nuggets of truth:

"Let us never negotiate out of fear, but let us never fear to negotiate."—*John F. Kennedy*

"If you are going to fight, don't let them talk you into negotiating. But, if you are going to negotiate, don't let them talk you into fighting."—*Abraham Lincoln*

"Always get to know the other party. Never negotiate with a stranger."—*Somers White*

"Have more than thou showest,
Speak less than thou knowest."—*Shakespeare*

"Always anticipate that the other side will use surprise as a tactic. You will come across as cool and collected no matter what happens."—*Jack Pachuta*

"As a rule, anything that is either shouted or whispered isn't worth listening to."—*Frederick Langbidge*

"Remember not only
To say the right thing
At the right time
In the right place,
But far more difficult still,
To leave unsaid
The wrong thing
At the wrong moment."—*Benjamin Franklin*

"Negotiations between conflicting parties is like crossing a river by walking on slippery rocks . . . It's risky, but it's the only way to get across."—*Hubert Humphrey*

"Life cannot subsist in society but by reciprocal concessions."—*Samuel Johnson*

"All government—indeed, every human benefit and enjoyment, every virtue and every prudent act—is founded on compromise and barter."—*Edmund Burke,* Speech on Conciliation with America, *March 22, 1775*

"A lean compromise is better than a fat lawsuit."—*George Herbert, Jacula Prudentium, 1640*

"We often repent of what we have said, but never, never, of that which we have not."—*Thomas Jefferson,* Writings *(c. 1800)*

And finally some of my own quotes which, incidentally, can be cited by our readers with appropriate credit:

Negotiation is like an athletic contest—momentum is paramount!

When a negotiation stalls—*change* something:
The Location
The Timetable
The Specifications
The Shape of the Money
The Negotiator or a Team Member

The strongest counter to the "Good Guy/Bad Guy" strategy is to point out its use to the other team.

When all else fails, the "Humble and Helpless" strategy often provides the best outcome.

Don't make the first concession on a major item.

Nothing moves a stalled negotiation like a little appropriate humor!

Rarely accept the first offer.
Most negotiators will concede something!

Look for things to concede that have *low value to you* but *high value to the other party*—
Look for things to ask for that has *high value to you* but *low value to the other party.*

Great negotiators always find a way to help the other party "save face."

Feelings are facts!
Treat them accordingly.
Then move on with the negotiation.

Forbearance is one of the strongest negotiation strategies.
The party with no deadlines has a tremendous advantage.

Give yourself room to make concessions . . .
Opening offers (or positions) are extremely important.

Ask to have an offer repeated.

It will often change for the better.

Rarely issue an ultimatum—
It backs either you or the other party into a difficult corner.

Do not assume you know what the other party wants for a concession—*ask!*
More is given away in most negotiations than need be.

Interact with the other party as if the relationship will last forever.
It probably won't, but your *relationship and the outcome* will improve!

If a negotiation stalls,
Introduce another issue.

Great negotiators always have something in reserve to sweeten the deal.
When the deal is close, the sweetener can make the difference.

Great negotiators see themselves as great negotiators.

When the relationship is right,
Details rarely get in the way.
When the relationship is bad,
No amount of skilled negotiation
Will bring about agreement.

About The Author

From Costa Rica to South Africa, from Australia to Saudi Arabia, Jim Hennig, Ph.D., is known as a dynamic keynoter, seminar leader, and business consultant. He is a past President of the National Speakers Association in addition to holding the two highest speaking designations awarded by the Association: CSP (Certified Speaking Professional), and the coveted CPAE: Speakers Hall of Fame Award. A frequent speaker and consultant to Fortune 500 companies and major national and international associations, his areas of expertise include Negotiations, Increased Productivity, and Managing Change. Dr. Hennig received his bachelor's degree from the University of Wisconsin and his master's and doctorate from Purdue University where he also taught for several years. At Wisconsin, he was a member of the University's 1962 Big Ten Championship football team. Jim's business background is diverse. He has been a national sales leader as well as president of four successful corporations in four divergent fields. An accomplished author, he has produced audio/video and interactive CD-ROM learning systems, as well as books and articles for business and trade publications worldwide. His training materials are available in fifty-two countries and have been translated into twenty-three languages. Dr. Hennig's energy and enthusiasm are contagious. Hundreds of organizations and thousands of individuals have attested to his ability to inspire, motivate, and educate.

Jim Hennig, Ph.D.
JF Hennig Associates, Inc.
721 N. Lisbon Drive
Chandler, AZ 85226
Phone: 480.961.5050
Phone: 800.654.5404
Fax: 480.963.7076
E-mail: jim@jimhennig.com
www.jimhennig.com

Chapter 2

Herb Cohen

THE INTERVIEW

David E. Wright (Wright)

Today we're talking with Herb Cohen. Mr. Cohen has been a practicing negotiator for the past four decades, intimately enmeshed in some of the world's headline dramas from hostile takeovers to hostage negotiations.

His clients have included business executives, entrepreneurs, sports and theatrical agents and large corporations, as well as governmental agencies such as the Department of State, FBI, CIA, the United States Conference of Mayors, and The United States Department of Justice.

While serving as an advisor to Presidents Carter and Reagan on combating terrorism, he was involved in the Iran hostage crisis and was credited with helping to shape the government's response to the skyjacking of TWA flight number 847 and the seizure of the Achilie Lauro. His input and advice has been sought by the White House on a myriad of problems such as: the Gulf Crisis; the seizure of the Japanese in Lima, Peru, and the Camp David Middle East Peace Talks. He is author of: *You Can Negotiate Anything*, which was on the *New York Times'* list of bestsellers for nearly a year and has been translated into twenty-one languages.

Mr. Cohen, welcome to our program today!

Herb Cohen (Cohen)

Well thank you, David!

Wright

Before we dive into some specific aspects of negotiating, I know our readers would appreciate learning a little bit more about you. Do you recall when you first discovered you had a gift or knack for negotiation, and how did you first begin using this talent to make a living?

Cohen

Well, strange as it may seem to some people, from my experience, negotiators are not born—they are really made. I say that because I come from a family who never negotiated anything. They paid full price—they always paid retail. They were just happy to be in the United States and so I really didn't negotiate as a child.

When I got married I was going to law school—I had come back from military service and married a college student. My wife and I, who are not big on long-range planning, figured out about a month after we got married that one of us had to work. I got a job answering an ad in the paper and I became a claims adjustor on the streets of New York, where I quickly heard more than eight million sagas in the "naked city." The key thing in my working for this company—Allstate Insurance—was that they gave me a company car. That influenced me a lot!

Every day I would be out there, in New York City, meeting people. One day I would be in Bedford-Stuyvesant, which was not a high socio-economic area and the next day I'd be on Park Avenue, or maybe both places in the same day. I learned a lot about interacting with people—how you persuade people, how you sell ideas—and very quickly. I was going to law school at night, doing this job in the day-time, working maybe twenty hours a week. It was supposed to be a full-time job and settling ten cases. Everybody else in the company was settling two. The company then asked me what I was doing. I didn't know. So I started to think about what I was doing. In those days there were no books on negotiation. In fact, "negotiating" was a bad word—you were engaged in some sort of manipulative behavior of other people.

Then I began to think about how certain things worked, certain things didn't work, and then in 1963 I went on to teach a three-week course on negotiation for attorneys. I developed my own material, but I've been doing this really a long time. That point was the first stop in my life where I realized, "Gee, I've got a knack for something."

Wright

You've been involved in some fascinating cases, both domestic and international in scope. Would you mind sharing with our readers some recollections from your work with Presidents Carter and Reagan?

Cohen

Well, first I worked for President Carter during the Iran hostage crisis. I was called to The White House because I had spent three years in Iran on all sorts of commercial matters. I knew a lot about the Iranian culture—I knew about Shiite Islam—and I had met people over there. They called me in because they said my job was to help them negotiate with the Iranian Mullahs. I remember coming in there thinking I was knowledgeable and saying to President Carter and Secretary of State Cyrus Vance that maybe we're not going about this right.

You may remember, the strategy at the time was that President Carter said publicly on television, "This is a breech of diplomatic tradition; this is a violation of International law; we need to get our people back right away." He also said that if the Iranians didn't immediately release these people he wouldn't campaign against Teddy Kennedy—this was during the primaries. He would have what he termed his "rose garden strategy"—in effect, he urged the American people to light candles and pray for the hostages morning and night, as he himself was doing, and to tie a yellow ribbon around trees. By the way, the "rose garden strategy" is a strategy we still use but which has never worked. In any event, I said to him, "This strategy is wrong," because we weren't looking at things from the other side's point of view.

How did Americans feel about negotiation, at least in those days? We regarded it as some sort of demeaning activity—we didn't even call it "negotiating," we called it "haggling" and "chiseling." My wife has even said to me on many occasions, "I do not lie for money"—the implication being that I did.

To the Iranians, negotiation is something done every day. Think of your own experience, David, or your listeners'. How many of you ever bought a Persian rug retail? Even if you wanted to, they wouldn't let you. The Iranians negotiate. From their perspective they've got fifty-two hot rugs for sale. They're trying to get as much as they can for their illegally obtained merchandise.

In effect, President Carter walks into the "rug seller's bazaar" and says, "I need the rugs. I want the rugs; they're the centerpiece of my foreign policy." So, unintentionally, he's making the hostages more valuable in the eyes of the Iranians and their value goes up. President Carter's a good man but unintentionally what he was doing was prolonging their captivity. When I told him this, by the way, he kind of stared at me and interjected at this point, "Herb, I don't think you understand. You, myself, and the mullahs, we're all from the same Abrahamic tradition." I didn't even know what that meant. I began to think about it. He and I may have been from that tradition, but not the Mullahs.

So, I went on and talked about when you buy a house, which is the most substantial purchase you make in your lifetime, how do Americans do it? Well, they go out somewhere to an area where they're selling homes and they see the big sign in the sky that says: $265,711. That's what we're paying—what it says up there in big block letters, even if we get screwed at that price, we don't care—everybody's getting screwed at that price—that's the American way—equality of screwing across the board. When we make that purchase, we're going to make it fast. Why? Because time is money.

Now, how about the mullahs? Well, they negotiate everything. That price on the sign means nothing to them. How do they deal with time? Americans go fast, but not the mullahs. Why? Because if you're a mullah, you're unemployed. Other than your obligatory prayers five times a day, the rest of the day you're looking to kill time (i.e., we're coming from a different place).

President Carter injected at that moment and said, "Herb, I don't think you understand Ayatollah Khomeini. He is a martyr who wants to die—he doesn't care about his own life.

I asked him, "How old is Ayatollah Khomeini?"

President Carter, who really knew details, replied, "Eighty-six years and eight months."

I said, "Look, I can handle an eighty-six-year-old martyr. The life expectancy of a martyr is about nineteen point two years. When you get to twenty, in your twenties or thirties you really need another career."

I would come home from those encounters, walk into my household and be greeted by my wife Ellen, who's an optimistic, enthusiastic person. She'd ask, "How'd it go?"

I would say to her, "Do we have any U.S. Savings Bonds? Sell."

Now, the point I'm making of course is a sound negotiating principle. What you want to do, always, is get into the world of the other side. You need to see negotiation as a problem-solving process. Try to get information from the other side. Why? Because the big mistake people make is they sell the technical features of their products, services, or ideas but what you want to do is discover the other side's underlying concerns, interests, and needs. There's a problem here. What you've got to do is help them to solve their problems while at the same time solving your problems. That's what negotiating is all about.

Wright

I was surprised to learn that you were involved with sports negotiations. I know you helped settle the NFL strike a few years back. Will you tell our readers something about that?

Cohen

Yes, I was involved in that. It was a situation where you're dealing with people on both sides who really didn't understand negotiating as a process. Each was trying to win at the expense of the other. That's a mistake because each side has a long-term relationship with the other side.

During the NFL football strike I happened to work for The Player's Association with Gene Upshaw and Ed Garvey (before he left), and the rest of that group. I was brought in to help educate the players and the players' representatives about negotiation. Professional football players, who have to support their leadership in a negotiation, really didn't understand what it was about. The owners were trying to intimidate them and you don't want to do that. So, I was involved and came up with some creative ideas for the players and strategies they should use.

Wright

If you don't mind, I'd like to focus on some of the basics of negotiation from your perspective. I'm sure that some of our readers do not consider themselves negotiators at all, but I have a feeling you could teach them some things that would help them be more successful in their personal and business lives. What are some of the fundamental principles involved in successful negotiation?

Cohen

One thing that would help anyone is the belief that you can negotiate anything—anything that is the product of a negotiation, and most things, by the way, are. Virtually everything is and can be negotiated.

What are the exceptions to that? Well, ethical, moral, and religious principles—aside from what Mel Brooks would have you believe. (The Ten Commandments was not a negotiated document.) The Sermon on the Mount did not involve negotiations. Christ did not get together with his followers and say, "Give me your input." He didn't form a couple of sub-committees, nor did He work out some compromise solutions for life. Since those things—religious principles, ethics, and morals—are not the product of negotiation, I can see they're not negotiable, but everything else is. Negotiation can involve a range of things from family dealings to business dealings to selling and to diplomatic relationships. All of these things are negotiable.

The second point I want to make is that what you want to do using negotiation is differentiate yourself. For example, why should I get more for my house? Why should I be paid more money? Well, because I'm differentiated from all the other people—keep that in mind. Your uniqueness can pay off for you. As I always say, "A nose that can hear is worth two that can smell." (I don't even know what that means, but I say it a lot.)

The next point is, with negotiations you want to have fun. Happiness is not doing what you like, it's liking what you do. The title of my second book is, *Negotiate this by Caring, but Not that Much.* This is one of the most important things you can do in a negotiation.

The two worst mistakes you make in negotiation, are: First, you care too much—you become emotionally involved. What happens when you become emotionally involved? The adrenaline starts to flow; you become doped up and dumbed down. You really do lousy. You want to care, of course, about this deal—but not that much.

The second big mistake people make, other than caring too much, is they go into a negotiation with too much authority. In other words, you always want to limit your authority. You want to use time. The other side says to you, "is that a deal?" You say, "It sounds good, but I'll have to check with my wife" (even if you're not married) or, "I have to check with my mother-in-law," or, "I have to get back to my Board," or, "I have to speak to my banker," whatever. Limiting your authority is important. You want to persist, because it takes a while for people to get used to a new idea.

Children understand the art of negotiation better than adults because children are really good negotiators. They're little people in a big person's world, so they're always negotiating with their parents.

Therefore, even when things look glum—when the other guy is closing his book on you and putting stuff away because the deal fell apart, you persist. Why? Because breakdowns are breakthroughs. Every blocked road is an alternate road to somewhere else. Pathology is opportunity, so persist and you'll make things happen.

Negotiating, as I said to you earlier, is a problem-solving process. Don't sell the technical features of products or services. You think your argument's going to be overwhelming. Rather than that, discover the other side's underlying concerns, interests, and needs.

Another point is that dumb—in negotiations and probably in life—is better than smart. Recognize that it's the Socratic pose of ignorance. Train yourself to say, "I didn't know. I didn't understand. Help me. Where are we?" This stuff tends to work because that's style and style in negotiating and in life prevails over substance. The singer—and your readers here are the singer—counts for more than the song. If you look at people who have been successful, whether it's Ronald Reagan in terms of getting what he wanted (policies prevailing), or being admired and beloved. Another example is Pope John Paul II—these people were admired and respected and influential and they exercised leadership. Not because people necessarily agreed with all their policies; it was their style.

If you look at Reagan, for example, he was optimistic. He was always smiling and waving—a happy guy, "Yea! Another great day for me and America and the entire free world." He was a man with a very old face and very young hair, moving toward that particular helicopter. Style is better than substance.

Always remember to start cooperatively as you deal with people because it's easy to go from cooperative to competitive than reverse yourself (i.e., to start out belligerent and try to change to cooperative). What you want to remember is you start your negotiations in an amiable, congenial fashion with a low-key pose of calculated incompetence, and that tends to work. What will this do for you? Well, the other side may think, "This guy's an easy touch," and they invest in the process. An investment will work for you because once you invest, it's hard to divest. Rats and human beings have this in common. The more energy expended in pursuing a particular goal, the more desirable that goal becomes. Off the top of my head, these are some ideas I would throw out to your readers.

Wright

They're great ideas! In your book, *You Can Negotiate Anything*, you outline three crucial variables to negotiating: power, time, and information. Why are these crucial and how do they play into the art of successful negotiation?

Cohen

Let's take power. People tend to underestimate their power. They always walk into a situation and look at the other guy or gal sitting behind a big desk and it seems to be that they're in a lower seat so they get intimidated by the other party. All of that's an illusion—things are not what they seem—even skim milk masquerades as cream.

What you want to do is understand where you always have power—and you always do. In fact, I point out in my book, *You Can Negotiate Anything*, and in my second book, *Negotiate This By Caring, But Not That Much,* fourteen sources of power that everybody has. When you go into a situation where you don't think you have power, it's a good idea to grab this book; I'll tell you where you *do* have power.

The reason we underestimate our power is we tend to be always tougher on ourselves. We measure the other side by what we think they've accomplished. We measure ourselves by what we could have accomplished. I show you where you always have more power than you think you have.

Power, by the way, is based upon perception. If they think you've got it, even if you don't have it, you've got it—that's something important. The other information I always want to know about you is: what your deadline is, how much authority you actually have, if you can make this deal right now, what your concerns are here, what you are looking for, and how I can satisfy your needs. Information is crucial.

The other factor is time, the last of the big three. Time is crucial, it's so important. Why? Because most concessions occur in proximity to a deadline. If I know your deadline and you don't know mine, that's a tremendous advantage for me. If I can get you to view a deadline literally and you really believe it, there's a tremendous shift of power in my favor. That's a summarized review of those three crucial variables that operate in every single negotiable situation.

Wright

You also talk about distinct styles of negotiating, which really fascinated me. I believe many people only think of one of these styles when they consider negotiations, especially when they're standing out on a used car lot. Anyway, you mention two things: winning at all costs ("the soviet style") and the style of "negotiating for mutual satisfaction." Will you tell us about these two styles?

Cohen

We live in a competitive world, particularly if you're talking about North America—United States. Many people approach you in a friendly way and they look like they're great guys. They have a smile on their face, their eyes twinkle, they use terminology saying, "Hey, let's make a win-win situation." Whereas in reality, they're what I call in the book, "Soviet style negotiators." You mentioned one example—when you're going to buy a used car, in a big city especially, hold on to your wallet. These people want outcomes where they win as much as they can; they don't care about you. I call this "the Soviet style," not the Russian style, because I first encountered that when I was involved in negotiations within the Soviet Union. This style is not just found in Moscow, it's found in Missoula, Montana, in Massachusetts, Maryland, wherever.

These are people who approach you with the eye twinkle, they have a Bible in one hand, holy water in their back pocket, and they say, "Bless you my son. May the Lord be with you." It's only after the deal when you realize there's blood trickling down your legs and there's a stiletto in your back. So I call this "the Soviet style." These are the people who are trying to win at all costs. It's hard to recognize them by the way they look or their name, but you can tell them by the things that they do and I outline those things in my first book. That style is the highly competitive style—the Soviet style.

The second style is the collaborative, cooperative style. It's a style that tries to produce win-win outcomes and solve problems—what you want to try to do, especially if you're in a continuing relationship with someone. An example is if you ask your boss for a raise or compensation increase. It's a good idea not to have this appear as a "you win, your boss loses" kind of situation. I think most people can understand this. You want the boss to think, "Gee, this was nice," and you get what you want. In my books I describe in detail how you do this. You don't want to be intimidated, but you can achieve a more profitable, enriched life using negotiations as the way to do it.

Wright

It's a fascinating title, *Negotiate This By Caring, But Not That Much.* You've mentioned it and it's a fascinating title. Sounds like the book will be a lot of fun to read, which I intend to do. I was curious about how you started your first major section in the book, "The Joy of Detached Involvement." What does that mean?

Cohen

That means, essentially how you want to train yourself to be involved, but be somewhat detached. You practice what I call "conscious inattention." If you look at great athletes in this world, or when we have the seventh game of the finals going on, whether it's the World Series or the NBA Playoffs, the guys who perform the best are the guys who care, they want to win, but not that much.

If you ever get down close, like at a hockey game—say the Stanley Cup Playoffs—and you look at these guys come out like Wayne Gretzky, or whomever, and you look at their face, they of course want to win—this is the biggest game of their lives. They know, however, that if they don't win it's not the end of western civilization—there will be a tomorrow. That's what detached involvement is. It works in sports; you want to play well, you train for it, and then you get out of the way and let the body go.

As a person who was quasi-golf I was not that good. I knew that because when I first started I'd see people watching me. I would tee off and I'd feel the pressure of the guys behind me and I'd try too hard. I knew in my mind I'd see the sand trap. When I would swing the club, in my brain I could see the ball flying and it would hit the sand and the sand would go swoosh! Then I'd get ready to do this with all that tension on me. What would happen is I'd see the ball and the ball would be hit exactly as I thought of it, but it would go right into the sand trap. I brought that about. I explain in the first chapter of my book what this is about. I have a writing style that is undoubtedly the way I speak which is, well, not too intellectual. People tell me I'm eminently readable. My sister told me *You Can Negotiate Anything* was a book for the ages—between about six and eight.

Wright

I love your sister already!

Cohen

I have a sister who's four years older than I am and was years ahead of me in school. She ruined my life. I was never able to measure up to her.

The second book is a little more sophisticated—I think it's for the eight to ten crowd. The point is, what I try to do is make the subject of negotiation fun and enjoyable for the reader. In reality, it *is* fun and enjoyable.

Wright

I hate to ask you out of context, but I was interested in one principle that you had—"the Titanic principle." What's that all about?

Cohen

Years ago, before the motion picture or the Broadway show came out, I named this after the vessel that only had one voyage. The Titanic sailed forth on its maiden voyage, struck an iceberg, and went down, but there were survivors. If it happened today those survivors would end up on The Larry King show or somewhere with a CNN coffee mug in front of them.

Larry would ask them, "What happened?"

They would say, "We hit an iceberg."

Larry would say, "Did you see it?"

"Yeah, but it didn't seem to be that much on top."

That's what the story of life is. In negotiations we deal with essentially what we see. We deal with demands.

Someone says I want to pay $20,000 and we say, "No, no, no, I can only give you $10,000."

They say, "$20,000."

"All right I'll compromise, this is my last compromise, $19,000. All right?"

"I'll give you "$10,500."

That's dealing with what's above the surface when you want to deal with what's underneath. Why do they want $20,000? Why does a guy need that amount? Why can you only offer $10,000? So you learn how to deal with what's below the surface and I call that "The Titanic Principle." By the way, no one has ever asked me about that in an interview. They ask me about a lot of other stuff, but not that. They'll ask, "What's this about hookers you got in the book or something?"

Wright

Boy, our time has just flown by today! Before we go, can you give us any news about upcoming books or projects you have? In other words, what's in the works for you?

Cohen

What I'm doing is going around speaking, because that's easy. Writing a book is hard. Various publishers want me to write about baseball—*Everything I Learned in Life I Learned through Baseball.* A lot I learned, but not *everything.* In any event, they think that would be a good title in trying to sell books.

I'm writing a play—I always wanted to write a play—and my wife says that due to my intellectual ability, I should be writing a children's book. My children would come up to me and they'd be afraid of something or they'd want a toy (this is a big thing, I think kids have too many toys). In many aspects of my life I don't know the difference between reality and illusion and I'd say, "Hey, when I was a kid I didn't have any toys.

These children today are bright, they say things to you like, "Well, what did you play with?"

I'd say, "Well I played with pots and pans and threw in forks and knives." Then I finally made up a story, which is somewhat true, but I've embellished it over the years. When I finally got my first present, my mother and father bought me a little red ball, so the story's about the little red ball. Every one of my grandkids—and I now have nine—like that story, so it'd be easy for me to write this book. I'm appealing now to an audience of two. I seem to lower the age of my audience the more successful I seem. This is what my next project may be.

Wright

You're probably going to live past 100 with an attitude like yours!

Cohen

Right now, if I can get to eighty, I figure an emissary of the Almighty may come to me one of these days and say, "Look, you want eighty, let's make a deal." I presumably will have some negotiating skill left. What I would probably say is, "Can you make it eighty-five?" Who knows? Remember, *everything's* negotiable!

Wright

Well, if I don't remember anything you've written or said, I'm certainly going to remember what your sister said about your "book of the ages"!

We've been talking with Herb Cohen, one of the internationally renowned negotiating experts.

Herb, thank you so much for being with us today and sharing such relevant and entertaining information!

Cohen

Well then, thank *you* very much. I really enjoyed it!

About The Author

HERB COHEN is considered one of the world's greatest dealmakers and has been a practicing negotiator for the past four decades. He has been intimately involved in some of the world's headline dramas, from hostile corporate takeovers to hostage negotiations.

While serving as an advisor to Presidents Jimmy Carter and Ronald Reagan, Herb Cohen was involved in the Iranian hostage crisis and credited with helping to shape the U.S. government's response to both the hijacking of TWA Flight 847 and the seizure by terrorists of the Italian cruise ship Achille Lauro. More recently, the White House has sought his input and advice on a myriad of problems, from domestic political strategy to the plague of international terrorism.

With his classic bestseller, *You Can Negotiate Anything,* Cohen has provided crucial negotiating tools to millions of people. The book was on *The New York Times* bestseller list for thirty-nine weeks, was translated into twenty-one languages, and has sold two and a half million copies. His latest book, *Negotiate This! By Caring, But Not T-H-A-T Much,* is a new, entertaining and indispensable look at the art and practice of negotiating beyond the business world.

Cohen's analyses, insights, and humorous view of world events have appeared in many national and international publications, and he has been the subject of articles in *Time, People, The Economist, The New Yorker, Newsweek, Rolling Stone,* and *Fortune Small Business.* Even *Playboy* called him the "world's best negotiator."

Herb Cohen
www.herbcohenonline.com

Chapter 3

Anne Warfield

THE INTERVIEW

David Wright (Wright)

Anne Warfield's unique ability to listen beyond what a person says and to hear what a person means makes her constantly in demand with Fortune 100 companies and the media for her negotiation insight. Her ability to show how to communicate proactively during adversarial conditions has attracted clients to utilize her for some of their toughest negotiations (saving them millions of dollars). She is in constant demand as a high level resource for her clients. She shows how to remove over 70 percent of what hits the negotiation table before the negotiation even starts!

Her expertise on communication, body language, and negotiation has been utilized by many of the nation's foremost corporations including media giants such as, CBS, NBC, ABC, *Business Week, New York Daily News, Investors Business Daily*, and *Forbes*. She has real-life experience that comes from running a $40 million dollar department, negotiating multi-million dollar deals in the U.S. and abroad, and running her own international company.

Anne Warfield, welcome to *The Masters of Impact Negotiating*.

Anne Warfield (Warfield)

Thank you David, I'm happy to be here.

Wright

So tell me, how does the Outcome Focus™ approach differ from traditional negotiation strategies?

Warfield

That's a great question, David. At a very young age I found myself negotiating multimillion-dollar deals across the table from someone usually twenty years older than I was. I didn't have their sophistication nor did I have their experience level. I realized I had to find a way for myself to get a little leverage in a negotiation.

What I found with traditional negotiation is that it often focused on strapping on your armor while trying to outmaneuver and outthink your opponent. You come in armed with "what I want" and "here's why you should give it to me." I found emotions ran high and the negotiation would get out of control.

The Outcome Focus™ approach comes from an entirely different mindset. The attitude this approach engenders is:

What is the outcome I want?
What is the outcome they want?
How do I see this from their perspective?
How do I achieve the highest level outcome?

It allows you to look at it as a dialog—you leave your armor outside of the room. Here's the pivotal key: what most people do not realize is that your thoughts and your language are so tightly woven together that if you think something, it shows in your body language. In a negotiation that can be deadly. You can learn tricks but your body language still reveals what your true thoughts are.

I show how to make thoughts and body language congruent so that you're authentic, you're in the moment with people, and you bring their ethics and their accountability into the room at the same time.

Wright

I'm fascinated with how you can learn to eliminate 70 percent of what hits the negotiation table prior to the negotiation so that it's more focused. Would you give our readers an example?

Warfield

Absolutely. Most people look at what is the pressing concern or need for them right now. They then panic and want to negotiate and eliminate that need. We rarely ask the question, is there a higher level negotiation I can do that, if achieved, everything else will fall in place?

Let me give you an example. Steve came to me and said, "We have a company we do about one million in business with and right now they are very difficult to work with. I want to negotiate with them on what changes we need in the way they set up the warehouse where they store what we currently buy from them so it is more cost efficient and effective for us. This warehouse is only utilized by our company."

As I asked Steve more questions, he told me that there was a low trust level between the two companies and that there was a new president at this vendor's company. On top of this Steve said that his major client was squeezing him to get lower prices. This meant that Steve had to get lower prices from his vendors as well. He felt that fixing this warehouse was just one of the things that could help. He said that his other vendors were letting him work directly with them on how to reduce their costs while preserving the vendor's gross margin so they could build a stronger partnership built on trust and loyalty. Steve said, "I don't want to financially hurt them, so that is why I want to work with them and reduce their cost so they can pass that cost savings on to us and still make their margin."

As I listened to him I said, "You're negotiating the wrong thing and a lot of stuff is going to hit the table that you don't want. Here's the higher level negotiation you should focus on: You currently do one million dollars of business with them and your business has grown 5 percent a year with them. You do not have another source to go to so they do have you a bit boxed in. What you want to do is move to the highest level of negotiation which is, how do we build trust that allows us to explode the business with you? Sit down with them, look at them and say, "We do a million dollars in business right now with you. I believe we could explode that business. In order to be able to do that, we need to look at the elements that need to happen so we can help grow that business with you." That's the conversation you want to have.

Now the president is going to be open to that discussion. That higher level negotiation will involve not only that warehouse but also allows your company to come in and walk their floor and change things such as their gross margin. I told him, "It's going to allow you to do things such as resetting up that warehouse, increase their line business, and look at whole new opportunities."

That's the difference. Not only does Steve's company get what they need, they cement the relationship that allows all future negotiations to move to a different level.

Wright

Sounds like you're also helping your vendor.

Warfield

Absolutely. It ends up being a very strong, non-adversarial negotiation and it allows you to ask very difficult questions. Every negotiation has very difficult questions and what most people try to do is attack back. Let's say you're negotiating with some people and you want to challenge them. You don't think they're looking at the problem right and you maybe disagree with what they said.

Most of us try to point out the other person's faults. We say things like, "David, that's not what you said earlier. What you told me was——" That's all adversarial. With the Outcome Focus™ approach I would say, "If you're saying this, then I don't understand how," or, "If this, then share with me how that relates to what we talked about here." This is allowing others to open the door where they can say, "Well, that's not what I meant." They can rephrase it and you don't get all the emotions in the room charged up, with people angrily pointing fingers at each other.

Wright

After all these years of experience and being as successful as you are today, what have you found is the number one thing to go wrong in a negotiation and how can you avoid it?

Warfield

The number one thing I find that goes wrong in negotiations is what people never manage before they get in the room. Let me step back and give an example. If you think of some of the best negotiators in the world, not many of them stand above four feet tall—children are fabulous negotiators. Children understand that there is an emotional tie people have to things and that's where they focus. As adults we try to remove the emotions and look at things logically. Well, logic makes people think—emotions make people act. When you don't manage emotions or even think of them from both angles before you enter the room, they're underlying and they just wait to burst forward. As soon as the logic isn't connecting with people, the emotion bursts out and it messes up the entire negotiation. I've seen corporations go into a negotiation that should have been smooth—it should have been a simple issue—but emotions got in the way, personalities mixed in, and people said things that could never be taken back. What was said and done damaged the relationship long-term.

Wright

So why is negotiating hard for some and easy for others?

Warfield

There are four different communication styles. Over 2,000 years ago Hippocrates was the first recorded Western thinker on personality. What I've found is that most communication profiles strictly look at what your personality is. What we look at is how you process information in order to negotiate or interact with others at a higher level. Each of these communication styles has a different way to process information and thus "hear what you say."

For example, "Producers" have in their base, power and control over their own situation. Therefore, negotiation is not scary for them. They welcome it because it gives them an opportunity to think creatively, put things out there, to gain more power and more control. So it's almost something they relish.

On the other hand, Connectors process everything through stability. How does it give me greater stability? A negotiation, by nature, absolutely knocks stability out of the question. For them it's a very fearful thing. They don't like it; they don't want to approach it. They feel like someone's going to get run over and it's not going to be a comfortable situation.

With the Outcome Focus™ approach, no matter what your communication style or what combination of the four styles you have, you can negotiate because you're always looking at a proactive, positive approach. You're always moving the accountability, trust, and respect of everyone in the room to a higher level. We find that people who are afraid of negotiations look up and say, "Wow! I'm not scared of negotiations anymore because I don't visualize them or think about them the same way." When you don't think about negotiations the same way, the way you listen and your body language changes completely because your thoughts and body language are so closely tied together.

Producers (who love negotiations) say they love the Outcome Focus™ approach versus the traditional approach because they are able to condense time, get finished faster, and they get much better results without arm-wrestling. They are absolutely floored by that.

I had one individual who was a very strong, Producer-driver personality model. After learning the Outcome Focus™ approach she said, "Anne, I just had a five-minute call and saved $100,000 for my company. It was so easy." That's the part that amazes people—it's so easy, no matter what style you are.

Wright

Are there certain words in the language that one should avoid when negotiating and if so, why?

Warfield

There are certain words you should avoid. Part of it is because people attach certain meanings to the words. Two of the key words to avoid are: "but," and, "however." These words automatically negate everything previously said. All the other person listens for is that "but" and he or she goes on the defensive. As a matter of fact, what you can do is watch the person across the table and anytime you hear the word "but" or "however," watch people's body language. Their spine will stiffen and they stick their head up—all saying, "Oops, I've got to listen for this. The shoe's going to drop at this point." You're far better off just simply using the word "and" instead.

Other phrases that really trigger people are, "you know," "you need to," "you should," and "you have to." All of a sudden people start saying, "Wait a minute! What about you?" People don't like to be told what they have to do. Often in negotiations, I see that we quickly flip because of the defensive words spoken and the emotions those words evoke. We quickly flip to telling people what they ought to do and the first reaction listeners have is an instinct to do the opposite. It usually ends up in very, very bad results.

A phrase I hear people say during negotiating that's a real killer is, "I'm not sure you understand what I'm saying." What you're really saying to the person is, "Excuse me, open up your ears. I said it properly and you didn't hear properly." What's better to say is, "Let me step back. I'm not sure I said that the way I meant." The response will probably be, "Okay, take your time."

Wright

I have trouble with colors and when my wife says, "That's a beautiful tie but—" I know I'm going to have to go back and change something.

Warfield

Exactly.

Wright

So what signs show that people disagree with you?

Warfield

This is interesting. Body language plays a huge part in a negotiation. I actually started studying body language because of a particular negotiation. I was twenty years younger than anyone else at the table. As I looked at it I thought I had to have a way to buy myself time, so if I said something that irritated them, I could change it around before it was too late.

Here's the most amazing part. I found that I could literally walk in a room, sit down to meet with a person, and within four minutes know exactly how the negotiation was going to go.

Wright

From body language?

Warfield

Yes, from the person's body language and by using Outcome Focus™ thinking. It was absolutely amazing. Most people are so focused on putting their arms around what they need that they totally ignore the body language signs in the room.

Let me give you an example of where someone disagrees with you. If it happens, you will see crossing or uncrossing of the arms, white knuckles, breaking eye contact, snorting or flaring of the nose, pursing of lips, and contracted pupils. By the way, contraction of the pupils of the eyes is one thing you cannot control. Therefore when you are upset, they automatically contract. This is one of the biggest ways in negotiating that you can tell if a person likes or doesn't like what you've said.

What usually happens is we ignore all those body language signs or we intuitively think people won't like what we will say but we are going to get our point through anyway. We finish and stare blankly at them and ask, "What do you think?" All they do is defend their position.

A great example of this is when I was a buyer and we were going to have a huge meeting with a company we did almost $25 million in business with. They came and sat down and were very upset with us because we returned all these defective shoes to their warehouse. They thought we were asking for too much money back for the defective shoes and for advertising dollars. They also thought the shoes we asked to put on sale weren't right.

So we sat down in the meeting and handed out our agenda. I watched their president and his eyes flared, he flipped his tie, he kept looking down, and finally he took our agenda and he flipped it over and he just stared at all of us. Our entire company got very quiet. I looked at him and thought, "You know what? He really is upset with something that was said." I took my agenda and flipped it over and I said, "Can we step back? Tell me about your vision for the company, where you're going, and let's chat about how we fit in that vision."

He started talking about the advertising campaign, all the things he was doing, and we weren't a part of them. He didn't want us involved. He saw us as adversarial and difficult. I asked him how we could be a partner and how we could support his vision. He agreed to put us in his major advertising billboards. Then I told him we have major sales and I would love to have his company involved in those sales. We would need to have a great buy price on the shoe that was in the sale. I knew that in the past it hadn't been something they had been comfortable with; but was there something we could do?

He said, "Absolutely." He started looking at his top three shoes and what price we could get for the volume we'd go through.

I said, "We'd love to run you in the ad. It would be about a quarter page of the ad. Here is what the advertising cost is."

He said, "Why a quarter page? Why don't we do a full page?"

"I'd love to," I said, "here's is the cost for that."

He agreed to the price. We walked through everything and we got to the last point that was about the defective shoes at his warehouse that he wanted us to take back. I said, "I realize we have some shoes at your warehouse that are defective. My understanding is that there is some discussion you want to have on that."

He said, "Yes." He sat back at this point and crossed his arms, which showed that he was pulling out of the conversation.

I sat back and thought about it from his perspective and thought about why that item on the agenda would irritate me. If I was that president and owned that company, it would irritate me because I would think, "I build a good quality shoe and you're now sending all these shoes back and telling me that they're defective. You're basically saying that I'm sloppy with how I'm doing business."

So I looked at him and said, "One of the things I love is that you have a great 'walk test' campaign. You have signs that we have put up in our department that say to people, 'This shoe is so comfortable, put it on and wear it and if you don't feel it's the most comfortable shoe you've ever had, bring it back.' We fully support that campaign. It does mean some people take advantage of it. They send their shoes back even when they're not really defective. What we need to know from you is which do you want us to support? I believe your advertising campaign drives sales but it will mean we occasionally get returns of worn shoes that we will return as 'defective,' or do you want us to take those signs down and carefully look and make absolutely sure it's a defective shoe before we take it back?"

He said, "No, you're right. Our walk test campaign is the right thing to do. Absolutely I want to do it. Let's continue with it; we'll take those shoes back." He flipped the sheet over and started laughing. He said, "I gave you more on the back of the sheet than you came to ask for and I feel really good about it." The kicker was when he got up, he said, "I want you to know one thing. I came here today for only one purpose and that was to pull your account. I no longer wanted to do business with you but I'm walking out of here a partner."

It was really watching those body language signs that made the difference. What was he telling me non-verbally? Once you see the signs, you've got to step out and address the emotion in the room. Don't ignore it and don't blow past it—you'll get people too upset.

Wright

What can a person do to challenge another person or show that he or she disagrees without the other person becoming hostile?

Warfield

Use open-ended, probing questions. I find that when someone wants to challenge a person, we want to first point out what the flaw is in what was said or was done. We don't want to use such statements as, "David, last time we got together, your e-mail recapping the meeting said one thing and now you're saying another." That is very adversarial and people will pull away. But if you say something like, "All right, how does that relate to the meeting we had a few weeks ago where we talked about this—?" I'm pointing out the difference but then they can say how it relates and there might be a new bit of information I didn't know about that you had gained. Now you're going to bring it to the table and relate it. If there isn't something new, you're going to have to step back and say, "Well, it doesn't relate, I guess I've changed it." Okay, so why are we changing it? What's the purpose behind changing it now?

So you bring that character and those ethics into the room but you do it in a very non-judgmental, non-accusatory way. You let people know you believe they want to handle this properly and you're going to give them the benefit of that, so let's look at it. The first way comes across to the person as, "You lied to me and I caught you at it, so now explain it."

Wright

Sometimes I've entered negotiations when I've tried my best to stack the deck in my favor and have everything going before I start. Other times I find myself in a weak position. In your opinion, could I still negotiate if I have no leverage?

Warfield

Absolutely. I think one of the biggest things people don't realize is that every negotiation does have leverage and the leverage is called the emotional tie. What does the other person have that is an emotional tie to whatever you're talking about? That is your leverage.

Let me give you a quick example of that. When my husband and I were looking to buy a new house we went into a neighborhood that had two spec homes being built. One I thought was lovely and the other I didn't think was the greatest. The one I didn't think was the greatest was actually $2,000 more than the other house. I really wanted the first house but it didn't have a great yard and my husband wasn't that wild about it. We kind of dragged our feet and the house I loved got sold on the day we called up and tried to buy it.

I knew the houses in this development were under-priced in the marketplace and the builder had done a phenomenal job. He was a very difficult, ornery type of person—a very driving-temper person. When we walked in to negotiate to buy the "not so great" house, he had us over a barrel:

1. We had been to the house many times and he knew we really liked it.

2. He had just sold the other house so he had all the money in his pocket—this was the last house in the neighborhood to sell.
3. He had two other parties interested in the house who wanted to buy it, so he had other buyers in the marketplace.

His desire to negotiate with us and give us any advantage was extremely low. On top of that, we didn't have a whole lot of leverage because we had already given away our cards on how much we liked his houses by touring them and asking constant questions, and by trying to buy the other house.

We walked into the negotiation and he looked at us and said, "So, you lost the other house because you couldn't make up your mind—the other people could. Hmm. So now you want this other house—you finally realize what a good deal this is." He then said, "You know, as a matter of fact, we want to get out of this project so we want to get this house closed within one month."

We hadn't even put our house on the market, and now he's trying to box us in with time and with the money.

I sat and looked at him. I tried to think from his perspective—what is his emotional tie? His son lives in the neighborhood so I knew that he wanted a great neighborhood—that was his emotional tie. I also knew he had a tremendous amount of pride in the houses he builds. He told us how great the market was and that we should be able to sell our house. He said, "As a matter of fact, the market is so great right now, if you don't buy this house today, someone's probably going to grab it." He used those emotional ties on us.

I looked at him and said, "You're right, you do build a great house and I can see the tremendous pride you have in that. As a matter of fact, it shows a tremendous amount of confidence that your son wants to live in the neighborhood. I'm sure you want a neighborhood that fits exactly with what your son wants. You want people in your house who appreciate it and that's us. I also hear you clearly telling us that the marketplace is really hot right now and we should have no problem selling our house. You sold out of this development; you want to move to a new neighborhood and you're ready to invest in a new development."

He said, "Absolutely, I'm ready."

"Great," I said. "We're going to make this really easy for you. What you want to do is get your money out of this house and be able to flip it into a new development. We have a house we have to put on the market. I'm going to gamble on your confidence in how great the market is. And we are fine moving into this house in one month and you will agree to carry our house for two additional months on the market. If the market is as great as you say, it's not even a gamble for you. Our house will sell immediately and you'll have your money. If it doesn't, you have our current house payments that are significantly lower and you've got someone in the house right away. My question to you is, where do you want to put that in the contract?"

He signed off on it right away.

Wright

This is great but what if I work in an industry where negotiating is a slimy business. Can this work?

Warfield

Absolutely. I've had people say to me, "All right Anne, we are usually across the table choking each other in negotiations—they're horrible." Most of the problems are based on the fact that most people assume the other side is trying to cheat or get something more out of you. So again, it comes from that adversarial point of view.

What I try to do is flip it around and manage the emotion and raise accountability.

Let me give you an example. One of the areas I work in is commercial real estate. The client said, "Often our negotiations get slimy because everyone starts pointing fingers, they get really harsh, and it just goes downhill."

I said, "All right, what's one of the examples where it gets really bad?"

"Anytime we have a re-trade," he said.

"What's a re-trade?"

"A re-trade is where you've gone in and looked at a building, you agree to buy it, and then later change the price you offered. For example, let's say they've priced it at $10 million and you say, 'I'll give you $9.5 million. And they say, 'Great, it's a deal.' Then we do due diligence where we send a team in. They tour the entire place and look at it to determine if repairs are necessary such as replacing flooring, ceiling leaks, etc. The tour is to determine if the property is really worth $9.5 million. Then we have to sit down at the table and if there are repairs needed, we have to do what's called a 're-trade,' which means we can no longer offer $9.5 million because of the condition of the building." He said, "Those are the situations where it gets really, really slimy."

I said, "All right, how many times are you negotiating against a seller who is a brand new seller and who has never, ever sold a building before?"

He said, "This is a small market. In this area, 90 percent of the time you're dealing with someone who has sold many times."

"Okay," I said, "how many times does a re-trade realistically happen? Are 80 percent of your deals re-trades? If so, you're dealing with a seller who knows a re-trade's coming and who has experience having done this before. So what you're really facing is the feeling the seller has in the process that you're going to lay out a dollar amount, then you're going to go to the property and you're going to try to rip the seller off by looking around for things and making things up or trying to just get the price down. And you're going to be attacking the seller's character and integrity saying the building was not kept up or that the seller tried to hide these issues."

I continued, "Realistically, how often does a person selling a building go climb up on the roof and check it out? It's just not going to happen. So is the seller trying to pull things over on you? Most likely not. If you are going to find problems with the property, most likely you will.

"What you want to do is manage the negative emotion that comes in the room when the seller figures you're going to try to rip him or her off. When you make the first offer, you look the person in the eye and say, 'We love your building. We'll offer $9.5 million for the building. We'll have our team come in and do their due diligence. What we commit to you is, whatever they find in their due diligence, we will let you know right away so you have the same information we do.' " "Now," I said, "when you call and say you've found a problem and want to give the seller a heads-up on it, do not negotiate it. The message you want to send up front is that you believe in the seller's character and integrity, you believe the building is fine, and you believe the seller is as surprised as you are that there's a problem and you believe he or she wants to take care of it. Now the seller is going to come to the table prepared to negotiate and lower that price."

He told me my advice worked phenomenally.

Wright

Brilliant. What a great conversation. I really learned a lot here today. You sure know what you're talking about and I'm glad you're going to be in this book. Our readers are really going to learn about negotiation.

Warfield

Thank you. I love it because when people use the Outcome Focus™ approach they are no longer afraid or intimidated by negotiations, they actually look forward to them! If you desire to dig deeper, please join us for an upcoming public seminar, or we can do a customized onsite seminar for you. Visit www.ImpressionManagement.com for more information.

Wright

Today we have been talking with Anne Warfield who is one of the foremost experts on communication. Her ability to show how to communicate proactively is amazing, as we have found out here today.

Anne, thank you so much for being here with us today and spending all this time answering these questions for our project, *The Masters of Impact Negotiating.*

Warfield

Thank you. It's been a delight.

About The Author

ANNE WARFIELD'S unique ability to listen beyond what a person says and to hear what the person means makes her constantly in demand with Fortune 100 companies and the media for her negotiation insight.

As a speaker, author, and consultant, Anne shares with you this new mindset that will move you from transactional to transformational communication.

Realigning your spoken and non-verbal message using the Outcome Focus™ approach, allows you to "say it right the first time." You will experience a new way of thinking that will transform how you present, negotiate, and lead.

Anne Warfield
Impression Management Professionals, Inc.
15768 Venture Lane
Minneapolis, MN 55344
Phone: 952.921.9421
Fax: 952.921.9420
E-mail: Contact@imp.us.com
www.ImpressionManagement.com

Chapter 4

R. R. "BOBBY" COVIC, EA

THE INTERVIEW

David Wright (Wright)

Today we're talking with Bobby Covic, EA. As an Enrolled Agent (EA), Bobby Covic is a federally authorized tax practitioner specializing in "crisis tax cases." He negotiates settlements for clients in IRS audit controversies, multi-year failure-to-file cases, and large dollar collection situations.

A former National Tax Practice Institute faculty member, Bobby is the author of the critically acclaimed book, *Everything's Negotiable!* He is also pens the popular weekly newspaper column *Negotiating Today's World!*

Bobby is a nationally recognized speaker and media personality known for his unique, entertaining, and inspiring perspectives on negotiation, overcoming overload, and creative conflict resolution. Bobby is also a member of the National Speakers Association and the International Association of Professional Negotiators.

Bobby, welcome to *The Masters of Impact Negotiating.*

Bobby Covic (Covic)

Thank you David, it's wonderful to be involved in this project with you.

Wright

So you're "the guy who wrote the book" on negotiation. How did you learn to negotiate?

Covic

That's a great question, David. As fate would have it, my father was a lieutenant colonel in the United States Air Force. And, needless to say, when he told his subordinates, "No," their response always had to be, "Yes, sir!"

Well, with good reason, my dad often told me, "No." I guess I must have begun learning to negotiate by daring to respond to his "no's" as if they were merely interesting opening bargaining positions.

Wright

So how valuable can negotiating skills be to a person in terms of actual dollars?

Covic

They can be phenomenally, yet not incalculably, valuable.

Wright

Could you give us an example of how to actually calculate the value of negotiating skills?

Covic

Sure, David. Here's an example from my book:

You've worked hard sharpening your bargaining and negotiating skills. Your car needs repair. Your local mechanic tells you to take your car to the dealership for a specialized job. Ouch! You know the pain of dealership bills—outrageous hourly labor rates and even more outrageous price tags on parts.

Are you just gonna take it? No way! You get ready to join the ranks of the financially successful. You posture yourself for the challenge, and you go for it.

You introduce yourself to the service manager, Al. He looks the job up in "the book." He then cheerfully quotes you $178.60 in labor and $400 in parts. He awaits your response. You gag; you're shocked. You use your logic: "labor—probably non-negotiable; parts—big mark-up, possibly negotiable. It's worth a try."

"Four hundred dollars in parts? Wow! That's a lot!" Pause. "Al, what kind of discount could you extend me on the parts?"

Silence. More silence. Al rustles some papers. "Fifteen percent is the best I can do for you, my friend," he says. Trying to contain your glee, you thank Al for his graciousness in extending you this courtesy. You don't feel too sorry for the dealership. You guess their markup could be anywhere from 100 percent to 300 percent.

Now, here's the math: 15 percent saved on the $400 part = $60. Right? Right! That's fantastic! You just saved $60. Congratulations. And, the good news is that there isn't any bad news. It only gets better. Stay with me now.

Next, estimate how long it took you to gag, be shocked, and think, "Labor, probably non-negotiable; parts, big mark-up, possibly negotiable. Worth a try" (thirty seconds).

Then, estimate how long it took you to say, "Four hundred dollars in parts? Wow! That's a lot!" (five seconds).

Then, estimate how long it took you to say, "Al, what kind of discount could you extend me on the parts?" (ten seconds).

And, finally, how long did you have to remain silent until Al gave you the discount? (fifteen seconds).

Okay. Let's add all the seconds up: 30 + 5 + 10 + 15 = 60 seconds. You've heavily invested in this negotiation to the extent of sixty seconds of your precious time—one minute.

Question: You just saved $60 in one minute. There are sixty minutes in an hour. In this case, how much are your negotiating skills worth on an hourly basis?

Answer: Well, how about $3,600? Yep! The $60 saved times the sixty minutes in an hour equals $3,600!

Three thousand and six hundred dollars an hour? That's right. Prorated, that's the hourly value of your bargaining powers. Not bad, huh?

Now, unless you're Bill Gates or Oprah Winfrey, I'm guessing that $3,600 an hour is more than your hourly wage. Am I right? Okay, that's what I thought!

Is this a little far-fetched? Maybe. Do the numbers work? You bet they do. Most people will never earn as much working in an hour as they can save by negotiating effectively for one minute.

And, the better you get at it, the more you'll save (i.e., earn), because you'll keep applying your valuable skills to bigger and bigger ticket items.

So, here's the summary: $400 part at 15 percent discount equals $60 saved in one minute times sixty minutes in an hour equals $3,600 per hour.

Wright

Wow! $3,600!

Covic

That's *right,* $3,600 prorated out on an hourly basis! That's just one example of how incredibly valuable negotiating skills can be. And, per your request, that's how to calculate their value in terms of actual dollars.

Wright

My wife says she feels like the bargaining deck is stacked against her. But, is a woman realistically at any disadvantage when negotiating with a man?

Covic

Absolutely not! As a matter of fact, the opposite is true. A man is at a disadvantage when negotiating with a woman. Why? Because from the time they are little girls, women learn how to use words and body language to get what they want.

Now, on the other hand, from the time they are little boys, men learn how to use aggression, power, threats, intimidation, and violence to get what they want, right?

So, as boys and girls grow up, a mastery of the more subtle nuances of persuasion gives the negotiating advantage to "the fairer" sex.

Wright

Bobby, let's shift gears a little here. I know you're a tax litigation consultant. Would you give any examples of the kind of money you've saved clients in your negotiations with the IRS?

Covic

Sure, David. Here's one example that comes to mind. One of our clients, a California architect, owed the taxman slightly over $297,000. Though it took quite a long time in negotiations, we eventually made a remarkable deal for him by utilizing the IRS Offer in Compromise program.

Unbelievable as this may seem, the Feds ended up settling for $19,292 against the $297,000. They accepted our offer of less than 6.5 cents on the dollar! We saved our client almost $278,000 in that case! Needless to say, he was a happy camper.

This is a prime example of the incredible results good negotiation skills (and patience!) can produce.

Wright

Was it mostly penalty and interest as opposed to actual tax?

Covic

The base liability was actually what is called a Trust Fund Recovery Penalty. That penalty is asserted when an employer fails to pay moneys withheld from employees' wages. Those funds are supposed to be held in trust on behalf of the government.

The IRS considers the failure to pay over those funds to be one of the most egregious offenses a taxpayer can commit. No wonder—it is effectively embezzlement from the United States government! So it is justifiably one of the most difficult liabilities upon which to get a sympathetic IRS hearing.

Though it is technically a penalty, interest does nevertheless attach to and accrue upon the base amount as well. To make matters even worse, the interest actually compounds on a daily basis as well.

Wright

Wow! That could be devastating. How about another example, Bobby?

Covic

Okay, David. Here's a different kind of example for you:

We represent a retired airline pilot against whom the IRS asserted and was originally attempting to collect well over $1,000,000 in delinquent taxes. That amount was based upon quite a number of years during which he failed to file tax returns.

The Feds had a levy in place of approximately $4,500 against his $5,000 monthly pension. After some intense negotiations we finally got it reduced to $500.

Over time, the ten-year statute of limitations for collections on many of the years involved lapsed. On May 13, 2007, the final year will become uncollectible by virtue of the expiration of this statute. Our client will then be completely absolved of the balance of the original seven-digit liability.

So, in the final analysis, he was saved from financial disaster as the result of this negotiation coup. Realistically, the $500 monthly levy proceeds were not even sufficient enough to service the interest on the million dollars plus in back taxes. Yet the IRS agreed that it was the most he could afford so the deal worked!

Wright

Amazing!

Covic

No question about it, David. That is yet another example of the kind of result that becomes possible with elevated negotiation skills.

Wright

I've heard you say Beatles' manager, Brian Epstein, made a critical error in the *Hard Day's Night* movie negotiations that cost the "Fab Four" some pretty big bucks. Would you tell our readers what happened?

Covic

Sure. Epstein was apparently intent on negotiating the Beatles' first movie deal for them all by himself. Unfortunately, he had no experience in the movie business—none whatsoever. History revealed that he knew the movie business about as well as Ringo knew quantum physics. Here are some excerpts from a *Rolling Stone* magazine article on the subject; I'll interject a few comments as well.

One of the producers by the name of Walter Sheldon recalled, "Bud [Orenstein] and I agreed it would be fair to offer Brian and the Beatles 25 percent of the picture. We put to him the fee of $25,000 to work the picture and he agreed to that."

[Now, here comes the kicker.]

"Then we asked him, 'Mr. Epstein, what would you consider a fair percentage of the picture?' Brian thought for a moment and then he said, 'I couldn't accept anything less than 7.5 percent.'"

Well, what was ironic was that the producers had actually decided in advance that they would go as high as 25 percent.

So, Epstein actually cost the Beatles 17.5 percent on the deal just by being the first to mention a number. As conventional negotiation wisdom dictates, it is absolutely crucial to avoid being the first to mention a number. Why? Because the first person who mentions a number usually loses.

Wright

So what do you find is the most powerful thing to say or do while involved in a negotiation?

Covic

That's another excellent question, David. Interestingly, to sum it up in one word, the most powerful thing you can say, or do, in a negotiation is—*nothing!*

To sum it up in two words, coarse as it may sound, it's—*shut up!*

For guys like you and me who make a living talking, that's a tall order. Yet silence is truly golden. The reality in any negotiation is: he who speaks most loses most.

Think about it. We were all blessed with *two* ears and only *one* mouth for a good reason. We should be listening twice as much as we're talking.

Talk is not cheap. It is expensive. Generally, the more you talk in a negotiation, the more it will cost you.

Wright

Some people are afraid to negotiate. They wonder, "If I negotiate, will people think I'm cheap or chintzy?" Does that concern have any validity?

Covic

It actually doesn't. However, many people certainly do think this way and that's why they have reservations about negotiating. The reality is that the wealthiest people—those with the least actual economic need to negotiate—are usually the very people most apt to do so. They are also typically the folks who are the most proficient bargainers.

People of the most substantial means don't let the lure of material possessions rule their thoughts and desires. They don't spend more than they have to. They do not buy on impulse.

So negotiation is, in the end, simply a balanced and honest discipline. It is a totally acceptable, realistic, and dignified approach to money management.

Wright

What is the mark of the best negotiator?

Covic

The best negotiator is, in my opinion, the person who leaves the table with exactly what he or she wants and with the assurance that the other party is leaving feeling like he or she got the best end of the deal. If you can accomplish this, you are always the winner. That's the best you can do in any negotiation.

As my co-author and good friend, Jim Henning, recommends: Follow the golden rule versus "the platinum rule." Take the win-win philosophy a step further. Treat people the way they want to be treated.

Always negotiate with another as if you are going to do business with him or her again in the future. Focus on long-term relationships and not short-term profits.

The best negotiator approaches each encounter in these positive ways.

Wright

While I've got you here, can I get you to help me solve a personal problem?

Covic

I'd be happy to.

Wright

One of the things that drives me crazy is the medical industry. I work hard, as I'm sure they do; but, sometimes I'm kept waiting in a doctor's office for two or three hours. How can I negotiate with a tardy doctor?

Covic

I love that question. I know I definitely feel the same frustration when that happens to me.

Okay. So, let's talk about it. How can you negotiate with a tardy doctor? Well, first of all, think about the mutual agreements.

You call and make an appointment. When the doctor's office sets a time, they make an agreement with you—a literal contract—albeit oral. It is called a bi-lateral contract and it is binding. The doctor contracts, not only to provide his services, but it is also implicit that he agrees to provide them in a timely manner. That's the whole key. He agrees to provide the services at the agreed upon time. In exchange, you agree to pay his fee and to do so in a timely manner.

If you're on time and he's late, he is technically in breach of the contract.

To rectify the situation, simply multiply the amount you earn per hour times the amount of time he was late, then subtract the product from his bill. This is powerful and it works. More than one court has held this strategy to be just and appropriate.

Here is an example. You have 3:00 PM appointment. The good doctor keeps you waiting until 4:30. You earn $20 per hour. One and a half hours late times $20 equals $30. Thirty dollars should be subtracted from his bill.

It is unlikely that this technique will fail to get a doctor's attention. I've found that after employing this tactic once, a doctor typically doesn't keep me waiting again.

Wright

Bobby, I know you're a negotiation coach. I'm not sure I know what that is. What exactly is a negotiation coach and how do you help people?

Covic

Overall David, negotiation coaching is a relatively new concept in the marketplace. However, it is a concept I began experimenting with in my practice many years ago. The benefits to our clients have been such that I've expanded on it more and more through the years.

Basically though, a negotiation coach is an expert in negotiating and who mentors other folks through any kind of negotiation situation. If necessary, the coach can "change hats" at any time and could actually end up negotiating on the client's behalf as a "hired gun."

As a negotiation coach, I help people in all kinds of transactional situations. I am available to my coaching clients on the telephone or in person to actually guide them through any kind of negotiation on an as-needed basis. I've helped people negotiate the best prices on hotel room rates, cars, homes, etc.

The negotiation coaching concept applies equally well to assisting clients in reaching property settlement agreements in marital dissolutions as it does to facilitating contractual agreements in the purchases of corporate jets, ocean liners, big city skyscrapers, etc.

Wright

So, if I decide to buy a business and I come up with a value that I think it is worth, I can call you and get your advice on the negotiation process along each step of the way?

Covic

You absolutely can, David. And the benefit to you is the power of one of the most effective tactics in any negotiation. It is called "resort to higher authority."

For example, you're a principle in a negotiation. You're negotiating to buy a business. You make an offer "conditioned" or "contingent" upon the "approval of your financial advisor." Now that could be me, it could be your attorney, your CPA, or your Certified Financial Planner. It could be anybody. (Come to think of it, it could just as well be your wife. As a matter of fact, let's be honest, David; you know it *would be* your wife. Kidding; only kidding!)

Wright

You know me too well!

Covic

Let's just say I appreciate the subtleties of marriage.

Kidding aside though, one of the most authoritative postures you can assume in a negotiation is one that obligates you to secure the approval of what we call the "missing man." It creates the safety net of a "boogeyman."

If you hire me as your negotiation coach, I become the higher authority to which you must submit any proposals for approval. You assert your obligation to consult with me. I am your missing man—your boogeyman. This is the ultimate "good cop/bad cop" scenario.

Best of all, this takes the pressure off you. You are relieved of the responsibility of negotiating with finality with the other party. You simply assert that you must resort to higher authority—consult with me and secure my approval prior to actually committing to anything in the negotiation. Many of my clients have found this to be a very constructive (and often hugely profitable!) approach.

Wright

So how does power come into play in negotiating?

Covic

Well David, power is one of the most important concepts in negotiation. Acknowledging the power you have in a negotiation situation is absolutely crucial. Many people are virtually unaware of the extent to which they actually possess power in a negotiation.

To be fair, in some situations the fact is that you may have little or no power. However, in most situations you are likely to have much more power that you might realize. So, when going into any negotiation, it's of paramount importance to assess how much power you realistically do or do not have.

One of the biggest mistakes people make in negotiation is underestimating how much power they actually do possess. And as a result they end up giving away much more than they should.

Wright

Will you give me an example of power?

Covic

Sure. As a matter of fact, Herb Cohen, one of the participants in our *Masters of Impact Negotiating* project here, mentions in his classic book, *You Can Negotiate Anything,* what he calls the "power of competition."

Here's how you would exercise the power of competition, for example, in negotiating the purchase of a new car: Contact dealership after dealership. Shop one's best deal against the other's best deal. And (here's the key) let them all know this is exactly what you're doing. Make constant references to the other dealerships you're in touch with. Continually express your concern about getting the very best price you can. Make it perfectly clear that you are effectively seeking competitive bids.

That's how you maximize the power of competition. The dollars you hold give you the winning hand when you properly use this power.

Wright

One thing is really striking me here! This negotiation thing is *very* practical, isn't it?

Covic

There's no question about it, David. In fact, as in the $3,600-per-hour example we discussed earlier, there are few people in our society who can earn as much money hourly as they could save in as little as a minute by being an effective negotiator. Again, you just can't earn money as fast as you can save money with good negotiating skills.

As Ben Franklin quipped, "A penny saved is a penny earned." It really equates to the same thing.

Wright

My impression of a negotiator is the guy who walks in and tries to settle strikes and those sorts of things.

Covic

Certainly, facilitating the settlement of strikes is a function that requires proficient negotiation skills. Usually in a situation like that it would be a specialist (mediator or arbitrator) rather than a generalist negotiator.

Parties enter into mediation voluntarily. The results are not binding upon either party.

On the other hand, parties enter into arbitration with the agreement that the results will be binding. They look to the arbitrator to come up with a final result for them.

Wright

So what is the biggest mistake people make in negotiating?

Covic

Being impatient has got to be the biggest mistake. As Americans we tend to want to rush to the bottom line. This is an unfortunate and usually very costly error. In any negotiation, the person who is under the least pressure for time usually prevails. So, try to find out at the very onset what the other party's time frame is; find out about their deadline or other sense of urgency.

The flip side of this is important as well. Try not to reveal your own time considerations. If it appears that you are in a hurry, it could easily create the impression you are overly eager.

Prudent negotiators play the opposite role. Savvy bargainers play the part of "the reluctant buyer."

Let's say you're out "kicking tires" on cars, for example, yet you're a legitimately qualified and truly motivated buyer. You've got the money in your pocket and you're ready to buy.

It pays to take a relaxed approach.

You might say to the salesperson, "Well geez, I'm just looking around. I don't really need to buy a car right now."

This puts you in a much more powerful position in negotiating the best price for a car.

Wright

So how can I maintain control in a negotiation?

Covic

Simply put, you maintain control by asking questions. The person who asks the most questions in a negotiation is the person who has the most power. The more you can get the other party to reveal about their real needs and goals in the transaction, the more likely you are to succeed.

Our primary job in a negotiation is to get, not give, information. It is to assemble, not disseminate, data. You've heard the old expression, "Information is power," right? Well, that's why we're actually in the negotiation in first place—to acquire information about the other party.

Learn to distinguish between their wants and their needs. Determine what undisclosed assets your negotiation partner possesses. What additional abilities does that person have to enhance the exchange equation? Always answer a question with a question. Avoid giving any information that you don't have to give.

Here is an example:

I pose the question, "David, what's the least you would consider accepting for your house?"

You answer my question with a question, "Well, gee, Bobby, I'm not sure. What's the maximum you would consider offering?"

Do you see how the dance goes? Avoid the "first person to mention a number" syndrome that Brian Epstein fell into to the extreme disadvantage of the Beatles.

Wright

What's the best way to relieve tension in a negotiation?

Covic

Use humor. When a situation gets tense, laughter cuts tension like a warm knife cuts butter. I call this the Foolishness Factor.

Humor humanizes. Self-deprecating humor is especially effective. Poke a little fun at yourself. It is disarming and endearing.

For example, let's say I am negotiating with Janie. The exchange heats up; it starts feeling tense.

I say, "Wow! It's getting pretty intense in here. I thought I had nerves of steel until I got eyeball-to-eyeball with you, Janie. Now I feel like a rank amateur. I've really got to say, you are *good!* Hey, what do you say we take a coffee break?"

People love levity; it tunes out the tension.

Wright

What is the power of personalization and how can it work in negotiating?

Covic

That's another very important question, David!

Okay. So for starters, let's set the stage. Today, we live in a world of technological anonymity. You try to reach somebody on the phone. More often than not, all you get is a recorded message or, worse yet, a digitized voice. People correspond more and more via e-mail. Instant messaging has replaced actual conversations. We send things overnight via Fed-Ex. No one even gets to wait for the mailman anymore.

Everything has become so impersonal; our communications have become increasingly depersonalized. We're all account numbers further distinguished only by our PIN numbers. We've become disembodied voices on answering machines, auto-responding e-mail recipients, statistics of a particular demographic, etc.

The power of personalization challenges us to break this tragic trend of technology. It challenges us to think of something unusual to set ourselves apart from others in the electronic void of facelessness.

Whether you're negotiating over the phone, via e-mail or through any other medium, harnessing the power of personalization can slant the odds significantly in your favor.

Here's how I used the power of personalization to make one of the best deals I ever made with the IRS:

My office represented a single mom; she was a hard-working restaurateur in Lake Tahoe. She was having a terribly tough time making a go of it. Her ex-husband left her with two young children, a floundering business and an IRS bill of around $30,000.

We offered the Feds $100. Needless to say, they laughed. They thought we were kidding. We weren't. I told them we were serious. They weren't amused, let alone impressed.

The case stalemated for well over two years. Eventually though, thanks to the power of personalization, the IRS Offer in Compromise Specialist ended up virtually handing me the case on a silver platter.

What happened? Well, one day I just happened to mention something to her about my cat. Come to find out, she was a cat lover herself. So, we engaged in a brief conversation about our mutual love for our felines. In the end, I promised to send her a color picture of my office cat, Mel, and me.

Now, I know this might be starting to sound a little ridiculous. And David, I know you might even be thinking, "Bobby, you're taking the Foolishness Factor one step too far on this one!"

Okay. I admit it—guilty as charged. My power of personalization philosophy is pretty liberal; it may even seem downright ludicrous. But regardless, I don't care how ridiculous a tactic may seem. If I think it will help make a better deal for a client, I will utilize it. As long as it is legal, moral, and ethical, I'll do anything I can for a client.

So anyway, in the next letter to my fellow cat-lover (as promised) I enclosed a color picture of Mel and me.

Bingo! The whole tone of that negotiation changed. The next time we talked, it was as though "Carla" and I had been the best of friends for our entire lives.

What happened? I took myself out of the depersonalized mode. I was no longer just another disembodied, silver-tongued sharpshooter trying to make an outrageous deal for a client. I became a real person—a soft, warm, and breathing person—a caring, kind, and cat-loving person.

I bonded with the person with whom I was dealing. The power of personalization leveled the playing field. It created a feeling of affinity between us. All kidding aside, it was truly a beautiful thing.

Finally, I got the call I'd been waiting over two years for. Carla said she was calling, first of all to say how beautiful she thought my cat was. After a little kitty-cat small talk, then came the zinger!

"You know, Bobby, I'm going to take your offer down the hall and run it past my group manager again. I really want to see if I can get it accepted for you."

And, guess what? She got it accepted! I was blown away. She got a $100 offer accepted against a $30,000 liability. Amazing, huh? People laugh when I tell them the story but I do things like that all the time. It works; so, why not?

Dream up something unusual that will set you apart. Power is yours for the taking when you personalize. So personalize, personalize, personalize.

Wright

I've got three cats; I'm going to try that one.

Covic

Yeah, with three cats maybe you could have made the same deal for $33.33!

Wright

I don't actually have any cats though, Bobby. I was just kidding with you. Anyway, as you probably know, cats don't have owners they have staff!

Covic

Oh yeah! I know all about *that!* I'm the supervisor of the cat staff in my office.

Wright

Okay, Bobby. Let's move on. You advise folks to "practice on the small stuff." What do you mean by that?

Covic

Well David, the secret to refining your negotiation skills is to convert every transaction in your day-to-day life into a negotiation exercise. So, regardless of how small the transaction, you want to use it as an opportunity to develop techniques that will come to your aid in larger transactions.

Think about it, now. Almost everything we do involves negotiating in one way or another. You've heard the expression, "I was negotiating my way through traffic." That's an example of yet another kind of negotiation—a physical negotiation.

Anyway, practice negotiating constantly. Utilize intention without reservation. You will succeed. It's like going to the gym—you build up muscles. Take professional football players, for instance. They exercise. They work out. They practice and they practice. They begin practicing well before the intensity of the competitive season even begins. So, when the big games do start, they're really prepared. They're in good shape because they practiced. So, in the same way, you want to hone your negotiation skills (i.e., practice on the small stuff). Practice daily! Practice at thrift shops; practice at garage sales. Keep practicing and practicing on higher and higher dollar items.

You will get better and better. You will become more and more sophisticated in each negotiation, regardless of the stakes. Sharpening your negotiation skills will save you a literal fortune over time.

Wright

Okay then, what would be an example of practicing on the small stuff, Bobby?

Covic

Here's a kind of silly, yet cute little story as an example for you, David. It demonstrates using something called "the flinch" as well as practicing on the small stuff:

My office manager's daughter, Katrina, came to work for us when she was young—sixteen or seventeen. I sent her down to the shoe repair shop with a pair of sandals. I instructed her to use the "flinch."

The flinch is a powerful tactic. You can use it in virtually any negotiation. It goes like this:

I ask you, "David, how much would you like for this car you're selling?"

You respond, "$15,000."

Now, watch this; it's deceptively simple.

I pause. I don't say anything; there's just silence. I let the tension mount. I look you in the eye. I tighten physically and exclaim with alarm, "$15,000!"

That's the flinch. I just feed your $15,000 figure right back to you—no other words—just the figure itself. I repeat it emphatically, unabashedly, and with incredulity. I express shock!

My physicality conveys my dismay just as if I had said, "How could you have possibly even come up with that number?"

Then, I'm silent again. In response, if you are like most folks, it is highly likely that you will start negotiating with yourself.

"Well, okay Bobby. I guess $15,000 does sound high; how about $12,500?"

Can you see how the flinch can make negotiating the easiest job in the world? When I've got you negotiating with yourself, it saves me the trouble. Talk about being in control!

Now, watch how Katrina practices on the small stuff using the flinch:

She walks into the shoe repair shop, plops the sandals down on the counter, and asks the owner, Ramon, how much the repair would cost.

Ramon: $12.

Katrina: (*flinch*) $12!

Ramon: Okay, $3.

Wow! He wanted $12. She flinched, remained silent, and listened. Ramon came back with $3. He wanted 400 percent more than how much he actually ended up agreeing to. And here's the best part of all: he negotiated the whole deal on Katrina's behalf.

You might rightfully ask, "Well, Bobby, who's got time to even listen to your dopey little story about saving $9 at the shoe repair shop?"

Well David, consider the 400 percent, not the $9. Think about the power of a technique like the flinch. Start learning how to use it on the small stuff. Your confidence will increase and you'll start getting better results on larger items almost immediately.

Again, I know this a story about small change. It's almost a throwaway—a gag. Yet, the principles (and the effect) are virtually the same even when you're dealing with things like real estate transactions in the six- and seven-digit figures.

Simple techniques like the flinch will seldom fail to come to your aid. They will work equally well for you in small and large dollar situations.

So, do yourself a big favor and make every small transaction a negotiating exercise. Keep practicing on higher and higher dollar items. And remember, the skills you develop by practicing on the small stuff will make you way more money in much less time than you could ever earn by working for it.

Wright

I've just learned another parenting skill I can use with my seventeen-year-old!

Covic

You need all the skills you can get, right?

Wright

What an interesting conversation. I have really learned a lot today, Bobby, and I really appreciate your taking this time to answer these questions for me. I can see why you're a national authority on this subject.

Covic

Thank you very much, David. It's been a pleasure talking with you and I wish you all the best for much negotiating success with the ideas we discussed today.

Wright

Today we've been talking with Bobby Covic. Bobby is a nationally recognized speaker and media personality known for his unique, entertaining, and inspiring perspectives on negotiation, overcoming overload, and creative conflict resolution. He's also a member of the National Speakers Association and the International Association of Professional Negotiators.

Bobby, thank you so much for being with us here on *The Masters of Impact Negotiating.*

About the Author

As an Enrolled Agent (EA), Bobby Covic is a federally authorized tax practitioner specializing in "crisis tax cases." He negotiates settlements for clients in IRS audit controversies, multi-year failure-to-file cases and large-dollar collection situations.

Formerly a National Tax Practice Institute faculty member, Bobby is the author of the popular book, *EVERYTHING'S NEGOTIABLE!* and the weekly newspaper column, *NEGOTIATING TODAY'S WORLD!*

He is a nationally recognized speaker and media personality known for his unique, entertaining and inspiring perspectives on negotiation, overcoming overload, and creative conflict resolution.

Bobby is a member of National Speakers Association and the International Association of Professional Negotiators.

R. R. "Bobby" Covic, EA
Bobby Covic & Associates
916 Southwood Boulevard, Suite 1-B
P.O. Box 6206
Incline Village, NV 89450-6206
Phone: 775.831.7694
Fax: 775.831.5328
E-mail: bobbycovic@aol.com
www.bobbycovic.com
www.negotiationcoach.net

Chapter 5

Bob Gibson

THE INTERVIEW

David Wright (Wright)

Today we're talking with Bob Gibson. Bob is a professional negotiator, consultant, and training expert. He's the founder of Negotiation Resources LLC, a San Francisco based consulting and training firm that began in 1987. His clients maintain he is masterful at teaching professional selling while maintaining profitability and integrity in the process. Clients appreciate the clear perspective, the insight, and business acumen Bob brings to his consulting and teaching assignments.

These abilities have made him an invaluable resource to corporate clients in North America, Mexico, Europe, Asia, and the Middle East. Recognized by the media for his expertise, Bob has written articles and has been featured in such publications as *Selling Power, Sales & Marketing Management* and has been featured nationally on CNBC television. His clients range from the financial community to manufacturing, from hi-tech to biotech, and he has taught business people worldwide to negotiate more effectively.

Bob, welcome to *The Masters of Impact Negotiating.*

Gibson

Thank you, it's good to be here.

Wright

Bob, tell us about Negotiation Resources.

Gibson

We're a consulting and training firm. I founded the company in 1987 to help people negotiate more effectively, and we accomplish that through consulting and training. On the consulting side of our business, we do the actual negotiation for our clients or we help teams prepare for a specific negotiation.

Our training seminars focus on teaching our clients to negotiate more effectively in a sales situation or in a work environment.

Wright

Do they come to you or can you take it on the road?

Gibson

Most of our work is done on-site at our client locations. Our work has taken us to North America, Mexico, Europe, and Asia. I went to the Middle East in April for the first time to Dubai and Oman. The principles of negotiation are universal, but the applications are specific. The principles we teach work anywhere in the world, but each assignment is tailored to the client's situation.

Wright

So why focus on negotiation as opposed to other business skills?

Gibson

I believe negotiation is the essential business skill, but one that is pretty much an untaught skill. That's true regardless of industry, regardless of geography, and regardless of culture. The one skill that must be in place for people to work together, for good business to happen, and to ensure profitability is negotiation.

Wright

All my life, when I've thought of a negotiator, I've thought of a back room filled with smoke and a bunch of guys with connections to some company fighting out schedules or deals; but that's really not what negotiation is all about, is it?

Gibson

Well it could be, but I don't believe that negotiation is limited to one situation or style. I believe that we negotiate all the time. The reality is, anytime someone feels a certain way about an issue and after a conversation they feel differently about that issue, a negotiation has taken place. It could be between a sales professional and a buyer, but it could be as simple as a mother and a child.

A negotiation is when someone moves emotionally from one point of view to another, and it could happen in a smoke-filled back room, but it's just as likely to happen in a business meeting. It's likely to happen on a golf course. It's likely to happen with two people talking at a water cooler.

After a good negotiation, you don't hear people saying things like, "He was tricky," or, "He had a lot of manipulations." You hear people saying phrases like, "I never looked at it that way before," or, "Oh, I never thought about that." When you hear statements like these, it lets you know a pretty skillful negotiator has been at work.

Wright

So what makes your negotiation training and methods unique?

Gibson

Four factors distinguish our work. To begin with, the training is down to earth—it's simple. It's not academic, and it's not theoretical.

I was raised in Texas trading horses and cattle. My Dad was in the construction business and I grew up listening to him trade everything from cattle to equipment. I've been the official route. I went through the Harvard Negotiation program; but the truth is, I learned more trading horses in Texas than I did at Harvard.

Our sales training is down to earth and it's easily understandable. When salespeople leave one of our sessions they're not saying, "That's interesting but how does that apply to me?" They're saying, "I can do this," and they can. We teach simple concepts and techniques that work well on the street.

Secondly, we're very good at teaching salespeople to articulate value. When they become skilled at building and communicating value, they can be great negotiators without having to resort to tricks and gimmicks and manipulations. We'll teach them tactics and tricks, but mainly so they can protect themselves when these are used against them.

Our process provides structure and specifics. This gives the sales force the ammunition needed to articulate value in the marketplace. Quite a bit of time is dedicated to practice. We drill the sales force until they have it.

Thirdly, we have created negotiation tools for the sales professional. Our "Street-Smart Negotiation Planner" is designed to reinforce the salesperson's thinking prior to a sales call. We have CDs and pocket reminders too. Changing behavior isn't easy and people need help implementing the new concepts and behaviors.

That leads us to number four. We follow up with a great coaching program to increase the "stick-ability" of the training. With e-mails, phone calls, and personal coaching, a salesperson has every opportunity to become a better negotiator.

Wright

I was very fascinated by your definition of negotiation being the point at which effort is converted into results. It really made sense to me. Will you explain the concept?

Gibson

Yes, let me give you an example. Someone will have a new idea for a commodity or a product. He or she runs it through R&D and decides to go with it. The time it takes to create and develop it could last from several months to a few years. Remember, there has been no money made on the product yet.

After the product is developed, it goes to marketing and they design a marketing campaign. They create an on-line campaign, they come up with brochures, and they turn it over to the copywriters. At long last, promotional materials are finally printed for the salespeople and still not a penny has been made.

After weeks, months, or even years, a salesperson is face-to-face with a potential buyer. We call this "the moment of truth." The negotiation in that meeting will determine, retroactively, the profitability of all the effort, all the time, all the energy, all the sweat, tears, and creativity. No one reaps a penny—there's no return on that investment until a salesperson sits down face-to-face in a selling situation, determines the customer's interest, and negotiates the deal. That moment is the point during which all the effort is converted into results!

Wright

I've really waited for this next question. You're well known for saying, "Sales ability determines gross receipts but negotiating ability determines profits." Would you explain that?

Gibson

Yes, this is an important distinction. I was a salesperson and a sales manager before I started this company and I learned from experience. If you are a good salesperson and a poor negotiator, you still aren't making your company any money. It's a problem that most sales managers fight.

I'll go into a company and we'll look at the sales numbers, and a profile emerges. A salesperson's gross receipts are good, their repeat business is good, their clients love them to death, and they're very good with people. But when you analyze the numbers, you might find the profitability of their accounts is below where it should be. That's a profile of someone who's a good salesperson, but a poor negotiator. While sales ability does determine the gross receipts, it's negotiating ability that determines the profitability.

I find most sales negotiations have a profit margin swing of at least two to five points. We've been able to affect some margins dramatically, up to twenty points. That money goes straight to the bottom line. When I say sales ability determines gross receipts but negotiating ability determines profits, I mean that in a very literal way.

Wright

You've just answered the question better than anyone else as to the difference between sales and negotiation.

Gibson

Sales is the ability to bring in business; negotiation is the ability to bring in profitable business.

Wright

Now I see it, so what's a common mistake that salespeople make in negotiations?

Gibson

Most salespeople leave money on the table. They give away too much, too easily, too fast. A client captured the essence of the problem recently when he said, "Bob, my sales force's greatest strength is that they're people-people, and their greatest weakness is that they're people-people." Because they have a need to be liked, and because they're afraid they're going to lose the account, they give away too much, too fast, too easily. They're driven by the fear that they're going to lose the business and they let a customer draw the box around price instead of value. That's the most common negotiation mistake I see in salespeople.

Wright

Absolutely. In your negotiation training do you teach methods of correcting that?

Gibson

Yes. We'll teach them how to build value, to position the company, the product, or service to get out of the commodity box. They must become masters at articulating value. That's key.

Wright

No wonder I bought that car! I promised myself for many, many years that I wouldn't drive a high-priced car. When I met someone extremely gifted at articulating value, that all changed. He never did talk price but he kept on talking value. I drove the car off the lot that day and am still driving it.

So how do you help salespeople negotiate when everything is so price driven these days?

Gibson

Let's go back to the point we were talking about before. It's only price-driven if you let the buyer make it price-driven, and that's their job. Procurement people and buyers are going to always tell you it's about price, and it will be unless you're skillful at changing that negotiation to a discussion about value.

First, salespeople have to understand how the game works. They must know what to do. Next, they must practice their skills and get good at them. I tell groups all over the world that negotiation is more akin to golf or karate than any other skill. It's not enough to know how it works. Negotiation is about practicing and improving your skills.

Wright

Would you say something about value? How does value manifest itself in the mind of the buyer?

Gibson

Here's a key concept we cover in our sessions:

There are always two negotiations taking place simultaneously—the obvious, conventional one on top of the table, concerning issues. Are they going to buy? How many are they buying? What are they paying? Which color? When do they need them?

But another negotiation—a subtle, complex negotiation—goes on "under the surface" and isn't just about business issues.

It's about *Who-You-Are,* and *Who-They-Are.*

There are always two levels of drivers. One level is for the company, and for the business. These are business drivers. Most negotiations take place at this level.

Effective negotiators go beyond just these business drivers and use personal drivers and issues as well. What's driving this person on the other side of the desk? To come to agreement with buyers, you not only have to give them what they want but you also have to give them what they want "under the surface." Many people say they want the same thing. The truth is they may want it for very different reasons.

Here's an example of three young women in Los Angeles who all want to go into acting:

Secretly, Amy may not enjoy acting per se, but wants to be famous and a celebrity. She dreams of stepping out of a limo onto the red carpet with the flashbulbs popping.

With Britney, it's the money. She envies the earning power of the stars on top of the heap. When she contemplates the possibility of earning several million dollars for a few months of work, she sees the road to security for herself and her young daughter.

Carol just enjoys the acting experience—the process of getting inside the head of another person and capturing the essence of that individual. She considers herself an artist and would act for nothing.

These young women all want the same thing—a career in acting—but for very different reasons. They are driven by different forces "under the surface."

They would all be open to enrolling in an acting class, and the specifics of that class—what's on top of the table—would be the same for each of them: what's being taught, class times, class size, where it's taught, and the instructor. What's under the surface is very different for them, and the skillful negotiator would use very different carrots to entice them.

Buyers are no different than this group of women. In business (and in life) we are driven by different forces. Many want *power* and *control*. Many want *wealth*. Many want *security*. Some want *harmony*. We live in a cynical world, but I find people everywhere who are driven by a need to be *fair*—to do the right thing.

To others, *being right* drives their actions. *Approval* is a motivator for many, as is *attention*. We've already said the Achilles heel of many salespeople is a *desire to be liked*.

Another example is my iPod. A technical person may be turned on by the number of gigs and battery life because they're driven by obtaining technical knowledge. That's not what turns me on. An iPod alters the travel experience for me. When I get on a plane and there's a crying kid, I don't sweat it. I just pull out my iPod, put on my noise canceling headphones, and I'm out of there!

Salespeople obviously have to be able to convey what something does, the technical features, and the business benefits. That's a given. In addition, a sales negotiator must be able to read people's drivers. Find out what's "under the surface" for someone and you have the keys to the city. You have access to the levers that work the top of the table.

Wright

That makes sense. I see exactly what you are talking about. So what key advice would you give salespeople who want to become better negotiators?

Gibson

You know, a couple of things. One, understand that it's a skill, not some God-given gift. It's like most things in life—if you learn how it works and practice, you get better. Just a little side note: you can continue to get better your entire life.

I'm a golfer, and I'm not as flexible as I was several years ago. No one confuses me with Tiger Woods. But you know what's great? Instead of declining with age, negotiation is a skill that should get better every decade of your life. Because it depends on judgment and insight and business acumen, you should be a better negotiator in your thirties than you were in your twenties. You should be better in your forties than you were in your thirties. There's no reason you shouldn't get better every decade.

The advice I give people is simple: read, listen, study, learn how negotiation works, and practice. You can get very good at this and it will affect everything in your life, not just your sales.

Wright

What an interesting conversation and I just can imagine how well you do with your clients. No wonder they rave about you. I really appreciate your taking all this time with me today Bob, to answer these questions and you certainly have added to our book. I know our readers are going to be really interested in your methods of negotiation.

Today we have been talking with Bob Gibson who is a professional negotiator, consultant, and trainer. Now we know why his clients appreciate the clear perspective, the insight, and business acumen Bob brings to his teaching assignments. His clients range from the financial community to manufacturing, from hi-tech to biotech, and he has taught businesspeople worldwide to negotiate more effectively.

Bob, thank you so much for being with us today on *The Masters of Impact Negotiating.*

Gibson

Thank you.

About the Author

Bob Gibson is a Negotiation Strategist. He is masterful at teaching businesspeople how to make deals work while maintaining profitability and integrity in the process.

Bob has assured the business success of his clients since founding Negotiation Resources in 1987. In addition to negotiating for clients in the corporate arena, Bob advises and coaches middle to senior level executives and has trained tens of thousand of business people. His STREET-SMART® NEGOTIATION SERIES has proven an effective vehicle to convey his decades of real-world experience to business people in America, Europe, Canada, Mexico, Asia, and the Middle East. "How to Negotiate High-profit Sales" is the most requested offering of the series.

Recognized by the media for his expertise, Bob has written articles and has been featured in such publications as *Selling Power, Sales and Marketing Management,* and *Your Company,* and been featured nationally on CNBC television.

His clients appreciate the clear perspective, the insight, and business acumen Bob brings to both forging business agreements and his teaching. These abilities have made him an invaluable resource to corporations in the U.S. and around the world.

Bob Gibson
Negotiation Resources, LLC
633 Ridgewood Ave.
Mill Valley, CA 94941
Phone: 800.572.8005
E-mail: bgibson@negotiationresources.com
www.negotiationresources.com

Chapter 6

BILL DOCHERTY BA (HONS) CA

THE INTERVIEW

David Wright (Wright)

Today we're talking with Bill Docherty from the United Kingdom (U.K.). Bill brings thirty years of experience in negotiation on behalf of the U.K. government and international businesses to business owners and entrepreneurs. Bill is a Chartered Accountant and was a U.K. head in one of the top four global firms of chartered accountants leading a specialist team of negotiators.

Bill has spoken to such groups as the Institute of Chartered Accountants of Scotland, The Institute of Directors, and The Academy for Chief Executives. He is a member of the Manchester Chapter of the Professional Speakers Association and the International Speakers Network.

Bill Docherty, welcome to *The Masters of Impact Negotiating.*

Bill Docherty (Docherty)

Thank you very much for that.

Wright

What is the essence of the new "Relaxed Panther Approach" to negotiations and how does this differ from the traditional approach to negotiations?

Docherty

The essence of the new "Relaxed Panther Approach to Negotiations" is that it incorporates a holistic approach to negotiations. The approach recognizes the interaction between the negotiator and the client and the importance of managing the physical and attitudinal aspects of the negotiation.

In negotiations, 90 percent of a negotiator's effectiveness comes from focusing on how the negotiation is presented physically and attitudinally. The approach then moves on to understanding how clients arrive at decisions in a negotiation and allows the negotiator to be able to predict their clients' decision strategies, which they will use in the negotiations before they meet them.

When the negotiator meets the clients the negotiator is able to identify the clients' first level processing patterns and how the clients use these patterns to arrive at their decisions. The negotiator can adapt the approach in real time to have the maximum persuasive influence on the clients he or she is negotiating with.

This ability to predict and react in real time to the specific approach being adopted by clients puts the negotiator at the cutting edge of negotiation.

This approach differs from the traditional approach where 90 percent of the preparation time for negotiations is spent on the negotiation issues. This new approach is focused on the negotiator's internal preparation and being able to predict the clients' decision strategies and patterns. The negotiator is able to make use of the information and signals coming from the clients in real time.

Wright

What is the importance of considering negotiations from "fixed pie" and "expanding pie" perspectives?

Docherty

The differences between "fixed pie" and "expanding pie" approaches to negotiation are vitally important. Whenever you consider negotiations from a fixed pie perspective, it means you are only negotiating on price. The consequence of fixed pie negotiations is that prices will be forced down over time and many businesses will go out of business.

An example of the fixed pie approach and its effect on business occurred in the accounting profession during the '70s and '80s where accounting firms started to "low ball" on the price of audits. I believe a direct consequence of that price war was the major catastrophe in the audit world contributing to major company collapses. We are now starting to see a move away from negotiating purely on price for audits and concentrating on other qualitative issues. As a consequence, audit prices have been increasing substantially in the last few years.

The expanding pie approach happens when, in any negotiation, both parties negotiate to expand both businesses. The result of businesses starting to think about how they can expand their clients' business and their own business at the same time is to create new and innovative ideas for both businesses. The negotiation is then about how they share in the enhanced profits and not on how they will battle over price.

Wright

Will you explain the importance of the use of a person's body to establish rapport and to interpret nonverbal signals?

Docherty

In workshops for The Academy of Chief Executives during the development of the "Relaxed Panther Approach to Negotiation" I established that there was a 100 percent correlation between the success of a negotiation in a team and the state of rapport being exhibited by the participants. I found that as I observed them in the negotiations I could tell, just by looking at the rapport and use of their bodies—their body language—whether they would be successful in achieving an expanded pie result or whether they would deadlock. In a room with negotiations being carried on simultaneously based on the same facts, independent observers could also predict the outcome of the negotiations by the negotiator's body language during the negotiation. They could do this without listening to the words used during the negotiation.

As a negotiator you should be aware of and take charge of how you use your body to convey multiple messages during a negotiation.

During negotiations, many levels of subconscious and conscious communication are being exchanged which have nothing to do with what is being said and which can be completely at odds with what is said.

In the course of observing and taking part in hundreds of negotiations, the conclusion I have reached is that people will listen to your body more than they will listen to your words in a negotiation.

The negotiator's body language will account for 92 percent of the communication in a negotiation and the words will only account for 8 percent. This is quite frightening for people who have passed through school, college, university, and professional exams where they have been taught that the words are all they need to succeed. Suddenly we're going into negotiations where we've now been told it's the attitude and body language which accounts for 92 percent of your effectiveness and only 8 percent is what is said.

The ability to interpret non-verbal signals and to control and understand nonverbal signals is of vital importance in any negotiation. Whenever you are able to build rapport with individuals you are negotiating with, it is more difficult for them to disagree with you.

Wright

Please tell us about any interesting research being done that has a high impact on current negotiations.

Docherty

There's been some fascinating work carried out at Arizona State University and Harvard University. Over the past ten to fifteen years they've been looking at the importance and the reasons for doing certain things during negotiation.

Robert Cialdini has published some fascinating work in this area on the importance of reciprocation and the timing of reciprocation in negotiation. What Cialdini has established is that when you negotiate and you drop your price, you set up a requirement for the other side to reciprocate back to you. This is one of the basic tenets of society—whenever you do something for others, they are obligated to do something for you.

The timing of when to move to a reciprocation price is contained in the concept of power moments. A power moment only occurs in the time frame of your current negotiation; you cannot leave and come back to a negotiation because if you do so, when you return it will be considered that you have started a new negotiation.

In any negotiation, therefore, you should have your ideal price and a reciprocation price that is slightly lower and you should move to the reciprocation price in the original session. The movement does not have to be large. It is the concept of movement that sets up reciprocation.

When they talk about their products or services during a negotiation, the majority of people emphasize that their product or service is the best. They never talk about a weakness in their product or service. When people are negotiating for a product or service they want to be working with an expert and not a salesman. They are looking for a valued business advisor. One of the defining elements of being an expert is the ability to say, "Yes, we are very good, but there is an area where we are not satisfied." Whenever you say you wish to improve an aspect of your product or service, you are considered to be acting as an expert. The person you are negotiating with will consider that you are being open and honest and that person will be more inclined to arrive at an expanded pie solution.

Wright

Will you explain what you mean by your concept of "power points" and "power moments"?

Docherty

In any room there will be a power point. If you occupy that power point you will have maximum power in relation to everyone else in the room.

When you enter a room you have to recognize and occupy the power point to establish your presence.

In any space, to occupy the power point you have to occupy the center of the available space. Your body should be equidistant from any solid objects around you.

When you are shown into a room to await the other negotiators, you should rearrange the furniture to maximize your power point. If you're sitting at a table, you should move your chair back from the table to create space around you. Whenever you are standing in negotiations you should occupy the center of the available space.

Whenever you occupy the power point, if you take a step backward or a step forward, you change the emotional reaction of the other people in the room to you and this affects the way you and they will negotiate. Once you calibrate the effect of power points you will understand the power of presence in negotiation.

Power moments occur in many negotiations. When you recognize a power moment and react in real time, you will gain a future advantage. A power moment occurs when you're negotiating with someone and that person challenges your price. Many people will say, "Let me go away and think this through and I'll come back to you with an alternative." Remember, whenever you leave the negotiation and return, you lose your moment of power. When you return to the negotiation the person you are negotiating with will consider the second meeting as the start of a completely fresh negotiation without regard to what has happened previously.

If you are aware of power moments you will have prepared a response which you can give immediately in the same negotiation and say something like, "Well, I've already thought about this and this is what I propose." When you modify either your offering or your price in the first negotiation without leaving the meeting you set up a power moment based on reciprocation. The immediate movement sets the client up for reciprocation in behaviour later in the negotiation. This power moment only applies in the moment, it does not apply if you leave the meeting and come back.

The second power moment occurs after you have made a concession in negotiation. The power moment presents itself whenever the client says to you, "Thank you for doing that for me." Many people will say, "That is okay, it's what we do." To make use of the power moment, after thank you, you should say immediately, "I know you'd do the same for me." You have to say the phrase *immediately* after you are thanked. When you use these words, the person will nod or say, "Yes." Later in the negotiation, when you wish something to be done for you, the person is obligated at a subconscious and conscious level to reciprocate because he or she agreed to it earlier in the negotiation.

Wright

What is the importance of the right-hand side and toes in negotiation together with the two-dimensional and three-dimensional body position?

Docherty

From working with thousands of people I've found that whenever you wish to have maximum impact upon an individual, you should always negotiate from his or her right-hand side. This applies to approximately 98 percent of the population. People feel most comfortable with you on their right-hand side. This goes back to the way they process information. For the majority of people, whenever they are processing new information or creating their future, they look toward the right. By placing yourself in that field of vision on their right-hand side, you are putting yourself effectively in their future and that's exactly where you want to be whenever you're negotiating.

When I talk about the importance of toes in my workshops many clients usually think I've lost the plot and left the planet. Toes give us vital information based on where they are pointing. Whenever you are negotiating you should have your left-hand toes pointing at the person on your left in the room and your right-hand toes pointing toward the person on your right. This stance includes all the people you're negotiating with. If you change your toe position and point both toes directly at a single individual you change the energy flow that's happening in a negotiation. You effectively produce a form of tunnel energy or vision between you and the individual. You can use this to create tension in your negotiations.

Where you place your hands in a negotiation affects the way people interpret your intentions. In any negotiation, whenever you are making statements and listening to statements from the other side you should have your hands open at all times with your palms pointing toward the people you are negotiating with. If possible, your client should be able to see the empty palms of your hands.

Whenever you bring your hands together you create tension across your shoulders and you appear to disappear within yourself; that tension will be picked up by the people you're negotiating with. Your client wants to negotiate with a relaxed, confident negotiator, not with someone who has disappeared within himself or herself.

The concept of two-dimensional and three-dimensional body positioning is important in negotiations. Actors and opera singers use three-dimensional body positions to interact with people onstage and with the audience. Whenever you are negotiating with a client, remember to stand or sit at a forty-five degree angle and not directly opposite. A forty-five degree angle is a three-dimensional stance; directly facing someone is two-dimensional. You should be careful about standing two-dimensionally—facing your client directly sets up tension. You should always stand at a forty-five degree angle. The person you're negotiating with will feel more relaxed. As you negotiate with your client, you will feel more relaxed. This relaxed state will help to provide an expanded pie perspective—you're looking for the best result and an enhanced profitability for both companies.

If you wish to make a serious point during a negotiation you should change your body position from three-dimensional to two-dimensional. This means you should point your body, toes, and hands directly at the individual. Whenever you become two-dimensional you will create a high amount of energy flow or tension between you and the individual. As a consequence you also exclude everyone else in the room from the negotiation for the time you are two-dimensional. You can use the two-dimensional position to make a specific or important point in the negotiation to a specific individual in the room.

Wright

You talk of the "physical filter" and "conversation filters" establishing the outcome of negotiations within seconds of meeting the individuals. Will you expand on these?

Docherty

As we live moment-by-moment, every one of us receives millions of pieces of information about our environment—about what's happening around us. The conscious mind can only deal with between five and seven pieces of information at any one time. Whenever you go beyond seven pieces of information, you go into an altered state.

In the first two seconds of meeting someone you identify between five and seven physical characteristics of the individual. If you walk into a room with your eyes looking down at the carpet, your hands clutching your papers in front of you, you'll be regarded by people in the room as being slightly timorous—someone who won't make decisions—even before you say hello.

How do people judge you in such a short time? Everyone identifies between five and seven five pieces of information about anyone they meet for the first time—where the person's eyes are looking, how the head is being held, how the shoulders are held, what the individual's hands are doing, and whether the person looked directly into the eyes of the people in the room upon coming through the door.

People take this limited information and at a subconscious level search their memories for how people behaved in earlier relationships where they had these specific physical characteristics. They extrapolate their remembered experiences and place them into the individual they are meeting. This process takes less than two seconds. In those two seconds a judgment is made about how the person is going to negotiate and whether it will be successful or not.

In our busy lives we tend not to think about the physical filter that is represented by the first two seconds of meeting. To maximize our success we have to manage these two seconds.

When you enter a room to negotiate, the first physical characteristic people look for is immediate and direct eye contact with everyone in the room. They then look for where your shoulders are—shoulders should be slightly back. You should manage your breathing so that it is originating from your diaphragm. People will also be looking to see how you are holding your hands. In any negotiation you should keep your hands apart at all times; ideally you should show the palms of your hands at all times to the people you are negotiating with. To maximize your impact upon entering a room, you should open the door, take a step and stop to scan the people in the room before you enter the room. You should also smile to soften the authoritative air you have just created by your pause.

Wright

Is it true that you become a "thirty-foot black panther" when you enter into negotiations and how can individuals use this technique in their negotiations to develop negotiation confidence?

Docherty

When I want to feel confident, I imagine that I am a black panther. Then I imagine I become progressively taller, becoming one inch taller, one foot taller, and then thirty feet tall. When I reach the height of thirty feet I imagine myself as having blazing red eyes and large claws. I look at people I am negotiating with and my internal reaction is that nothing can affect me as a thirty-foot tall relaxed panther. Additionally, a thirty-foot tall, relaxed panther does not have anything to prove.

In my workshops I have found that female executives like to become thirty-foot tall giraffes. I think this has something to do with long, elegant necks and being quite gentle yet able to frighten off tigers and other menacing animals with their hooves.

A number of people who imagine becoming thirty feet tall find that they magnify some of the characteristics they don't like about themselves. It is for this reason that the alternative of becoming a black panther or a thirty-foot tall teddy bear or a giraffe or an American football player allows them to shift their perspective and leave behind their fears and unwanted characteristics during the negotiation.

The concept of conversational filters applies in all negotiations. We have already considered the "physical filter" which occurs in the first two seconds of meeting. The "conversational filter" immediately follows once we start talking. Your first three to five sentences determine how you will be treated during the course of the negotiations after the physical filter has been established.

The first three to five sentences should be about upbeat topics—topics that have energy and that deal with things which can be seen by both parties in the room. If the first three to five sentences are downbeat or discouraging, the conversational filter will apply and the person you are negotiating with will want to stop the negotiation as soon as possible. That person will also predict how you will react either in a positive or negative way later in the negotiation based on the conversational filter.

Wright

The use of time is an important concept in your approach to negotiations. How does this work and what is the background to this?

Docherty

Using time in negotiations mirrors the training undertaken by Olympic athletes. When they are training for the Olympics they imagine how they will feel after they have won and analyze how they performed in their competition. They go forward in time to a point just after they've competed and then look back in time at how they achieved their performance.

Applying this time-based approach to negotiations changes your perception during the negotiation process because you are subconsciously negotiating from a perspective of success. From this perspective you have already achieved the end result you wished for from the negotiation and you are able to look back on how you achieved the end result. This gives you a fresh perspective—a confident, relaxed perspective.

When people think about a forthcoming negotiation and look forward from the present into the future, many people tend to see the obstacles and objections together with all the things that could go wrong in a negotiation. This causes a reduction in calm self-confidence when they start to negotiate. By changing the time perspective and looking back from having achieved success, people know that no matter what the obstacles are, they have already achieved a successful outcome. They will then work to achieve a solution to any problem they are faced with during the negotiation on the basis that they have already solved the problem.

Wright

You have developed a "negotiation wheel" that identifies the main decision patterns used by negotiators. Will you explain the concept of the wheel and the main decision patterns?

Docherty

I became fascinated by the processes involved in negotiating with people over the past thirty years. I realized there were specific patterns in negotiations and specific decision strategies used by different types of people in organizations.

When these strategies were analyzed it became clear there were fourteen main strategies that covered the majority of negotiating situations. As the strategies emerged it became clear that the strategies were grouped in patterns that could be predicted and applied to individuals who occupied specific roles in organizations. The exciting discovery was that, without having met the individual, and only knowing his or her position in the organization, that individual's decision strategies could be predicted and the pattern that he or she adopted could be identified using the "Negotiating Profiling Wheel©."

Everyone uses these decision strategies and groups them to create a negotiation pattern. The Negotiating Profiling Wheel makes identifying the strategies and predicting the patterns easily accessible for negotiators so that whenever they enter into negotiations they will be able to recognize the particular decision strategy and predict the pattern that will be followed by the person they are negotiating with. This allows them to structure the way they will negotiate and to react in real time with the correct approach to satisfy the strategy of the person they are negotiating with.

Negotiation Profiling Wheel©

THE MAIN STRATEGIES ARE:

"Don't wanters"

These people know what they don't want. They know what they wish to avoid, however, they may not have a clear picture of what they want.

"Wanters"

These people know exactly what they want. In their desire to achieve results, many of them do not know what they should avoid in order to minimize risks.

"Jobsworth"

These people's concern is for procedures. They will want to know exactly what they have to do at every step of the negotiation. You should advise them of the procedures you use in your firm when negotiating with them.

"Explorers"

These people are always exploring for new and different ways of doing things. They will change procedures just to see what happens.

"WIIFM" (What's In It For Me)

These people are always interested in what the result will be for themselves. They typically only hear what they want to hear. They are usually short-term managers with organizations.

Wright

Do you mean what's in it for them personally or what's in it for the company?

Docherty

WIIFM people are only concerned with how the proposal or negotiation will affect them personally. They will typically be people who are in organizations at the managerial level for a short time before they move on. They base their decisions on the effect it will have on making them a more experienced or better businessperson. They hear the points you make that affect their personal position and tend not to hear or pay attention to issues that affect the company as a whole.

"WIIFO" (What's In It For Others)

These people are interested in the good of the organization rather than what's in it for themselves. They are typically long-term managers with organizations.

"Traditional"

These people base their decisions on what has happened in the past and like small changes because radical change frightens them. When negotiating with them you always have to refer to what has happened in the past.

"New"

These people are always looking for new ideas and notice what is different in a situation. They base their decisions on introducing new concepts and new ideas into the organization.

"Broadbrush"

These people only want to know high level conceptual descriptions. If you present them with very detailed arguments they will be turned off.

"Detail seekers"

These people need to have lots of detail provided to them before they come to any conclusion about the concept as a whole. If you do not have the detail immediately at hand you will not be successful with them in your negotiations.

"Quick-time"

I really enjoy negotiating with quick-time people because they are always prepared to conclude the negotiation at the first meeting. Invariably they will be late for meetings and the meetings will run beyond the allocated time but they will make a decision.

"Slow time"

Slow-time people start negotiating in January, continue the negotiations through spring, summer, and fall. It may take them years to conclude a negotiation. When negotiating with slow-time people you have to be prepared for a long drawn out process before concluding the negotiation. Slow-time people will always be on time for their meetings and will consider it a personal insult if you are late for a meeting with them.

"Networkers"

Networkers will only arrive at a decision after they have talked to other people in the company and obtained external references. They need to hear other people's views before they will arrive at a decision. When dealing with Networkers you should ensure that you have a client list and reference sites where they can talk to the Chief Executive Officer of a number of companies.

"Commanders"

Commanders want to be given the facts in any situation. They resist other people's opinions because they consider that their role is to make their minds up based on the facts. When negotiating with commanders ensure that you keep your opinions to yourself.

Wright

I understand that you are able to predict how individuals in companies will negotiate, even though you have never met them. How is this done?

Docherty

The fourteen decision-making strategies can be grouped into patterns that attach to specific positions in a company. The strategies have been placed on the Negotiation Profiling Wheel© which allows you to identify and predict between five and seven strategies that will be adopted by an individual occupying the particular position in a company. Once you have worked your way around the Negotiation Profiling Wheel© you will be able to structure your negotiation specifically for any individual. When you meet with them you will find that you are between 80 percent and 100 percent correct in the way you approach the negotiation.

In this chapter we have been able to touch on some of the key characteristics of the Negotiation Profiling Wheel©, however, there is additional material on its use and application.

Applying the Negotiation Profiling Wheel© we can predict how a chief executive officer (CEO), a managing director, a finance director, a senior manager, and a junior manager will negotiate. We can also predict a variety of other job positions and occupations.

As an example of the pattern prediction from the Negotiation Profiling Wheel© we will look at the predicted pattern for a CEO.

Recent research established that the operating life of a CEO in a quoted company in the U.K. was eighteen months. The decision strategies of CEOs will, therefore, be influenced by this short timeframe.

The decision strategies and resulting pattern of a CEO will be as follows:

They will be "Wanters"—knowing exactly what they want.

They will be "Explorers"—always exploring new ways of doing things.

They will be "WIIFOs"—always thinking about what's in it for others.

They will be always searching for what is new in technology and thinking. In addition, they will always be searching for what can be different in their organization.

They will be "Broadbrush" in their approach, wanting to discuss the high level strategy and leave the detail for their managers.

They will be "Commanders" and will only want the facts to make their minds up about how they will act. They will not want to spend any time on considering other people's opinions.

They will be "Quick Time" in making their decisions. Once they start considering an issue they will work at it until they come to a conclusion.

Another example would be the pattern adopted by an accountant or banker. Their decision strategies and final pattern will be as follows:

They will be "Don't Wanters."

They will be "Jobsworth" in that they will abide by their procedures and expect you to do the same.

They will be "WIIFOs"—interested in what's in it for others.

They will be "Traditional"—looking for how things were done in the past and only supporting new approaches if they incorporate the traditional procedures.

They will be "detail seekers" who will require you to have a solid grip on the fine detail of any proposal or negotiation.

They will also be "Commanders"—looking for the facts and rejecting opinions that are offered to them. They will make up their own minds based on the facts.

They will be "Slow-time" people in arriving at their decisions. When negotiating with them they will see the negotiation as being over a long period of time.

When you look at each of the positions people have in business—a managing director, executive manager, a sales director, a long-term manager, innovators, people in certain industries such as media—you can predict, with a high level of certainty how they will negotiate by working around the Negotiation Profiling Wheel©.

By adopting this approach a negotiator can enter into negotiations having predicted in advance how the people he or she will negotiate with will arrive at their decisions and the overall pattern that they will adopt.

The Negotiation Profiling Wheel© will allow negotiators to structure the way they present their negotiations to have the maximum persuasive effect on the decision strategies of the person they are negotiating with. With the Negotiation Profiling Wheel© approach we are moving away from the traditional negotiation approach of having opening and closing strategies, to one where a negotiator can understand and predict how people will negotiate and how to negotiate with them to achieve expanded pie outcomes to negotiations.

Wright

What an interesting conversation. I really appreciate your taking all this time with me. I know you're in the U.K. and I'm in the United States—are we a day apart, or hours apart?

Docherty

We have a six-hour time difference.

I really enjoyed talking with you; it's been a pleasure.

Wright

Thank you so much.

Today we've been talking with Bill Docherty who brings thirty years of experience in negotiations on behalf of the U.K. government and international businesses to business owners and entrepreneurs.

Bill, thank you so much for being with us today on *The Masters of Impact Negotiating.*

About the Author

BILL DOCHERTY brings thirty years of experience in negotiation on behalf of the UK government and international businesses to business owners and entrepreneurs. Bill is a Chartered Accountant and was a UK Head in one of the top four global firms of chartered accountants leading a specialist team of negotiators.

Bill has spoken to such groups as the Institute of Chartered Accountants of Scotland, the Institute of Directors, and the Academy for Chief Executives. He is a member of the Manchester Chapter of the Professional Speakers Association and the International Speakers Network.

Bill Docherty BA (hons) CA
Persuasion
1 Linden Road
Didsbury Manchester M20 2QJ England
Tel: 00 44 161 434 6292
E-mail: billdocherty@persuasion.uk.com
www.persuasion.uk.com

Chapter 7

CAMILLE SCHUSTER, PH.D.

THE INTERVIEW

David Wright (Wright)

Today we're talking to Camille Schuster. Camille has a Ph.D. from Ohio State University. She's currently a full professor of Marketing and International Business at California State University, San Marcos. Dr. Schuster has also taught at Xavier University, Arizona State University, Garvin School of International Business, Virginia Polytechnic Institute and State University, and Indiana University Northwest. Dr. Schuster co-authored a book titled *Global Business: Planning for Sales and Negotiations* with Michael Copeland from Procter & Gamble. She also co-authored a book titled *The Consumer . . . Or Else! Consumer-Centric Business Paradigms* with Don Dufek, retired senior vice president and officer of The Kroger Company. Dr. Schuster wrote *The Rise of Consumer Power: Adopting the Right Marketing Strategies,* published in Singapore. Dr. Schuster has conducted seminars and given lectures to over sixty companies in more than twenty countries around the world.

Dr. Schuster welcome to *The Masters of Impact Negotiating.*

Camille Schuster

Thank you very much.

Wright

Does the business negotiation process work the same way all across the world? If not, how is it different?

Schuster

The basic process is the same in terms of the steps that are used, but they're not used the same way, they're not emphasized the same way, and the implementation is hugely different.

Wright

You mean from culture to culture?

Schuster

Yes, from culture to culture. The model that Mike Copeland and I have developed looks at the difference between the emphasis on tasks and relationships. There are some countries in the world that emphasize getting the job done, getting the job done on time, on budget, and on schedule. There are other cultures around the world that look at making sure you understand who the people are with whom you're working, making sure that you feel comfortable with the people, that you trust the people, and that you know them. The Japanese talk about it being heart-to-heart communications—making sure you have basically the same understanding, values, and goals, and then you attack the task. And to all those people who emphasize the task, this whole beginning part is a waste of time. So both sides don't really use the process the same way and there ends up being a lot of confusion and frustration.

Wright

So what's the biggest mistake people make when going to another country to negotiate a business deal?

Schuster

The biggest mistake is assuming that the way people in other countries do business is the way that everyone else does business. As a result, expectations are very often not met. If you take people from your company who are the best at negotiating in your country and send them somewhere else where the culture is very different, they come back very frustrated and the business deals generally don't work out very well. As a matter of fact, in the United States about 70 percent of the joint ventures with companies in other countries in which we get involved don't work out after about a year and a half.

Wright

Just not on the same page?

Schuster

They're not on the same page because their goals are different. In the United States we assume that people are in business to make a profit and we expect that all decisions are made with generating a profit as the major goal. Not everybody around the world does that.

Wright

I remember someone told me years ago that his company was doing business with China and he made the mistake of saying something dumb that had to do with asking them why they didn't understand whatever it was that they couldn't understand. The Chinese businessman told him, "You know, your country's been doing business for 200 years and we've been doing business for thousands of years."

Schuster

Yes.

Wright

That puts it into perspective—

Schuster

And so when you ask why don't they do it the way we do it, people in other countries have developed their traditions over a long period of time and things work well in their environment using their methods.

Wright

Right, so how can someone prepare for negotiation in every country?

Schuster

It's important to try to figure out how people from that cultural perspective think, how they view business, and what values are important to them; not so you learn how to do business in the way they do—that's not really the point. You're never going to become a cultural native and you don't really want to, but, if you understand how they view decision-making, how they view business processes, and what the goal of doing business is for them, you can adapt your strategies so you can be more successful.

A businessperson who was in a seminar that I was doing spent a week in Canada with a client. At the end of the week his client looked at him and said, "You know, this is the first time someone from the U.S. has spent some time with me and I haven't gotten pissed off."

Wright

Oh my! Isn't the World Trade Organization creating a standardization in transparency in business all around the world?

Schuster

It's trying but it's not there yet, and it's going to be a long time before it happens; but that is the goal. That goal works really well in North America and Northwestern and Central Europe. For the rest of the world, transparency is a huge change because for transparency to work it means there needs to be a rule of law, a well established government and financial process. In most of the world that does not exist, so you can't really rely on the regulations to protect you.

Wright

You know, it didn't occur to me that there were differences. I learned one lesson when I took a pleasure cruise; it had nothing to do with business. I went on one of these deals where they let you off the ship and you go in and buy things at some island. I saw this shirt hanging up in a shop and I asked the proprietor how much it was, he said $14 American so I just reached down in my pocket and took out the five and the ten and handed it to him. By the look on his face you would have thought I killed his puppy! All of the sudden he got angry and I had no idea that it was insulting him not to negotiate.

Schuster

Right. In a number of areas of the world negotiation is part of the transaction process and not negotiating is offensive. In other areas of the world, trying to negotiate is offensive. It's useful to know which is which.

Wright

Well, I grew up here in this culture—in the United States—where no one negotiates. If I go into a men's clothing store to buy a shirt, tie, pants, or whatever, no one there has the authority to drop the price so it would never occur to me to negotiate with anyone, so even on that small level, it gives some insight.

Schuster

Yes.

Wright

Is it true that women should not be a part of the negotiating team in some countries?

Schuster

No, I don't know of any country where women should not or could not be part of a negotiating team, even in the Middle East. I know women who have been very successful as part of negotiating teams and there seem to be two characteristics that make a difference.

One characteristic is how well the other men in the company are going to back up the decisions the woman makes. If a woman is negotiating, people in other countries think, "Okay, she's from the United States and it may be a little weird but that's the way they do things in the U.S." However, they will immediately go behind her back to a higher authority in the company to get her decision changed. If the men in the company change the decision, then she no longer has any ability to negotiate in that country. If, on the other hand, the men in the company back up her decision, they realize they have to deal with it and they will.

The other thing that makes a difference is that the women who are negotiating need to be sensitive to local nuances. Generally it's useful in other countries to negotiate as part of a team because the other side very often will have teams. There may well be occasions when evening entertainment comes along where the woman should say she's very tired or needs to call home that evening and declines to participate in some specific evening activities. However, when the man or the men on her team come back from the evening activity, there needs to be a meeting in the hotel among the members of the team so everybody knows what happened at the social event, what the conversations were about that night, and plan for the next set of business meetings. In this way, a woman can work very effectively.

Wright

So there are countries where women socializing is not acceptable?

Schuster

Certain kinds of socializing, yes.

Wright

What are the traits or characteristics of the most successful international negotiators?

Schuster

Patience and flexibility. You realize that not everything is going to get done on the same time schedule everywhere and you plan that into your process. You need to be willing to wait to have some things happen and to have some flexibility. One good friend of mine, who was in charge of worldwide sales for a company said, "When I go into a country and get off the plane I need to click my mind to find the right page and say, 'Okay, this is where I am now, this is the kind of behavior I need to use.' " Then he'd go to his next stop and get off the plane and have to click his mind again and say, "Okay, this is where I am now and these are the behaviors I have to use." If you can be flexible, that's good. If you have the patience to live with ambiguity and variances towards time that's also very good.

Wright

I use to hear a lot of funny stories about dealings with the Japanese. I would go to seminars to hear speakers tell such amusing stories. Are the Japanese deemed Westernized today, or are we still that much different?

Schuster

You know, that's a really interesting question because all around the world there are more and more people who wear Western clothes, who eat Western food, who speak English—at least as a second language—and we assume that they're becoming Westernized and they're using the rules of the World Trade Organization. But when it gets down to making decisions, people very often make them based upon the values they've traditionally held. Most psychologists say that people's values are formed by the time they're somewhere between the ages of seven to ten and those values tend not to change unless someone confronts a major life crisis. So what people wear might change, what they eat might change, how they behave might change, the language they speak might change, but the values they use for decision-making tend to change very slowly. To me this means that expectations are often not met because we assume people are going to make decisions the way we do because they're looking and acting and talking like we do but in reality they don't have the same mindset.

Wright

What is the basis of your knowledge and information?

Schuster

Part of it has been reading, part of it's been traveling, part of it's been interviewing businesspeople, part of it's been negotiating with businesspeople around the world, and part of it is based upon the knowledge my co-author gained, especially from his work in the countries I haven't been to.

Wright

I'd say Procter & Gamble goes everywhere.

Schuster

That's right.

Wright

So what does it take for someone to be adept at international negotiation?

Schuster

Willingness to learn and to realize that differences aren't good or bad, they're just different and there isn't one right way or one best way to do anything. There are different ways of doing things. Very often we assume that our way of doing things and our set of expectations are the "right way," because they've worked for us. It's hard to realize there can be other ways of doing things that also work. Other ways may even work better in different situations. So, being accepting of ideas not invented in the U.S., being open to understanding why somebody might want to do something differently, and then being able to work with differences are really critical for success.

Wright

Our company does a little bit of international business, not to the extent that you're talking about. You used the word "flexibility" and I like that word; but I think that if I were going to be an international negotiator, learning about the cultures and being flexible and all that would really amount to one word—respect. Respecting the other person's culture and where they're coming from, their history, would be really important.

Schuster

I would agree that you can be as flexible as you want, but if you don't demonstrate respect for the other culture and point of view, you're not going to be taken seriously.

Wright

And they'd know it right quickly I would think.

Schuster

Yes they would. You know, I've seen situations where it's gone both ways. Somebody might be very smart and trying to do all the right things that they were taught but not demonstrating respect. People end up deciding they don't want to do business with you.

Wright

Right. This idea of being the greatest country in the world—it's a great political statement but it's really not all that true, is it?

Schuster

We're great in very many things but it doesn't mean that the way we do things is the best way to do things everywhere and it doesn't mean that everybody wants to do business with us just because we're great.

My co-author has a really good example he likes to use. In a number of countries you may have been doing business with someone very successfully for a number of years, but if another product comes along that's even close to being comparable—not even as good as or better, but close to being comparable—if the people from that other company show more respect, adapt better to the culture so that the customer feels more comfortable with them, you lose your business, even if your product is better.

Wright

I hope this is not unrelated but it reminds me. I've read articles about mothers and fathers who have deaf children and they did not learn sign language, I can't imagine that.

Schuster

No.

Wright

It would be like operating in a different country—everything would be different.

Schuster

Right, and not understanding because the language you use is related to the way you think; if you don't understand the language or you don't understand the way people think it's really hard to communicate with them.

Wright

So what's the relationship between the rule of law and international negotiation?

Schuster

The rule of law has very much to do with contracts and the enforcement of contracts as well as the idea of transparency that you mentioned earlier. In North America, Australia, New Zealand, Northwestern and Central Europe, the rule of law is a very important tenant of how society is ordered and how business activity takes place. In a system where there is a set of regulations and a court system that enforces those regulations, everybody abides by the same regulations so work is going to be transparent. Everybody needs to report the same information in the same way, which also helps transparency and, if it's not done, then the courts will enforce the correction of any deviation, and there's some kind of penalty or punishment.

In countries where there's not a strong legal system and where the political system isn't independent, then the rule of law doesn't work very well. If the political and legal systems are not independent, it's very easy for people to buy off law-makers or to buy off judges in the courts. Then you can't depend upon government or the courts to enforce any regulations.

In a place where that's true then what does a contract mean? Well, you can't depend upon the contract being enforced. In the places where the rule of law is strong, getting the contract signed is the goal of negotiation because once the contract is signed you know who's going to do what, when, by what deadline, and with what consequences if it doesn't happen. In a country where there's not a rule of law the contract can be signed, but when you walk away you can't depend upon things happening the way they're stated in the contract. If things don't happen that way, who is going to enforce them—the judges someone can buy off? Probably not; so contracts don't work the same way everywhere.

In China there's a saying that once the contract is signed, it signals the beginning of negotiations. So, if you walk away assuming that the contract is signed and now you think you know what's going to be delivered, when, and with what level of quality, and you don't follow through, guess what? You're not going to get what you thought you were going to get.

I know many companies that have ended up being very surprised that deliveries of goods either don't come on time, or the quality isn't there, or the order delivered is not what they expected. Then people say, "Well, if I can't depend upon the contract what do I do?" There are lots of countries around the world where contracts cannot be relied upon, and those people have managed to figure out a way to deal with it.

One of the ways you deal with it costs more time and money because you have to show up often. You have to be there and, given the language differences, you can't always just ask a nice direct question. If you ask, "Is the delivery going to be on time?" the answer is always yes, but it means nothing. You have to show up and you just can't ask if the delivery is going to be on time, you need to go to the factory, you need to see what's going on, you need to see what kind of quality is coming out at the end, and you need to see how quickly they're working. Then you can make a decision about whether or not you think this contract is going to be fulfilled. If it's not likely to happen, you need to begin conversations about what else the people need to make the process work better or what assistance you can provide.

Wright

I have a really good friend who's an international businessman. He builds multi-million-billion dollar projects. He was operating in Russia and really lost a lot of time, effort, and money. I asked him,

"What is the bottom line? You've always made money, why did you fail this time, what was different about Russia or the Soviet Union actually?" He told me in their legal system nothing could be enforced. He said the greatest thing about the United States is our legal system.

Schuster

It makes a huge difference.

Wright

I had never thought of it before.

Schuster

Because the legal system is so much a part of the fabric of how we do business, we just take it for granted. In places where you can't take the system for granted, business doesn't operate the same way. As a result, there is usually a lot of corruption, deception, and surprises in these places. Some companies have been able to sue companies in the former Soviet Union or in Southeast Asia and win, but it takes tremendously deep pockets, a lot of time, and a lot of effort. A company like Procter & Gamble can do that but a small or medium-sized company can't afford to do that—they have to find another way to be able to make business work. It means spending more money on travel, which is also expensive.

Wright

Well, what a great conversation! You've taught me a lot here today and I know our readers are going to get a lot from this conversation. I really appreciate your taking this much time with me to answer all these questions.

Schuster

Obviously I enjoy talking about it very much; I could talk about it for a long, long time.

Wright

Today we've been talking with Camille Schuster who is currently a full professor of Marketing and International Business at California State University, San Marcos. And as I have found out, and I'm sure you have too, I think she knows what she's talking about.

Thank you so much, Dr. Schuster, for being with us today on *The Masters of Impact Negotiating.*

Schuster

Thank you very much; I've enjoyed it a lot.

About The Author

CAMILLE SCHUSTER holds a Ph.D. from Ohio State University. She is currently a Full Professor of Marketing and Management at California State University, San Marcos and is President of Global Collaborations, Inc.

Dr. Schuster co-authored a book titled, *Global Business: Planning for Sales and Negotiations,* with Michael Copeland from Procter & Gamble. She has co-authored a book entitled, *The Consumer . . . Or Else!* with Don Dufek, retired senior vice president and officer of The Kroger Company. Her most recent book, *The Rise of Consumer Power: Adopting the Right Marketing Communication Strategies,* was published in Singapore. Dr. Schuster has authored over thirty articles in professional and academic publications.

Dr. Schuster has conducted seminars and worked with over sixty companies in more than twenty countries around the world.

Camille P. Schuster, Ph.D.
Global Collaborations, Inc.,
Phone: 760.877.2897
E-mail: info@globalcollaborations.com

Chapter 8

CIARAN MCGUIGAN, B.A., M.BUS., CSP

THE INTERVIEW

David Wright (Wright)

Ciaran McGuigan, B.A., M.Bus., CSP, is one of Australia's leading professional speakers when it comes to inspiring and training under performing sales teams. He is an expert in fixing the number one problem facing most companies—lack of sales. He has the proven ability to help people increase their performance and empower them with unique and valuable business-winning techniques to drive their sales curve higher with less stress. Ciaran is also the author of *The World's Best Sales Tips* which has been described as the "Swiss Army Knife" of sales books.

Ciaran McGuigan, welcome to *The Masters of Impact Negotiating*.

Ciaran McGuigan (McGuigan)

Thank you, David. It's a pleasure to be here.

Wright

So, what do you think is the most important aspect of negotiating to remember when preparing to negotiate?

McGuigan

That's a good question. There are a lot of things to remember. Most people don't do this, but the most important thing to understand is what the consequences will be of *not* taking action for your client or customer. For example, if you're preparing to go into a negotiation, you need to understand the point of view of the person sitting across the negotiating table from you; that is, your potential customer or supplier. Most importantly you need to understand what the consequences are for that person of not taking action—not investing in your idea, your product, your service, or not agreeing to your terms. If they don't understand the consequences of not taking up your offer, then you're not going to get leverage at any time throughout the negotiation.

Wright

What is a common weakness business owners or salespeople may have in their approach to a negotiation?

McGuigan

Probably the biggest weakness that small, medium, and large business owners and all salespeople have in their negotiations is not recognizing that they're in a negotiation from the very start. As they begin their initial conversation, they tend to concentrate on building rapport, but the smart negotiator has already begun to negotiate.

It is common to only plan for negotiating strategies when we get down to talking about price. Most of the time price is *not* the core issue—it is important but understanding *value* is often the key.

At a conference recently I asked the delegates to write down what they thought was the value of a recent product or service they had sold. This was at the start of my presentation, not at the end. Without exception they wrote down the price. I then said, "Hang on, is that the *value* or is that the *price*?" Most people are confused between the two. In fact, some of the delegates had written down the discounted price, which is an even greater mortal sin!

The key thing here is to understand you can't go into the negotiation unless you understand your value and approach each conversation, each engagement, as some form of negotiation. Not all of it is hard negotiation, but negotiation nonetheless.

Wright

I often get frustrated when, later in the negotiation, I find that I'm talking to the wrong person. Would you give me a simple way to ensure I am negotiating with the right person?

McGuigan

It's not uncommon to find out, perhaps 70 percent of the way in or maybe after three or four meetings, that the person you're talking with is doing what is called "deferring to a higher authority"—they are not the decision-maker and they'll have to "take it upstairs to management" where, of course, price pressure is going to come back. It is essential that you find out during the first conversation if they are the decision-maker or if there is anyone else. That's as simple as asking something like, "Is there anyone else in your team or in your business who will be involved in this decision?"

Then listen to what is said because this is an opportunity for them to either tell you the truth or not. Most people will say they are the right person to talk with and, if that's the case, that's great. At the same time it is not unusual for there to be several people involved in a decision. When you get a number of people involved, ask your contact what his or her relationship is like with the others. Often this question will come as a surprise and the person will ask why you need to know. When in this situation, explain that it is important to know whether the person's colleagues will act on his or her recommendation or whether you will need to include different information for specific people. As negotiators we need to know what other people are involved and who the key influencer is.

Wright

Some people say language is the currency of negotiation. If this is so, how can I use this resource more effectively?

McGuigan

Language is not only the currency of negotiation but it's the currency of our lives. The more effective we are at communicating, the happier we are and the wealthier we are. Think about it: if our quality of life improves at the same rate as our ability to communicate, shouldn't we communicate as if our lives depended on it?

Let me explain to you how we can use language more effectively when dealing with different people in negotiations. Imagine you're a business owner, or a sales director, and suddenly you are called in and told that your client list had been divided into four segments. Twenty-five percent of them now speak only German, 25 percent only French, 25 percent only Spanish, and 25 percent only Italian, what would you do?

It's pretty obvious that if you wanted to stay in business you wouldn't have a choice—you'd have to learn German, French, Spanish, and Italian. In a lot of ways, when you're dealing with different negotiators, you need to be able to speak their language. You need to be able to discern their perspectives, understand the words that motivate them, what sort of metaphors they are using, and how you can use their language and relate to their fundamental issues.

It is important to consider the relative seniority of the person you are negotiating with. If you're speaking with someone who is a member of the support staff rather than management, what would be the key drivers for this person, and how can you address him or her in terms of that person's language? For support staff the words that are going to get them to sit up and take notice are most likely going to be around making their life easier. For the next level up—managers—they're driven by features and benefits. So, how are the features of your service or product going to make their management easier? As a general rule directors are motivated by controlling costs and building revenue, so if you can show how your product/service is going to drive revenue and increase customers, you are likely to get their attention. For "C" class executives—chief executives, CFOs, CIOs, etc.—their major concerns are competitive market share and future trends. If you can show during your negotiations that your product or service is going to position their business to be ahead of the market in a few years' time, that's what's going to get them to take notice. This is a big topic in itself and worth more detailed analysis subject to the strategic value of your negotiation.

Wright

What are some of the challenges for business development executives when they are negotiating?

McGuigan

The number one challenge is time. We all increasingly have less time than we've budgeted for. The tendency is to "fire-fight" which means there is less time to plan. Projects and negotiations tend not to stay on track. If you're in business development, the most effective way for you to negotiate is to consistently prospect. If you're consistently trying to find new prospects or new clients to negotiate with, you are in a much better position to leverage a better outcome.

If you know customer A doesn't agree to your terms and conditions in your negotiation, your confidence is boosted when you know you've got customer B, C, D, and E in line. If you're not continually developing new clients, this will become a key weakness. If you've got just one prospective customer you're negotiating with, and that person gets a sense that he or she is the only one, that individual is going to leverage the hell out of you!

In terms of business development, executives often negotiate with their boss rather than the customer. The executive has gone out and found a prospective client. Now if the potential client is streetwise, their initial offer will be ridiculously low—perhaps terms 30 percent below the asking price. If the prospective client does a good job, the business development executive goes back to his or her manager's office and starts negotiating a discount for the client. This appears backwards to me. I know a lot of team managers complain about this constantly saying, "Hey, I pay this guy $80,000 a year and he spends most of the time negotiating with me rather than negotiating with my clients."

Wright

Trying to sell you on what's best for the client?

McGuigan

That's it in the sense that the person will come into their manager's office pitching, "We really need this client on board," and, "It'll get us leverage to sell to other clients." That all may be true but it's indicative of a negotiating weakness. If not managed the chances are high that the executive is going to continue to negotiate like this because it has worked in the past.

Wright

What is it that the best negotiators do to load the game in their favor?

McGuigan

The best negotiators prepare. They know what questions to ask. They know what motivates each client, they know the challenges for that particular industry, they know the typical yield and revenues, and they know what's going on. They don't go into the room without knowing. To their opponents they may not always appear to know this information, but you can be sure they've done their research and have prepared properly.

This is what I call "upstream marketing" rather than "downstream ambulance chasing." The difference means being at the right place at the right time ahead of the pack rather than chasing one piece of business with five or six other vendors competing. Don't allow your customer to treat your product as a commodity and just negotiate with you purely on price.

Good negotiators always make sure they are talking with someone who can make the deal. They don't want to waste their time talking with someone who really, at the end of the day, is going to defer to a higher authority or who doesn't have the power to say yes. If the person you're negotiating with can't say yes—close the deal because you're not really negotiating at all.

Wright

You're just practicing.

McGuigan

And that's fine *if* you know that you're practicing. I know people who've really worked hard and whose skills are great but they're just practicing in front of the wrong people. Practice in front of people who can say yes and you'll find your income goes up substantially.

Wright

What I hear you saying is that people who really prepare, really know their clients, and know them before anyone else, find that knowledge is power.

McGuigan

Knowledge is power in the same way that a power station has power to direct where needed. There's no point in having power in one place when you need it somewhere else.

Wright

Many people try to keep emotion out of their negotiations. Should emotion play a part in negotiations and if so, how can we best use it?

McGuigan

Yes, most definitely. You'll find the best negotiators create balance between the rational and the emotional elements. If you're just negotiating a one off deal, you can be rational and keep it to facts, figures, and numbers and you're going to appear much tougher than you really are. But the truth of the matter is that people make decisions based on what they want rather than what they need. They will make decisions in stages.

I have broken these down into what I call the "REACT" model. This is a simple model everyone can use: Rational, Emotional, and ACT (Activity). Begin by looking at what their rational drivers are—what the objective concerns are in terms of this particular offer that's being made. Then look at what the personal (Emotional) drivers are in getting decision-makers moving. What are the things they want? In a perfect world, what would they like? What would make them happier? Finally find out what *action* will satisfy those two things.

If it is a more complex negotiation I look for more detail and use a model that can reveal even more. I call it the "Tipp Top" model. It's a simple acronym, which makes it easy to remember. Below I have illustrated examples of a few questions that encourage investigation. The first four elements are:

Time	What are ours/their deadlines and milestones? What are the consequences for missing a deadline?
Information	What do we know about the other party's customers, suppliers, staff, etc., and what does that person know about us?
Personality	Who has the dominant personality? Is the other party influential or not? Do we need to adjust or change our personality to fit?
Power	Where is the decision-making power? Do we have power to walk away? (BATNA—Best Alternative to a Negotiated Agreement)

Followed by:

Tone	The tone of the conversation, the tone of the room, the tone of the market at that time
Outlook	What is the person's personal and corporate outlook on the future? Is it positive, more protective, or other?
Pace	Who is controlling the pace of meetings, conference calls, and the sense of urgency?

The key thing here is you need to have a balance and be in control of it sometimes without the other party being aware.

Wright

If I know that my offer is far superior to my competition but I'm still on the outside, what do you suggest that I do?

McGuigan

This isn't uncommon. If you feel you're on the outside, you more than likely are and you're probably on the shortlist just to leverage a better price or aspect of the deal from another more preferred supplier. If you suspect this is the case you need to basically step up to the line and qualify your customer. The easiest way to do that is just say, "Mr. Customer, we are really excited about working with you. As you know, we haven't done business before and I know from my research that you've worked with company X and company Y in the past. I know our product is extremely competitive with what they're offering but before we go any further, would you mind telling me why you're interested in speaking with us?"

There's a golden rule in negotiating and dealing with customers. If the customer tells you something, it's the truth, whereas if you say something, they can choose to believe it or not.

Also, I believe you can outsell or negotiate anything if you personalize it enough. If you make it personal you can sell anything at all. There's a story that's relatively well known about Florida resident, Diane Duyser, who, according to a November 2004 BBC News report, sold a ten-year-old piece of toasted cheese sandwich for $28,000 on eBay. It was a pretty regular toasted sandwich, the only difference being that it supposedly had the image of the Virgin Mary on it. That seems like a lot of money for toast but the simple fact was that the purchaser, the Golden Palace Casino, didn't buy it because they wanted toast, what they were buying was the fact that this piece of toast would peak visitors' curiosity and drive people into their casino.

So personalize your offer and by default make it superior to that of your competition. When you know your product is superior to your competition's and you're still outside, you've got to find out where those points of leverage are that will get you in. If you don't get in, however, make the decision to step back and get the customer to sell you on the idea of why you should be involved.

Wright

How can I stay calm and in control during a tough negotiation?

McGuigan

It's very easy to get emotional, even angry at times during negotiation. Certainly becoming frustrated is an everyday part of negotiating but if your frustration spills out during the negotiation you are weakening your position. It is essential to approach the negotiation from a position of strength in terms of the knowledge and research and the work you've done beforehand and qualifying all the way through.

Probably the key thing to remind yourself all the way through the negotiation is that it's their *problem* but it's your *project* and don't let them make it your problem. When you're negotiating with someone, if you approach it from the perspective that it's that person's problem it will assist you to present solutions. Your project is to present those solutions in a compelling and persuasive way. Your opposing player, on the other hand, is trying to make it your problem because when you perceive the issue as your problem it's going to give you a greater amount of stress and it's going to create an imbalance in your respective negotiating positions.

If you're negotiating with a potential purchaser of your product or service, it always works well to think about how many alternatives the purchaser has versus how many alternatives you have. For example, if you're one of four widget manufacturers on the East Coast and you're dealing with someone who needs to buy those widgets, you know that person only has four alternatives. The alternatives you have are pretty much endless in the sense that you can just pick up the Yellow Pages and identify all the other organizations that need widgets. You're going to have substantially more alternatives than they have. That gives you leverage to stay calm and in control.

Another aspect to understand is the customer's critical issues. Do you really understand your customers? Here's a simple way to find out: Draw three columns on a single page. In the left hand column write down your customer's (or your negotiator's) critical issues. It sounds simple doesn't it?

The biggest mistake that most people make when they do this is they're writing down the critical issues *they* perceive. It is only natural for most people to relate the "problem" to their products or service. That is not the case. That's only the case about 5 or 10 percent of the time. Most of your potential customers' critical issues have nothing to do with what you're offering and you have to approach it from their point of view and how you can help them. Most of the time you will not be able to help them directly.

Let's assume that after a little work you have a list of *real* issues that are critical for your client. Now in the next column write down how you can help your client, either directly by providing a solution or indirectly by referral to another provider. A major factor in how you're going to win the negotiation is how you can help your client across a range of areas, most of them unrelated to your business. In the third column for each issue write down how you can prove it.

Wright

Even when I've presented a great deal and my prospect still says no, what am I doing wrong?

McGuigan

Just because *you* believe it's a great deal doesn't mean the prospect does. It sounds as if the key issue here is probably a lack of trust. If the other party is just stonewalling you and increasing price pressure, you've got to go all the way back and let the negotiations start all over again. Redress your analysis of perceived risk and reward.

Most people will make decisions based on consequences rather than on hopes and fears. If you've presented a great idea to a decision-maker or a panel of decision-makers and you've walked away, I want you to imagine the decision-makers sitting there thinking, "What happens if we don't get company X's widgets on board?" If they think that nothing will happen, then they will believe they don't need to negotiate with you. People are driven more by consequences—the fear of something happening or not as the case may be—than by hopes and aspirations.

Think about this: two salespeople go to a suburb and start marketing on two separate streets. Each street has the same demographics and they talk to the same type of people. Salesperson A knocks on the door and says, "Good morning, Mrs. Smith, my name is Joe Soap from Acme Roof Insulation. Do you know that by insulating your roof you can save more than $5 a week in terms of your heating costs?"

Salesperson B on the next street knocks on the door and says, "Good morning, Mrs. Jones, do you realize that by not having your roof insulated you could be losing up to $5 a week on your heating costs?"

There are only a few differences in the words used by each salesperson but there is a substantial difference between the two offers. People are more likely to say yes or get involved in negotiation if they understand the consequences of losing something they perceive they already have rather than something they might get. Salesperson B will be substantially more successful than A.

Wright

I've heard that called "fear loss motivation."

McGuigan

Absolutely, that's exactly what it is.

Wright

Often panels and committees will make faceless decisions. How do you negotiate with a group?

McGuigan

Let's go back to a couple of points I made earlier in terms of upstream or downstream marketing. Working with a panel usually involves working with some kind of document that has also been sent through to a number of competing vendors. You have to come back and present to the panel, or perhaps you're not even allowed to present.

When you're negotiating with a group there are a couple of things you've got to do. You've got to find out and identify a likely or actual champion for your cause—someone who is driven to sell on your behalf when you're not in the room. Again, this goes back to your research and homework.

You really need to break down each of the players and the people who influence those players on a worksheet. Work through each panel member one by one and find your most likely champion. Then focus your efforts on them one at a time in order of priority and start building relationships. If you are successful they will give you the inside track on what's going on within the panel or the group. They will also act as leverage for you internally. This is hard to achieve when you are "ambulance chasing"—trying to build relationships after the tender or request for proposal is announced.

You also have to make a decision whether you want to win this and how badly you want to win it. The degree to which you're driven is going to affect your potential to negotiate so there's a double-edged sword there. You need to build what I call the "emotional leverage model," which is looking at the emotional, the rational, and the political drivers because the group itself may be pulled together without having ever worked together before. In that case you can "divide and conquer."

The final thing I would say on that is you need to create what I call a "Gravity Position." A gravity position is focused on what the most likely line is that they want to follow. What are they driven by? What is it, with the minimum amount of support, that they will lean toward? Be honest with yourself. Most people will say to themselves, "Our product is the best in the marketplace." That's nice but if that isn't in the customer's mind or potential customer's mind, you are kidding yourself.

Wright

What an interesting conversation. I have taken copious notes here today, Ciaran. Today we've been talking with Ciaran McGuigan. As I can tell by his answers to these questions, readers are really going to learn a lot from this chapter. I think one of the most important lessons I learned (it sounds sad but I think it's true) is what Ciaran said about people being driven by consequences instead of hopes and dreams. What a shame but what a truth.

Ciaran, thank you so much for being with us today on *The Masters of Impact Negotiating.*

About the Author

CIARAN MCGUIGAN is a Certified Speaking Professional and a recognized sales and negotiation expert. He has a master's degree in Marketing from the University of Technology in Sydney, Australia, where he has also lectured. Born in Ireland, he migrated to Australia in 1991 where he now lives with his family on Sydney's Northern Beaches. Leading organizations and corporations use his motivational keynotes and unique facilitation skills to turn resources into results and ordinary employees into extraordinary winners.

Ciaran McGuigan, B.A., M.Bus., CSP
Early Coaching and Communication Pty. Ltd.
Level 6, 38 York Street
Sydney, Australia
Phone: (+612) 9222 9112
Mobile: 0404 852 347
E-mail: ciaran@earlycoach.com

Chapter 9

JOHN PATRICK DOLAN

THE INTERVIEW

David Wright (Wright)

Today we're talking with John Patrick Dolan. As a criminal lawyer, John Patrick Dolan has handled everything from traffic tickets to death penalty murder cases. Dolan is a California State Bar Certified specialist in criminal law and a true courtroom veteran. As an author, John Patrick Dolan has written twelve best-selling books, including his classic *Negotiate like the Pros™*. He is a recognized international authority on negotiation and conflict resolution. And, just to show that he does not take himself too seriously, he is also co-author of the wildly popular *Lawyer's Joke Book™*.

A communications veteran, John Patrick Dolan is a radio broadcaster and television legal news analyst appearing frequently on Fox News Channel, MSNBC, and Court TV. He has also been honored by the National Speakers Association as a member of the Professional Speakers Hall of Fame.

A trial lawyer, best-selling author, and communications expert, John Patrick Dolan has combined his many talents to become a favorite presenter for countless diverse clients, including the American Bar Association, PricewaterhouseCoopers, and the Texas Rangers baseball team.

John Patrick Dolan, welcome to *The Masters of Impact Negotiating.*

John Patrick Dolan (Dolan)

Thank you, David. It's a pleasure to be involved in the project.

Wright

So how in the world did you ever get involved in negotiation?

Dolan

There are a couple of answers to that question. The first one would be, I suppose, we always teach people what we need to learn ourselves. I'm a criminal trial lawyer and on my way through college and law school I was involved in sales and marketing. I've always been fascinated with the process—how you solve problems, how you resolve disputes, and how you work back and forth when you have disparate interest in the outcome of any particular transaction. That led me to the discussion, analysis, and review of the field of negotiation.

Concurrently with that, I've always found it interesting, just as a person observing human behavior historically, that there are some times when disputes are resolved by violence and there are some times when disputes are resolved by orderly processes. I've always thought the latter was much more civilized. So, I've always wondered, how could you cut down on the amount of violence? This is probably because I come from the '60s when we were all about peace and love and that kind of thing. How do you cut down on the violence and increase the affinity and good feelings and still deal with challenges that everyone has to deal with on a regular basis, in personal life and business life? That's, I guess, the genesis of my interest in the field of negotiation.

Besides practicing law for a little more than thirty years, for the last twenty years I really studied the subject because I've noticed that when people don't have the skills to follow an orderly process, things tend to degenerate into uncivilized behavior, sometimes bordering on and even entering into violence. It has always interested me to watch people have conflict and see how they resolve it.

In the legal field, negotiation is a huge area now called "alternative dispute resolution," and that really grows out of understanding the skills of negotiation.

Wright

I've always been fascinated by the strategy of negotiating. You see a lot of it on television. The last time we talked you mentioned something about misconceptions of negotiators.

Dolan

I think many people misunderstand the process. When the word "negotiation" comes up, they think in certain ways that are not always the most accurate. The first myth that I see people embrace and that I deal with all the time is that you have to be a real tough guy to be a successful negotiator. Really, nothing could be further from the truth. The best negotiators in the world are civilized, pleasant, affable people. That doesn't mean they can't be zealous in representing their interest or their clients' interests, but it does mean they can see the difference between the problem and the person. The people who act like tough guys are usually amateurs in the field of negotiation. When you deal with the high level professionals, it's always professional. That's the first myth I think people need to disabuse themselves of. Decent, right-thinking, ethical people are very good at negotiating, once they understand the skills involved.

The second myth/misconception people have is that negotiating is fighting or synonymous with fighting. While there are some similarities with fighting, of course, such as there are two different sides—opponents—the best negotiation is collaboration. That's the opposite of fighting. It's people who have disparate points of view coming together and saying, "How can we resolve these disparate points of view so that we can both come out of the transaction or give-and-take situation with a meaningful result?"

When negotiating becomes fighting, it's no longer negotiation.

The third myth is that only high level "Philadelphia" lawyers and the Henry Kissinger types know how to negotiate and are the only people who can use the techniques. That is absolutely false. Most people know that if you carefully look at your childhood, mothers are probably some of the best negotiators in the world. Mothers and fathers sometimes are good negotiators. Sometimes children use negotiation skills to set the mother against the father.

Almost everyone has the capability and the intelligence to learn the tools to become a skilled negotiator and many people will often intuitively use some of the things we'll talk about. The high level executive types have experience on their side when it comes to high level negotiation, but for everyday give-and-take, there are many people in the world who know how to make their way through life without as much difficulty as otherwise would be by smoothing off the edges and understanding the skills of negotiating.

The fourth myth I see all the time is that somehow negotiation is ruthless, unethical behavior and the real negotiators really don't care anything about integrity or honesty—they get away with anything they can get away with. That's another caricature. The best negotiators are people who give you their word and keep it. They are people who maintain ethical standards—standards of integrity—they refuse to compromise integrity and ethics simply to get a result. There's nothing inconsistent at all with being an ethical person with integrity and being a good negotiator.

The fifth myth is that somehow you need to have a position of strength in order to negotiate. Actually, negotiation skills are most important and most useful when you don't have a position of strength. Many times the use of skill in a negotiation scenario can allow you to come out in a situation where otherwise you'd be crushed if it was just managing who has the greatest leverage on which side of the table. So negotiation skills are really, really crucial, especially when you're in a weak position.

The sixth myth is that negotiation is a time-waster; it's just a bunch of useless haggling—why don't people just agree with what they're going to agree on and quit messing around? Of course, if we were all in perfect harmony and there was perfect trust among all people, there wouldn't be a need for negotiation skills. The problem is, however, there is almost always a disparity in trust, so it's hard for us to reveal what our real bottom line is. Also, if we were to venture into that territory, revealing our bottom line, it's not always interpreted as our real bottom line because so many people have their defenses up. What we think or what we say our bottom line is (because we don't want to engage in the give-and-take process) becomes the ceiling rather than the floor because people interpret it as just our opening gambit. It's really important to recognize that negotiation is a time-saver, *if* the participants have the skills.

The last myth is that negotiation is a formal process. Of course you can understand that. When people hear the word "negotiation," what do they think of? They think of labor-management and they think of union strikes or whatever. Negotiation is a formal process but that's not all negotiation is. Every time we meet with another human being and we engage in any kind of communication, the principles of negotiation apply. So it's husbands and wives, parents and children, people at the airport, people at the hotel, people we meet for business transactions, people I meet in the courthouse, witnesses on the witness stand, when I'm trying to get the judge to give me an evidence ruling, all of those scenarios involve the process of negotiation—it's just not the formal process.

Those are the kinds of problems I run into all the time—the kinds of myths that people embrace about negotiation. I think the most important thing we can do is understand the process, learn as much as we can about the process, and use the skill we learn to create results for others and ourselves.

Wright

Given all these seven myths that negotiation is not, would you share with our readers a little bit about what negotiation is?

Dolan

My definition of negotiation is working side by side to achieve mutually beneficial solutions. It's not mortal combat. It's not a contest. It's much better characterized as collaboration. You have two or more parties trying to resolve a dispute, bridge a gap, or figure out a way to overcome some differences and if you treat the relationship with the other parties as a collaboration rather than a contest, it creates all kinds of different dynamics.

On a continuum of everything that could happen between us and someone else, on the extreme end would be just giving up. There's something at stake and we just give up saying, "I'll just take whatever you give me. Woe is me."

At the other extreme end of the continuum is literal, physical violence where someone gets punched in the nose. Rarely is that part of negotiation, in fact, as soon as it becomes violent it's not negotiation anymore.

Most of us spend most of our lives between those two extremes. We're not going to let someone walk all over us; we're not going to punch someone in the nose. We're going to figure out a way to get the job done and that's where this definition "collaboration"—working side by side to achieve a mutually beneficial solution—makes the most sense to me. If you think of it as a contest, it becomes a contest. If you think of the process as a collaboration, it changes the dynamics of the process.

Wright

Would you distinguish for us the difference between strategy and tactics?

Dolan

Absolutely. I think this distinction is probably the most important distinction anyone can learn if they have a sincere interest in learning how to negotiate and create better results for themselves and those they represent.

A strategy is an overall mindset or approach to negotiation. It's the general way we approach any give-and-take situation.

A tactic is a tool we use within the context of that process. Many people never make that distinction. They think if you use a tactic, then that's a strategy, or if you use a technique, that means you're negotiating. The big picture, the dual vision—what's in it for everybody in the transaction, what are the agendas, not only my agenda but that of my counterpart(s)—is how I am going to approach the process each and every time I get involved in the process is the strategic discussion.

Within the process there are all kinds of techniques we can use to move us toward our end. In that context I always like to say strategically, first of all, you want to be able to develop this dual vision as I mentioned—you want to see what's on your side of the agenda but you want to see what's on the agenda of your counterpart(s). Then you want to take the attitude where the answer is always yes. What I mean by this is there will be requests for concessions in every negotiation. Sometimes there are just ambient requests for concessions where people will just walk up and ask you for something. Sometimes it's within the process where you're going back and forth on a give-and-take.

I like to always at least begin strategically saying yes. You can begin strategically to say no if you want to and most people are oriented that way. For example, someone could ask, "Could you pay us an extra 15 percent?" And you say, "No." You can see that when someone says no to a request for a concession, it cuts down on the flow of the process. Usually how it works is you say, "No, I can't give you an extra 15 percent unless you give us business for two years and you pay the shipping," and whatever other conditions are placed on the request. You can make the same conditions by saying, "Yes, we can give you a 15 percent discount as long as you're willing to give us a two-year commitment and pay the shipping, etc." Saying yes initially changes the relationship; it builds affinity by saying yes rather than no. That's a skill you develop regarding your strategic approach to negotiation—to always figure out the answer is yes and to figure out how you can support the answer.

I always suggest to people to take a big picture approach, look at both sides of the transaction, understand your own agenda, understand the agenda of the people on the other side of the transaction, look for areas of mutual interest, and the answer is almost always yes.

Wright

How do different people negotiate? You can't be of like mind and call it negotiation, can you?

Dolan

Tony Alessandra wrote a book called *The Platinum Rule*. It's a pretty simple concept. The "golden rule" is, "Do unto others as you would have them do unto you." The platinum rule in Tony's book is, "Do unto others as they want to be done unto." The truth is, in any kind of negotiation, you're going to have to deal with people. Sometimes there's some filter between us and the other person, but most of the time it's eyeball-to-eyeball or at least ear-to-ear on the telephone.

So you have to evaluate who's on the other side of the transaction and what's important to them. There are all kinds of landmark work that's been done—the DiSC profile and the Larry Wilson profile—where you look at different personality styles such as the dominant or the driver kind of style, the socializer or the influencer kind of style, the steady or the process oriented kind of style, and the detail oriented style, etc. While I've heard different descriptions of these styles (and I'm sure many readers have heard about them also), I rarely see these descriptions applied to negotiation. I have to say, if you're trying to get concessions from your counterpart(s), giving them opportunities to make concessions, working and collaborating with your counterpart(s) to get concessions to make sense, it's critical to know what kind of person is on the other side of the table. Some people just want to get to the bottom line so you have to be able to negotiate that way. Some people want to deal with friends and build affinity and have relationships, so you have to be able to be light on your feet and do some relationship building—do your howdy do's sometimes. Sometimes people just want to follow a step-by-step process, they want to have an agenda and they want to follow the agenda.

Sometimes people want to have lots of details and large amounts of time to absorb those details.

We need to evaluate who the person really is when we deal with him or her on the other side of a transaction because this is part of our strategic approach. The dual vision we develop has to deal not only with the subject matter but also the personalities on the other side because that helps us modify the way we offer what we offer into the process. That can then position us to use the tactics we know or skills we have developed to get to the point where we get a resolution to a transaction or we put together a deal where we settle a dispute.

Wright

You distinguished strategy from tactics so I would be interested in hearing more about tactics. What are some of the most commonly used tactics?

Dolan

There are many tactics we can talk about, but let's make sure we understand this. Strategy is like your game plan—it's like winning a football game. A tactic is any particular play you use in that game, whether it's a running play, a passing play, or a reverse, or a quarterback sneak. All those plays are intended to move you toward a touchdown—the resolution or the end result of a game plan. That is the overall approach to the football game.

Tactics are techniques we use to implement our plan of looking for a solution that works for all parties, making sure that everyone is committed to the outcome, and making sure we deal with the objectives on both or all sides of the table.

There are three most commonly used tactics:

1. *Take it or leave it.* Everyone knows that one. Most people don't recognize that as a tactic. When someone says to me in a negotiation, "Take it or leave it, I don't negotiate," they are really saying, "This is a tactic I'm using, let's see if it works." "Take it or leave it" just means the person has given you a position now within the negotiation, what are you going to do about it?

Usually the best answer to that tactic is to say, "Why do you say that?" You use an open-ended question to smoke out what the real reason is behind the take it or leave it statement. Almost always the reason behind it is a limitation on authority, exasperation because of the amount of time the negotiation has taken, a personality flaw, or a disinterest for the ultimate outcome, given the parties and the circumstances. Take it or leave it is a very common tactic, and many times it's at the front end of the negotiation. However, sometimes it's given later on at the frustration point in the process.

2. *Split it down the middle.* Everyone in the world knows this one. I've been around the world, I've talked with everyone I can talk to in seminars, in person, in telephone conversations and you don't have to explain that to anyone. Usually it comes at the end of a negotiation, and it's usually one party or the other making an offer to see if you can bridge the gap because it's not too much of a distance.

Usually the answer to that is, "Gee, that sounds fair to me," and you split it down the middle. That's a very commonly used tactic. This is an interesting distinction and as a tactic it works very well.

If you don't distinguish in your mind between tactics and strategy, you can get yourself in trouble because a strategy is a big picture approach in which someone says, "Here is my extreme offer, it's ridiculous, it's high and more than anyone would ever realistically pay for this particular product but let's see if you're an idiot or if you recognize that." When we get an offer like that we tend to make a lowball response and then there's this back and forth discussion. When you finally reach a mutually accepted deadline, you split it down the middle. That is a very bad approach to negotiation because it creates all kinds of friction and ill will. But the split it down the middle tactic at the end of a negotiation is a good one. So understanding that distinction between strategy and tactics can make a big difference.

3. *The wince.* Someone asks you how much you want to sell your car for. So you say, "Well, $2,000." The person who is on the other side of that transaction says something like, "Two thousand dollars! My gosh, that's more than any car would cost!" The wince is intended to get sellers to bid against themselves. The intent is for the other guy to say, "Well, maybe I could sell it to you for $1,500." This is getting him to bid against himself. Everybody knows how to do that. Everyone knows how to say, "The price is too high, or, "The bid is too low," or, "I'm sorry, that's unacceptable," or, "I never thought we'd have to pay that kind of money," etc.

The real problem for most people is what to do when they get the wince? It's interesting—we know it's coming—whatever we say as a positional statement in negotiation is almost always objected to by our counterparts because it's a behavior that's built into our genetic code. Another example, by the way, is people don't like to make the first offer. Why is this true? Because someone is going to say the offer is not acceptable, it's too much, it's ridiculous, etc.

Once you understand how to handle the wince, it's not that big of a deal. Here is a good example: I went to get some printing for my printer recently. I asked how much the printing cost is and she said, "Fifteen hundred dollars."

"Fifteen hundred dollars!" I said.

She said, "Oh, that's right—you're the negotiation guy. I'll give you 10 percent off."

Now, you see, just by saying fifteen hundred dollars in a surprised way, I got a $150 discount. What if she hadn't given in to my wince? What if it didn't work? Here are five things people can do when they get winced. If you practice this and you get this—if you can just get the five responses to being winced—it'll make a massive difference in the end result you get in any negotiation.

1. Okay. So now I'm at my printer's office and I ask, "How much is the printing?" and the response is, "Fifteen hundred dollars." I say, "Fifteen hundred dollars!" The first thing she does is nothing—just complete silence. The reason she does that is she wants to see if I'm serious. Many people have developed a behavior pattern, which is just to wince at anything. As soon as someone says anything to them, they just complain about it and they can usually get a better result. So you see if they're serious.
2. The second thing is, if I say, "Fifteen hundred dollars!" she can just restate her position by saying, "Yes, $1,500. That's what we agreed to when we gave you the estimate." It's the same thing—she's not bidding against herself but she's not being confrontational.
3. The third thing she can do is intentionally misinterpret my statement. I find this happens more in the southern part of the U.S. but it happens all over. I say, "Fifteen hundred dollars!" And she says, "I knew you'd like that price. A lot of people pay $2,000 to $3,000 for this kind of job. Aren't you smart to recognize what a marvelous deal I've just given you?" That's not what I meant at all, but if she can get me to laugh and I'm still standing there, I'm probably paying the $1,500.
4. The fourth is escalation. My colleagues in the legal profession know this one well. You make your position more extreme so that the original statement doesn't look nearly as bad as it did when you first heard it. So I ask, "How much is the printing?" and she says, "Fifteen hundred dollars." I say, "Fifteen hundred dollars!" She says, "Well,

$1,500 is what's written on the quote. I notice here that your printing is actually more like $2,000 but somebody made a mistake and put $1,500, so you'd better pay it now or you'll be paying the $2,000 next week."

5. The fifth and final technique to use to respond to the wince is called "feel, felt, found." It recognizes you can commiserate with people, and you can help them understand that their surprised reaction is not uncommon and you can help them to come to closure as far as the original price that was quoted. So I say what's the price and she says, "Fifteen hundred dollars." I say, "Fifteen hundred dollars!" and she says, "Well, I understand how you feel." That's the commiseration step. You're expressing surprise or concern and you should. The second is the generalization step: "Many people who haven't purchased printing have felt the same way." So now I'm not a cult of one—I'm actually someone who has had a surprised reaction and it's an understandable and predictable surprised reaction. Now she gives me the features and benefits: "But when you understand the quality of the paper—when you recognize that this is acid-free, recycled paper—most of our customers have found the price is not so bad and it is $1,500." So there you have feel, felt, found, plus you did a repeat.

Those five techniques: (1) silence, (2) repeat your position, (3) intentionally misinterpret, (4) escalation, and (5) feel, felt, found, are powerful. If you get those, you can state a position in any negotiation and defend your position to the point where you can actually improve the results you will get.

Wright

Well, I can see you're passionate about negotiation. Would you share with our readers why you are so passionate about it?

Dolan

I think it goes back to what we said in the beginning of our conversation. I really believe people don't have to fight with each other in order to solve problems or resolve disputes. If people have just a minimum understanding of the skills necessary to engage in the negotiation process, all kinds of ill will, hurt feelings, and attacking behavior can be eliminated from the formula making it so much easier to solve problems.

The challenge here is that it's not part of the curriculum. Nobody takes a negotiation class in high school and very rarely in college, though I have to say now that some colleges are buying books from me and they're teaching classes—it's usually in an MBA program.

I'll tell you something else most people don't know: Most lawyers don't get any training in negotiation. Lawyers get out there and learn it on their own by experience, which explains why lawyers tend to be a bit abrasive. I teach lawyers—I teach continuing legal education. I've done it for more than twenty years. I can tell you that in a group of a thousand lawyers you'll have maybe ten or twenty who have ever had any skills training in negotiation. Most have learned on the job and because they don't have skills, the natural fallback position for most people is aggression. There's so much aggression in the legal profession, which translates back into the business world. It just doesn't need to be there; it's just that we haven't had this set of skills as part of the curriculum. I'm all for it.

As I mentioned, I've been involved for more than twenty years in writing and speaking on the subject of negotiation. I'm right now in the process of putting together some business plans that may eventually put me in the law school business because I'm working with a small law school out here where I live now in La Quinta, California, that we would like to expand. One of the things I want to do is found a center for negotiation and mediation skills training. That's on the horizon as we speak.

I can tell you, that's really where I see the future of our country and of our planet going. If we continue to resolve disputes by using aggression and force we'll eventually blow ourselves out of the solar system. If we figure out a way to solve our problems without letting them degenerate into fights, we have a very bright future.

Wright

Well, what a great conversation. I really appreciate all this time you've with me talking about this important topic on the art of negotiation. It's always a pleasure talking with you, John.

Dolan

Thank you very much, David. I hope we've given the readers something they can use.

Wright

Today we've been talking with John Patrick Dolan, trial lawyer, best selling author, and communications expert. He's combined his many talents to become a favorite presenter for countless diverse clients including the American Bar Association, PricewaterhouseCoopers, and the Texas Rangers baseball team.

So, John, the next time I see you, you'll probably be on Fox News or MSNBC.

Dolan

Keep your eyes open. There's always something going on.

Wright

Thank you so much for being with us on *The Masters of Impact Negotiating*.

About The Author

As a California criminal trial lawyer with over twenty-eight years of courtroom experience, John Patrick Dolan has handled everything from traffic tickets to death penalty murder cases. Dolan is a recognized California State Bar Certified Specialist in Criminal Law and a true courtroom veteran. He is AV (highest) Martindale-Hubbell rated. As an author, John Patrick Dolan has written twelve bestselling books, including his classic *Negotiate like the Pros™*. He is a recognized international authority on negotiation and conflict resolution. And, just to show that he does not take himself too seriously, he is also co-author of the wildly popular *Lawyer's Joke Book™*.

A communications veteran, John Patrick Dolan is a radio broadcaster and television legal news analyst appearing frequently on Fox News Channel, MSNBC, and Court TV. He has also been honored by the National Speakers Association as a member of the Professional Speakers Hall of Fame.

In addition to his professional legal experience, John Patrick Dolan served as CEO of LawTalk™ MCLE, Inc., a continuing legal education company from 1992–2004. John Patrick Dolan is a native Californian. He grew up in Huntington Beach, California—"SurfCity USA." He is a life-long drummer. His rock and roll band "The Wild Ones" was his passion during his younger days. His undergraduate studies at California State University Fullerton yielded a bachelor's degree in Speech Communication and Political Science. During his college years, John Patrick Dolan was recognized as a nationally ranked debater. His debating performance at one national event was described by Professor Laurence Tribe as a "tour de force."

John Patrick Dolan attended Western State University College of Law, from which he graduated in 1977 with a J.D. degree. During law school he served as a law clerk and sat second chair on numerous criminal cases including two murder trials. Additionally, he supported himself during law school as a stockbroker for Merrill Lynch. Dolan passed the California Bar Exam and was sworn into practice in 1978. He is admitted to practice in California and numerous Federal jurisdictions. Additionally, he is admitted to practice before the Supreme Court of the United States of America, originally sponsored by renowned defense attorney F. Lee Bailey.

John Patrick Dolan
79-505 Via Sin Cuidado
La Quinta, CA 92253
Phone: 760.771.5490
Fax: 760.771.3198
E-mail: negotiatelikethepros.jpd@gte.net

Chapter 10

BOB DANZIG

THE INTERVIEW

David Wright (Wright)

Bob Danzig grew from a childhood spent in five foster homes to two decades as nationwide head of The Hearst Newspaper Group and vice president of The Hearst Corporation. After graduating from high school with no family support, he took a job as an office boy at his local newspaper, the *Albany* (New York) *Times Union.* Nineteen years later he became publisher of the *Times Union*, before heading to the helm of The Hearst Newspaper Group.

Now an author and motivational speaker, Bob is also a member of the teaching faculty at the prestigious New School University and the guiding hand of The Hearst Management Institute. His goal is to be an instrument for renewed affirmation that every single person is worthwhile.

A civic leader, Bob has served on the boards of directors of Albany Medical College, Siena College, Russell Sage College, St. Peter's Hospital, Sunnyview Hospital, Albany Institute of History and Art, and Caldwell College, and on the executive committee of the Saratoga Performing Arts Center. In addition to graduating magna cum laude from Siena College, he received the college's Outstanding Alumni

Award, as well as an honorary Ph.D. Bob was also recognized as a Knight of Malta.

As an industry leader, Bob has served the Newspaper Association of America, Newspaper Advertising Bureau, New Directions for News and the American Press Institute, and has earned industry-wide respect for his innovative marketing leadership. Bob was also awarded one of twelve professional journalism fellowships at Stanford University, the only business executive ever to be accepted into this program. He now serves on its board.

Bob is the author of *The Leader Within You, Vitamins for the Spirit, Angel Threads, Every Child Deserves a Champion,* and *There Is Only One You.* He is also working toward adapting his adult-focused program, "The Confidence Academy," for children.

Bob's net speaking and author fees are donated to foster children (his passion) and gifted young musicians (his wife's passion).

So tell me, Bob, are there any skills that you believe a negotiator must have to insure his or her success and if so, will you give our readers a couple of examples?

Bob Danzig (Danzig)

I believe one of the most important skills is genuine empathy for the other party that induces you to really seek those combinations of value benefits that are of use to both them and you.

An example that comes to mind is the following: When I was a young advertising salesman in Albany, New York, we had *zero* business with the leading grocer chain in that area. Numerous salespeople had called on him repeatedly offering the general demographics and other information about our newspaper. I studied his ad—he ran ten pages a week, every week in the competing newspaper. When I examined his ads I found a pattern of his not including any kind of frozen food merchandise to any large extent. I researched the frozen food category to find cooperative advertising monies that could be available for users if they exceeded a certain volume of sale. I then eyeballed the frozen food sections of his grocery stores to come up with an estimated volume of sale. I then redid his ads to include a large section of frozen food merchandise on every single page. I identified the monies that would flow from the manufacturer for his including those items on each page. I showed him how the inclusion of those frozen food ads could free up enough money for him to run his ads in my newspaper free!

In other words, all our other salespeople had negotiated with him previously only about what we had to offer. What I did was the extra homework to demonstrate what he had to gain. So we ended up with a negotiated result that had me getting the same advertising volume as our competitor but at no extra cost to the advertiser because I gave him the solution. What I had was a genuine empathy for the reality of the economics of his business and sought out a negotiation that would be a gain for him and a gain for us.

By the way, when he made the move to our newspaper, because he was the "bell cow" all the other advertising in the whole market followed him and we went from zero business to 55 percent share and in eighteen months we bought out our competitor. That's what I call a win-win *big* win—when you start with a genuine empathy for a value for the other person.

Wright

When considering the salient steps in negotiating, how important is time as a factor in successful discussions?

Danzig

I think time is a very important factor because if you're in the act of negotiations then reasonable celerity has to be your objective. If you let this thing slip into sluggishness and a time delay I think you run the risk of losing interest by the other party. That doesn't mean you rush into the situation but you're conscious of the fact that the other party is giving you one of their most precious commodities—their time. Therefore you should be using their time with recognition of how valuable it is to them.

Wright

Some negotiators I've talked with have told me that body language and non-verbal signals play an important role in establishing rapport and interpreting what the "other side" really means or wants. Has this been your experience?

Danzig

Well, I guess that might be pertinent for poker players but I don't think that is a vital factor. I don't think it's so much the body language as it is the intensity of listening to the other person. That to me is much more important than the subtleties of body language. But I'm not a good poker player so I may not be the best one to bring that answer into sharp focus for you. I think body language is overplayed and what's much more important is to be a genuinely aggressive listener to the other person.

Wright

That also shows a tremendous amount of respect, especially in this culture.

Danzig

I agree with that.

Wright

During a negotiation, what have you found to be the number one thing that can go wrong and how can it be overcome in most cases?

Danzig

Emotional turbulence, usually by the other party and sometimes these eruptions need to occur in order to get down to business. It's a very, very subtle point of balance, to be able to withstand it and show some courtesy when the other person is going through an emotional outburst. Let them get it out of their system so you can then respectfully bring them back into focusing on the issue at hand.

I don't think your own emotional turbulence is permitted at all. But you're going to find that on occasion.

I remember we bought a newspaper in Laredo, Texas. The people who were selling the paper to us were a very successful Mexican-American banking family who were very wealthy. They got into the competitive newspaper business as a hobby. They took great pride in what they had achieved but they were also losing a ton of money. We represented a solution for them but we had to understand the emotional challenge for them to be dealing with their severance from the newspaper they had started from scratch. There were several times during the course of our discussions where they had to just blow off steam. And we let them—we just sat there—we didn't say anything, we were respectful. They came back to the table and we got it all done.

Wright

I have heard most negotiators say they're really seeking a "win-win" situation between the parties involved. Do you agree with that and if so, how would you define a "win-win"?

Danzig

I think the term "win-win" is a cliché; I think what really matters is giving the other person a clear sense of winning. If you make the other person's comfort your objective, that doesn't mean you're going to do something hurtful to yourself but I think what matters most is their comfort and their sense of winning. I think the whole idea of win-win is just a business cliché.

Wright

I would tend to agree with that. Most of the win-wins that have happened down through my business life have been that somebody won and somebody lost. And the winner came away saying he had a win-win situation.

I have always thought that the best tool for negotiating with anyone would be leverage. Is that true or are there better ways?

Danzig

I'm concerned about clichés, David. I think having leverage over the other person implies some sort of power advantage; you're not negotiating then, you're just ramming something down someone's throat. I think that's an overused idea. I don't think leverage is the most important thing. In fact, when you used the word I thought you had said "levity." (I'm not sure I don't think levity is as important as anything else.)

If you're seeking a fair negotiation with another party where your objective is their winning, then you're not seeking your greatest tool to be *your* leverage—your greatest tool is seeking *their comfort.*

Wright

That would just about negate leverage as a win-win, wouldn't it?

Danzig

I think so.

Wright

When people disagree or become hostile, how do you calm them down so that agreements can be reached?

Danzig

Use terms such as, "Help me understand this more clearly. I don't want to misinterpret what's important to you." "Would you just walk me through your position so I'm really clear on all that surrounds it?" I think you should ask gentle questions to help clarify things to bring a conflict from passion to clarity.

Wright

In the example you gave earlier about the people who owned the newspaper, if you couldn't have calmed them down they probably had enough money to run it without you and lose money forever, didn't they?

Danzig

That's true.

Wright

Before you go into a negotiation, how much preparation time do you require and are there any standard principles you use to reach your desired goals?

Danzig

I think it's wise to spend whatever time that is required to try your best to understand what the value proposition is in terms of importance to the other party. I think it's important to study out those things that are important to them. You know it's important to you—you don't need a lot of time to deal with that. But I think it's vital to take the time to do the homework to try and get a feel for what is genuinely important for them. You take whatever time necessary to do that—I don't think there's a formula for that.

Wright

The time you took to get the grocer's business was well spent.

Danzig

Actually, there's a bit more of a story there, David. I had been a classified advertising salesman and the display advertising salesman, where the grocery accounts were, made ten dollars a week more salary. So I applied for that job with zero business and offered to keep my job in classified advertising and not be paid the extra ten dollars a week unless I did some business. The ad director, a man who ultimately would work for me and became publisher of our newspaper in Baltimore, took me up on my offer.

The very first week I was there, one of the advertising salesmen came to me on a Friday morning and said, "All the Sunday ad copy is in. We have a tradition—we go to lunch late, around two o'clock, on Friday and then we shoot darts at the Kenmore Pub. Since this is your first week, we'd like to invite you to join us."

I remember thinking to myself, "Here I am, I've got a six-month trial, I have zero business, and no money. I'm not going to go shoot darts!" However, he was telling me something. Friday afternoon is too late and you can't call customers—they have no interest in talking to you. So how could I use my Friday afternoons more constructively? I decided to make myself a student of the grocery business on Friday afternoons. That's what I did—for weeks and weeks. That's how I stumbled across the frozen food equation and opportunity.

Wright

What advice would you give someone who is faced with a negotiation situation for the first time?

Danzig

Allow your natural tension. It can become an ally. Do not fret about some nervousness—let your nervousness be an ally. Spend your time ferreting out what is important to the other person. And let the progress of the dialog dissipate your tension.

Wright

All through these questions I've heard a common theme—you actually believe in what's best for the other person, don't you?

Danzig

I think that has to be your focus, David. I'm not talking as a professional negotiator; I'm just relying on my general business background.

Wright

What are the most common mistakes people make when negotiating a sale or negotiating anything?

Danzig

Expecting too much too quickly. Not having some patience. Not allowing some levity.

People want to go in there and have things done by sundown. Sometimes you need a few sundowns.

Wright

Levity can calm down almost anything.

Danzig

Well, it sure doesn't hurt.

Wright

I don't trust people with no sense of humor.

What an interesting conversation, Bob. I always have interesting conversations with you.

About the Author

After growing up in five foster homes Bob Danzig's corporate career began as a teenage office boy at the *Albany* (New York) *Times Union.* Nineteen years later he was named publisher of that newspaper. During his later twenty-year term as nationwide head of the 6,000 employee Hearst newspapers, the group had a renaissance of talent, technology, reputation—and cash flow grew 100 fold. Bob stepped down early to share his insights with audiences and readers. All of his speaking fees and book royalties are donated to charity. His greatest satisfaction is sharing ideas, which stimulate the wisdom within you.

Robert Danzig
Phone 973.761.6389
E-mail: bdanzig@hearst.com

Chapter 11

David and Martin Sher

THE INTERVIEW

David Wright (Wright)

An interview with Birmingham, Alabama, brothers David and Martin Sher gives new insight on what negotiation skills are essential to collecting past-due debt. David and Martin share their wealth of knowledge on bill collecting, with an emphasis on maintaining a positive assumptive attitude, learning how to ask for money, and really developing the information-gathering techniques to get the hang of it!

What are the major things that are different and unique about the negotiation process while collecting money?

David and Martin Sher (Sher)

There are three differences that come to mind. First of all, most collection work is done over the telephone. Face-to-face collection activity is very rare because of the expense and time involved. Second, it is an unwanted telephone call. The person receiving the call is not thinking, "Hot diggity dog! It's the bill collector!"

There is one other major difference in collection negotiations: in a typical negotiation process, the parties negotiate to create an entire contract, whereas in a collection negotiation the collector facilitates for his client the final details of the contract with the debtor—when and how the debtor will pay. There is already a valid contract in place when a debtor and a collector begin their negotiations. The debtor has already created a debt, owes a debt, and needs to find a way to pay the debt. It is a collector's objective to help make this happen.

Wright

What are the basics of collecting?

Sher

As with other types of negotiations, successful collections are a little bit of an art, but mostly a science. Just like in anything else, with knowledge, training, and practice good things will happen. In our book, *Championship Collections: How to Squeeze Blood From a Turnip*, we start off with what we consider the big picture, the objective of "championship collections." The objective of "championship collections" is to:

1. Collect the most money,
2. As fast as you can,
3. Net of expenses,
4. While maintaining the goodwill of the customer.

The most important objective in a successful collection negotiation is number four, maintaining the good will of the customer.

Wright

Maintaining the goodwill of the other party is important in other negotiations, too. What are some other similarities between collections and other negotiations?

Sher

That's correct! In my view, trust is at the heart of both collections and other types of negotiations. That's why we think of debtors as customers and treat them with the same respect as customers, just as parties in other negotiations relate to each other as equals. After all, they are *someone's* customer, and deserve to be treated like a customer. In addition, it is the key to being an effective collector.

We've seen that the way the collector treats the customer separates the effective collector from the non-effective collector. With trust, customers know that collectors are there to help them solve their problem, which in most instances is helping them figure out how to raise the money to pay the past due debt. Isn't development of trust one of the most important keys to effective negotiation of any kind?

Wright

You mentioned that almost every collection call is an unwelcome telephone call, so how do you develop trust?

Sher

This is the most important part of being successful in collections. If you can develop trust, you can be successful—it is that simple. In our book, *How to Collect Debts and Still Keep Your Customers*, we use the acronym A-S-K to help our collectors remember the components of successful collecting. After all, you have to ask for money in order to collect it.

The A in A-S-K stands for the collector's Attitude. When we effectively train collectors to develop the proper collection attitude, 80 percent of our job is done. With the proper attitude, it is not only possible, but also probable that you can develop trust and therefore succeed.

The S in A-S-K stands for Speed. The collection process happens fast. It's urgent. It has a beginning, middle, and an end. Accounts receivable is not like a fine wine—it does not get better with age. Developing this sense of urgency is something only the collector can do, and the customer has to trust you in order to feel this sense of urgency.

The K in A-S-K stands for Knowledge. You have to know what you are doing to be a professional and effective bill collector. This is where the science of collections comes in.

Wright

Martin and David, will you tell me more about developing the champion collector attitude? It sounds like it is the important first step in effectively negotiating and collecting money.

Sher

Sure. There are four steps to developing a champion collector attitude.

1. *Number one is to Believe in Yourself.* It takes a lot of confidence, energy, enthusiasm, and most importantly, an assumptive attitude to be successful. Martin and I grew up in a family business called Mr. King Furniture. Our target market niche was to sell to people no one else wanted to sell to.

We financed customers for twenty-four months without any down payment. Almost all of these customers had either no credit or bad credit. Obviously, we had to be exceptional in our credit and collection techniques in order to be successful with this particular market.

Let me tell you about Margaret, a new collector we hired at Mr. King Furniture. Margaret had tremendous confidence and believed that she could collect anything from anybody. She truly had an assumptive attitude.

During her first week, the collection manager mistakenly gave her the wrong group of accounts to collect. Margaret was supposed to get accounts that were thirty to sixty days past due, but instead got accounts that were two to five years past due. These were accounts that we had tried for years to collect but were not successful. The past due customers were out of work, had skipped town, or were just being evasive. We always called these accounts "the uncollectible group." But Margaret did not know this. We forgot to tell her.

In her zeal to prove to us how good she was, she collected thousands of dollars on accounts that we considered uncollectible. Margaret did not know they were uncollectible and we forgot to tell her. Her belief in herself and her assumptive attitude is what helped her to succeed. She assumed she was going to collect every single account because she knew the customer owed the bill and the customer was going to pay the bill. This is the first step of being an effective collection negotiator.

2. *The second step of developing a championship attitude is to Believe in Your Company.* You must believe in the service and/or the product you provide. If you do not feel good about the service or product, it is going to be extremely difficult to ask for the money and negotiate a good result. David and I started AmSher Receivables Management in 1986. We have received well over a billion dollars of accounts to collect in that time period. We have helped hundreds of companies recover hundreds of millions of dollars, and thus have helped those companies as well as the economy overall. We have kept businesses open, saved people's jobs, and have helped keep the prices of goods and services down. After all, when bills are paid it keeps the

pressure to raise prices down. Everyone pays for bad debt through increased prices.

We feel very good about the service that we provide. I believe it is a noble cause and I make sure the collectors know we wear the white hats. This makes it very easy to train our employees as to the importance of their jobs. Collectors protect our credit system. Can you imagine a world without credit? Keeping the importance of credit in mind is very helpful while collecting. Since being an effective negotiator requires art, skill, and science, it helps greatly, when negotiating, to believe in your company.

3. *The third step is to Treat the Money You're Collecting as Your Own and Build Urgency.* One of the fun and useful exercises I do in our seminars is to hold up a $5 bill. I say, "The first person to come up to the front of the room and put $5 in my hand wins. I will give them their $5 back plus my $5." It just takes a few seconds until people are in a mad rush running up to the front of the room to put their $5 in my hand. Before I give them back the $10 I promised, I ask them to please go sit down. They are always a little bit uncomfortable about my instructions, but in most cases they work their way back slowly to their seat.

I wait another few seconds before I talk. I tell them I did say I was going to give them back their money, but I did not say when. I want them to feel a little bit uncomfortable so I can make my point, and it is an important one. In order to effectively collect money, you have to treat the money you are collecting as your own, whether it is or not. This is the only way to build urgency, and building urgency is critical to being a successful negotiator. Of course I do not wait too long to give them back their money, but I make a point of waiting just long enough to make sure they feel a good bit uncomfortable. That tension they feel is necessary in order to collect money. You have to build urgency, and if it is your money on the line, it feels a lot more urgent.

4. *The fourth step is to Take Nothing Personally.* When you ask people for money, they might not want to pay or be able to pay right then. They might get upset and say things that can be a little bit personal. It is a natural reaction for them to be upset and behave angrily. What should become natural for an effective collector is to deflect this anger. This person is not angry with the collector. He or she is angry at the situation. I would like to mention a couple of techniques that are helpful when this happens.

It is important to be cool and maintain control. The customer's anger will subside if you do things right, and then you will be able to get down to business, which is to make arrangements to get the bill paid. If someone starts to get loud or even abusive over the telephone, talk softly. The louder the person gets, the softer your voice should get. Many times that will startle the person and catches him or her off guard. You might just stop the venting and have a chance to get the conversation under control.

If you have accomplished this part, then you have the opportunity to begin to gain trust and therefore have a chance at developing a solution together. While people are venting, suppress your own feelings, and divert that energy into being an active listener. There will be many things they say that you can use to your advantage to demonstrate your empathy and helpfulness. Statements such as, "I know how you must feel," "That is very unfortunate and I am so sorry," and "I had no idea that you were having that problem," are some examples of these types of statements. Empathy is okay, but sympathy is a ticket to disaster.

You can steer the remainder of the call to a successful conclusion by using post-empathy phrases such as, "Now that I know your problem, I have some ideas on what we can do together to get this solved," or, "Thanks for sharing that with me, Mrs. Jones. Would you allow me to work with you to help us find a solution?" or, "It sounds like you have so many problems, Mrs. Jones. Would you allow me to help you solve this one and get it out of the way?"

You want to listen actively, show empathy, and then gain control back and move toward a solution. After all, it is so exhilarating to get a bill paid in full. Help the customer find the money needed so he or she can enjoy that wonderful feeling of relief when the bill is paid off.

Wright

The S in ASK is for speed. Why is it important to build a sense of urgency in the negotiation?

Sher

Keep in mind that if it is not urgent to you, the bill collector and negotiator, it sure is not going to be urgent to the customer who owes the bill. As a collector, you want the payment today. If a bill is past due, you want the entire past due amount *right now*. The customer might want to pay the bill over a long period of time. This is the challenge. It is a documented fact that debts are less collectible over time.

Over time many things can go wrong in a customer's life that can reduce your chances of getting paid, whether your customer is an individual or a business.

Let's see what different things can go wrong in a consumer's life as time passes that can lessen your chances of getting paid:

Consumers could:

- be fired, laid off, or quit. Another breadwinner in the family could lose his or her job;
- retire;
- experience illness, have an accident, become disabled, or die;
- relocate leaving no forwarding address, or join the military;
- experience a natural disaster such as a hurricane, a flood, or earthquake that would seriously affect the consumer's ability to pay;
- have marital problems could occur, get separated or divorced, or have twins;
- have unexpected bills such as medical, transportation, etc., incurred by someone else in the family or the consumer;
- file for protection under the bankruptcy laws, or
- be sued by other creditors, which would affect his or her ability to pay you.

Now, let's identify what can go wrong in a business over time that would affect a business's ability to pay. David and I have been very fortunate over the last thirty years and have always paid our bills. We have had many good things that have happened to us, but we have had to survive many catastrophes or near catastrophes also:

We have had a fire, a flood, and a problem with termites that have disrupted our business.

We have been burglarized and vandalized.

We have had a computer conversion that has disrupted our business.

There was a change in the tax law that forced us to change our business model overnight.

We have had large new competitors come into our market and we have lost a major client who went out of business.

We also have had to move on short notice because of unexpected growth.

Let's identify a few other things that can go wrong in a business that are not part of our experience, but that we have seen happen:

- Businesses have lost their source of financing.
- Businesses have had their assets seized by the IRS or have been closed down because of unpaid city or state taxes.
- A key owner or top management person has died or become disabled.
- A natural disaster has occurred in the area where their business is located.

What catches many business people by surprise is not being able to collect from a business that is growing too fast and runs out of cash. Businesses pay their bills with cash, not paper profits.

We have identified just some of the things that can go wrong in an individual's life or in a business that can seriously affect ability to pay over time. So be sure and make the money owed you as the most important and urgent item in the world. If consumers say they can't pay you because they have other bills, I would always convince them that yours is the most important.

David and I have talked with many different groups of people over the years about how to best negotiate with customers. Many times we will start off with the question: what is the last bill people always pay? It does not matter which group we are talking with, they always feel that they are the last to get paid. When we have asked a group of CFOs from hospitals, they say that people pay their medical bills last. When we talk to utility executives, they say that people pay their power or gas bills last. When we talk to cellular administrators, they say that people always pay their cellular phone bill last. How can everyone be paid last? The person who is paid last is the last one to *ask!*

Wright

One last question about speed and urgency. You mentioned earlier that a debt becomes less collectible over time. Would this affect its value in a financial way?

Sher

The best way I know to answer this is to relate it to business. I have been in the receivables business all of my life. I remember when Martin and I were talking to a group of bankers and we asked a group of people, "If a business wanted to offer up their $1,000,000 accounts receivable that is ninety days old or older for collateral on a loan, how much would you lend against that collateral?" It did not take long for the group to yell out "Nothing!" That should answer the question of how important it is to collect your accounts receivable as fast as you can.

Wright

I see now why you use the acronym A-S-K in outlining your negotiation training. We have covered A for Attitude and S for speed. What about the K in A-S-K?

Sher

K is for Knowledge. I mentioned earlier that collection negotiations are a science as well as an art. If you study and practice and read and learn and listen, you can develop the skills you need to execute the science of collection negotiations successfully.

There are two major components to collection knowledge: information and technique. To help you organize your thinking, the acronym to remember is I-T—Information and Technique. When you finish this section you will have gotten I-T!

Let's start with Information. When I refer to information, I am going to help you with some information you need to know as the collector, and more importantly how to listen for and gather the information you need from the customer in order to collect the bill.

Here's the big picture: I think it all starts with three basic groups of people. There are well-intentioned honest people. I believe this makes up about 80 percent of the population. These people pay their bills and you should have no trouble collecting from them.

Group two consists of the credit criminals. These are people who have no intent to pay. You do not want to waste too much time on these people. They will not pay no matter what you do. Luckily this is a very small minority, representing just 2 percent of the population.

This leaves about 18 percent of the population where most of the collection activity and negotiation takes place. These people generally have good intent, but are young and immature, disorganized, or run into an unplanned circumstance that makes it difficult for them to pay. These percentages work the same whether it is a consumer account or a commercial account. I think you can assume though that roughly 98 percent of the population can be reasoned with, negotiated with, and collected from. They have good intentions.

You then have to consider a person's ability to pay. Does he or she have enough money coming in to take care of bills owed? With good questioning, listening skills, and a little bit of experience you can determine this rather easily.

There are basically three methods of collections. The personal visit is the most effective and the most expensive. This should be utilized when trying to collect very large commercial or consumer accounts. Sending collection mail is the least effective and the least expensive. Letters do not collect much money on their own, because they are one-way communication. By far, the most cost-effective and productive method of collections is utilizing the telephone. It is a two-way communication and it is very efficient from a time standpoint.

Wright

David, are there certain basic steps you have to go through to be an effective negotiator on a telephone call?

Sher

Yes, there are eight steps to an effective telephone negotiation. Let me outline them for you and briefly discuss:

1. Identify the Customer
2. Identify Yourself
3. Ask for Payment in Full
4. Pause and Listen
5. Determine the Problem
6. Find a Solution
7. Close the Call
8. Document the Call

Steps one and two are very easy. Just make sure you are talking to the right person on the other end of the phone and tell him or her who you are and who you represent.

Step three is also easy, but important. Always ask for the *total amount* past due. When this is done you have officially opened up the negotiation process.

Step four is the simplest step and definitely the most important. All you do is listen. Do not say anything. You must use tremendous self-control. The customer will talk in 100 percent of the cases, even if there is a long silence before he or she starts. But you must listen. Remember, we are discussing the two parts of the knowledge section: information and technique. You are about to get a ton of information that will help you collect that bill if you actively listen and question.

Step five is to determine the problem. It is almost always about not having enough money—still pretty easy.

Step six is where the rubber hits the road—find a solution. This is where you help the customer figure out how the money needed can be raised in order to pay the money owed you.

Step seven is to close the deal, which simply involves reviewing the solution you and the customer have both agreed upon in step six.

And step eight is to get it documented in a computer, on a piece of paper, or on a napkin if necessary—just get it documented. The information you learn and document from this important phone call might give you the edge you need to get this debt collected. In a significant number of cases, the customer will not pay from this first phone call and commitment. Being able to call back the day after the commitment is missed, and being able to review the information you learned during the last phone call will let the customer know that you are persistent, knowledgeable, and are going to follow up until this bill is paid.

Wright

Well, Martin and David, you have covered a lot. What are some of the most effective negotiation techniques you can describe that will help us collect more money?

Sher

We will share with you some of the most important and useful ones we use at AmSher in our training. David and I have trained thousands of collectors over the years and we will outline and describe a few that have helped us build one of the best collection businesses in the world!

Before we describe the techniques, we still have to remind you about the importance of the championship collector's attitude—it is vital. You must assume that the customer owes the bill and is going to pay the bill. You also have to have that assumptive attitude that the customer has the money or can raise the money to pay you today.

To drive home this last point—that people have money—David and I will share with you one of the examples we use in our Championship Collection seminars.

First of all we try to find someone in the room who needs every penny of his or her paycheck each week to make ends meet and does not have additional disposable income. I ask, "If I called you today and told you that I need a payment of $1,000 on a medical bill you incurred, would you be able to pay me today?" In almost all the cases, the response is, "Absolutely not! Impossible."

Then I describe the following situation about my imaginary multimillionaire friend who loves to give away his expensive $100,000 plus cars every month for just $1,000. My job is to find people who can come up with the $1,000 for that valuable car. So, since I have this customer on the phone (who did not have $1,000 for this medical bill), I decide to ask the following question, "Can you give me $1,000 by this afternoon at 5 o'clock in exchange for a $150,000 Rolls Royce?"

How many of these people who just said they could not come up with $1,000 for the medical bill would come up with $1,000 for a $150,000 Rolls Royce? You guessed it: almost everyone. The point is that more people have money or access to money if they know how to find it and are motivated to find it.

I am going to give you seven of my favorite negotiation techniques and a brief description of how you might use them. There are a lot of different kinds of debtors/customers and many different circumstances. I feel certain that any one of the following techniques will collect more money, and more than pay for the price of this book.

Suggest that the customer not pay a competing bill: When you call someone and he or she says that your bill cannot be paid because there is a more important bill to be paid, say that your bill is more important and not to pay the other one. If you are (or feel like you are) collecting your own money, this is easy to do. The squeaky wheel always gets paid first!

Appeal to a higher authority: Remember, your job is to ask for the total amount past due to be paid today. If the customer does not agree, and gives a counter offer, always say you have to get permission from a higher authority. You can almost always get additional money above the counter.

Good Guy/Bad Guy: This is similar to the above. The point here is to always let the customer know that you are on his or her side and are trying to help get the best deal possible for the customer. Let the higher authority be the bad guy.

Refuse a Payment: In certain circumstances where you know a customer has the capacity to pay and is trying to pay too little, it can be very effective to say no, that you absolutely cannot take a payment that small. I would recommend this mainly in situations where if you guess wrong, you can enforce collections legally.

Incremental Negotiating: Remember, it is important to ask for the entire amount past due today. The customer might want to pay a very little amount over an extended period of time. Always avoid splitting the difference. Do not go to the middle of the two offers. If a customer cannot pay you the entire amount today, the next question should be, "What is the closest you can possibly get to the amount I am asking?" If you accept less, let it be in tiny increments. Let the customer come up faster than you come down. It is worth taking a little extra time to accomplish this. Remember, every counteroffer made by the customer can be discussed with the higher authority.

I would like to mention one other component of incremental negotiations that might be useful. It deals with negotiating length of time to pay as opposed to an amount of payment.

Let me give you an example. Let's assume you are trying to collect from a person who owes you $5,000 and you are not going to be able to get payment in full. You realize you are going to have to set up a payment plan. Never ask, "How much can you afford to pay a month?" You might get an answer that is way too low and might take way too much time. Always ask, "What is the least amount of time you need in order to get this paid?" In the $5,000 example, if you ask how much is affordable, the amount might be, "Ten dollars a month." That would take over four years. Instead if you asked, "What is the least amount of time you need in order to get paid?" I doubt they would say, "a little more than four years."

Yes Questions: Ask a series of "yes questions" that will help set up the payment you want. This type of questioning can work with people who have good intent to pay. Let me give you an example or two of the types of questions you can ask. A series of properly scripted and sequenced "yes" questions can help maintain the customer's self-esteem, give him or her a reputation to live up to, and create trust.

- *"Mr. Smith, wouldn't you pay this bill if you possibly could?"*
- *"Mr. Smith, I know you always do the best you can to pay your bills, and I know you would pay this one if you possibly could. Isn't that true?"*

- *"Mr. Smith, I know your credit and reputation are important to you. Would you allow me to help you maintain your good name and get this bill taken care of?"*
- *"Mr. Smith, would you allow me to work with you to help you get this past due bill taken care of?"*
- *"Mr. Smith, I know you will be relieved when we get this bill paid. Will you allow me to help you find a solution?"*

Create Anxiety: When all else fails, sometimes you have to create a little anxiety. I would only use this if nothing else seems to be working. One technique I teach is to ask a series of questions that the customer might feel uneasy about. You want the person to wonder why you are asking these questions. The entire phone call might go something like this:

- *"Mrs. Jones, I know we have talked previously and you have not been able to follow through on your commitments. I would like to verify a little information, please."*
- *"Mrs. Jones, your address is 2816 Hickory Oak Drive, isn't it? I also show that your social security number is 555-555-5555. Isn't that correct?"*
- *"Are you still employed with ABC Company?"*
- *"Thank you very much and have a nice day."*

Hopefully you have created a little anxiety with the customer by asking these questions. I would not be surprised if the customer calls back a little later to see why you asked this information.

Wright

I have one final question. What advice can you give us that would summarize what someone would most need to know to be a successful collection negotiator?

Sher

Be the first to ask for the money, have an assumptive attitude, and help the customer figure out how the money can be raised to pay the entire amount past due, today!

About the Authors

DAVID AND MARTIN SHER have literally grown up in the credit and collections industry. From their childhood experiences working in their parents' credit clothing store in Birmingham, Alabama, to their current daily activities running AmSher, a national debt collection agency, David and Martin have learned the value of negotiations in all their endeavors. David is a recent past President of the Birmingham Chamber of Commerce and Martin has served the American Collectors Association International in many capacities, including as Chair of the Ethics Committee.

David and Martin Sher
AmSher
600 Beacon Parkway West
Suite 300
Birmingham, AL 35209
Phone: 205.322.4110
E-mail: negotiate@amsher.com
www.amsher.com

Chapter 12

T. MAX HAYNES

THE INTERVIEW

David Wright (Wright)

Today we're talking with T. Max Haynes. For almost twenty years T. Max Haynes has trained, consulted, and shared his expertise with banks, resorts, associations, technology companies, and real estate executives. He tackles such diverse topics as simplifying sales strategies, creating corporate culture, financial management in tough times, and implementing outstanding customer service. A graduate of the University of Southern California's Entrepreneurship Program where he also studied international relations, Mr. Haynes led U.S. business delegations abroad to Russia, China, and Japan. He has produced entrepreneurship educational videos and national conferences with Michael Dell of Dell Computers, Steve Jobs, Apple Computer founder, and Ted Turner, CNN founder. He has been featured in more than 500 television, radio, and print interviews. He served on national advisory boards of the U.S. Small Business Administration, and the U.S. Department of Commerce where he deliberated U.S. economic and competitiveness issues. His experience, interactive style, straightforward approach, and bottom line business savvy are the qualities that make him impactful.

T. Max, I'm intrigued with one of the titles of your presentations, "Negotiating Your Future." Will you explain the title to our readers?

T. Max Haynes (Haynes)

Before you can be a great negotiator with others, you must first be able to negotiate with yourself. We tell people you must have a clear picture of what you want out of life. That may include your dreams, your goals, your priorities, and values. You can learn all the secrets of great negotiators but until you can negotiate with yourself and understand what *you* want out of life it's going to be very hard to accomplish your goals.

Wright

That makes a lot of sense and that makes for a perfect title.

In your contact with highly successful people have you found any important assets that are shared by all?

Haynes

Absolutely. I'll list the top three winning assets:

1) They never give up,
2) They tend to have great leadership skills, and
3) They somehow always have access to capital.

These are three critical ingredients found in my experience with successful people. These experiences tend to go across the board from entrepreneurs to corporate executives to those who have started impactful nonprofit organizations. They all tend to have these qualities and they know how to utilize their skills for their particular goals.

To review these assets in a little more detail, the first one is probably the most important one—*they don't give up*. This involves again, negotiating with yourself and understanding why you are doing what it is you are doing. You must really know yourself and what you want from life. Is it money? Is it to help others? Is it independence? What's your driving force? You absolutely must believe it; if you don't, others will not. The first thing is they don't want to give up—they believe in their dream well beyond what anyone else believes.

Wright

As you teach people to become the best negotiators or salespeople possible, is there a magic formula that you recommend?

Haynes

We often look for a formula to help us become a better negotiator or a better salesperson. There are numerous books on these topics and there are many formulas—ten habits, ten theories, or ten methods. Oftentimes these can work but in my experience it again begins with a belief in yourself together with leadership basics. It's not that these formulas don't work, it's just that some people find it difficult to use them and others don't need them because they already have those skills. They're not secrets, they're just basics. They may sound too easy but they're really not. It's all about the implementation of leadership concepts and basic ideas. The concepts are simple, yet making them happen every day is very, very difficult.

The advanced formulas will work and they are great for some people but until you understand the basics and you're committed to those it's going to be very hard to go on to the advanced concepts.

Wright

You speak often of "Back to Basics leadership concepts." Will you summarize these for our readers?

Haynes

Probably the essentials in "Back to Basics" leadership involve some simple principles. Number one, I would say is that *people don't want to be managed—they want to be led.* If you want to manage someone, we say you should manage yourself. You want to manage your tasks but you really want to inspire people. If you can do that well, then hopefully those people will find a way to manage themselves in a way that benefits the organization. It comes back to inspiring those around you—selling them on your vision, making them understand what you are about, and what the organization is about.

The second principle is that we must believe *the carrot always wins over the stick.* Again, that's a very simple concept. You must praise those who work with you or your partners, at least four times for every reprimand. That is very difficult to do. It means you have to compliment people four times as much as you criticize them. Interestingly enough, this applies to your personal life as well. We all know how hard that is to do with a significant other—a spouse or a child. The positive feedback is what allows people to listen to the negative and make themselves better and do more of what you want them to do.

The third concept we teach is to *catch people doing something right.* Great leaders always take the time to find the greatness in every person. Leaders and managers often only meet or talk to their employees when there is a problem. We must spend more time catching people doing the incredible things they do because then they'll want to do more of those things.

There are many basics but the last essential principle is that we need to *correct the behavior, not the person.* We have to focus on the inappropriateness of an action performed, not necessarily that you feel a person is inept. You don't ever make it personal.

Those are some of the basics that highly successful people have found can dramatically change an organization. They may be simple to understand, but a challenge to implement every day.

Wright

Is it really possible to never give up?

Haynes

I am asked that all the time. Of course there is a point where you must set a dream or a goal aside, however, in my experience, if you are willing to let go too early you'll never be able to make it through the difficult times. In almost every story of success there were many, many hard times. It's how you handle those hard times that defines success for those highly successful people. If you don't believe yourself and your dreams it's going to be very hard to bring others around to that dream. You have to believe that you're never going to give up. In reality, there may come a time when you need to know when to let go but that comes much further down the line; you can't go into a challenge believing that you're going to get out if it becomes difficult.

Wright

Is it possible to learn great leadership skills? And if so, why do more people not do it?

Haynes

Absolutely. You can learn leadership skills. I've met many incredible, special people who learn people skills each day. It takes a strong desire and tremendous self-discipline to master those skills. I think the key is to realize that without others the size of your dream will be limited. You need to inspire others to see your vision.

People who are great at something but not great at leadership tend to know this deep down inside and they know that they need to work on people skills. A lot of the skills we teach are designed for those who say, "Okay, what are the basics I need for the rest of my life?" Once they understand they have to do them and that they're not hard, yet require discipline and focus, then they'll do them. After thirty days, sixty days, six months, and a year, those skills start to set in and they become more of a habit so they can truly change and apply those skills.

Wright

T. Max, I've read that you suggest that leaders should correct the behavior not the person. Will you give us an example?

Haynes

Yes. In order to survive you must focus on the behaviors of people, not whether they're right or wrong or good or bad. This is probably one of the most difficult leadership skills. If you have someone in your organization and he or she is not doing something in the way you want, or someone in a relationship is not doing what you want, you can't think of that person as bad. If you do, you won't be able to change their behaviors. You must find a creative and sincere way to talk to the person about what they are doing that needs to change. Usually it starts with a belief that people are good, they want to be there, and they want to do a good job. In reality, people want to do a great job. If they're just shown the way to do it and they're complimented, they're willing to have their behaviors corrected.

I often use a technique called "*Tell, Show, Practice, and Feedback.*" It is so basic, yet it can change an entire organization. It's one of those "Back to Basics" that people say, "I can't believe this is so simple." You tell people how to do something, you then have to show them how to do it, and then you have to have them practice that action. While they are practicing, you've got to give them feedback of what they're doing correctly and where they need to improve. It doesn't matter whether they're learning how to pour a water glass or if they're learning to run an entire department in your company, it's the same basic concept. It's not complicated; it just takes a lot of work as a leader. Most bosses only "tell" people what they want them to do; they rarely "show" them and hardly ever give immediate "feedback."

I believe that you can correct behaviors, you just have to take your time, be focused on it, separate the personality of a person or what you think about that person, and focus on what it is he or she is doing.

Wright

I wish I had met you in my twenties. I probably could have saved myself from a lot of managerial mistakes I made.

How much time should leaders spend in self-development?

Haynes

Self-development never ends. The most successful people I've met are open to learning and improving every single day. Probably one of the best things they realize is that they're limited in their own knowledge. My "Back to Basics" concepts are simple, yet even I must relearn them constantly every day. Every time I read these concepts I think, "My gosh, I need to do a better job at this. Oh, I'm not doing this or that."

Great ideas require great execution not just knowledge. Often in our society today we focus on knowledge rather than implementation. There's plenty of knowledge out there. There are plenty of concepts out there. It's all about practicing and remembering those concepts and applying them every day.

I believe great leaders never stop developing themselves. They tend to make mistakes and they tend to realize they're making mistakes and they tend to improve. They tend to admit they're making mistakes, not only to themselves but also to people around them.

Wright

Is it really possible to motivate others? I've been told that motivation comes from within.

Haynes

Indeed we must motivate ourselves, however, we can inspire others. We like to focus on inspiration. Inspiration is leadership that will lead to self-motivation. Everyone wants to be part of a vision, a dream, a goal, an organization, family or something great. A great leader has to paint that vision and he or she has to use every negotiation skill available to help others "see the light." It takes a lot of work, however, and as a leader that is your job. Motivation is the goal and I'd say that inspiration is how to get there.

Wright

You've said that successful people have access to capital. How does one go about developing that characteristic?

Haynes

People don't speak a lot about capital and money as skills. People say things like, "Money makes the world go around" or "it takes money to make money." The reality is that great leaders have access to capital—maybe their own money—but often it's not their own money. Often the goal requires a lot more than you have. I talk a lot about having your own capital or your own access to credit, but you must know how to go out there and raise money as well. Your ability to negotiate will really come out when you have to raise money.

Martin Luther King did not say, "I have a budget."

It all comes down to selling a dream. People talk to others about business ideas but will they believe enough to write a check? That's the question to ask. *A business idea is just an idea until someone is willing to write a check!* That's a concept that never goes away. It doesn't matter if you're starting a lemonade stand—you have to borrow enough money to buy lemonade—or if you're going public and you need to raise capital. My experience is you've got to sell your dream, you've got to master your leadership skills, you need negotiation skills, and access to capital is essential.

More importantly, you have to practice the skill of fundraising. People say, "Well, when I have a great idea I'll go raise the money." Well, you've got to learn to raise money along the way and you need to know where to get that money. There are many sources of money and you have to be creative. Usually they will be people who know you—friends, family, investment groups, it may be venture capital. It may be other creative strategies that we teach such as seller financing or supplier financing.

It amazes me how little personal financial education we receive growing up. Building capital and managing credit are keys to always having money available for your future. There are three key steps to paying for your dreams:

1. Establishing and maintaining great credit
2. Controlling your life with a budget
3. Building a personal endowment

First, credit is a way of life in America today. You need to *establish credit*, but you need to use it wisely. You must always protect your credit and payment history. In emergencies, most entrepreneurs have used credit.

Second, you must always *control your life with a budget*. You must focus on needs not wants until you reach your dreams. If your world is out of control, you can't be successful! You must focus your resources on goals that really matter. Most self-made people have at times skipped expensive dinners, new cars, and other items that only give short-term pleasure. Once you reach your ultimate goals, the small things will follow.

If you are just starting out, you must master the concept of a *personal endowment*. This is your war chest to use to finance your dreams. It is not a savings account; it is your endowment for success. This kind of fund is the basis for your financial freedom. It is money that you invest, grow, and always find a way to contribute a portion of all your earnings. If protected, it will provide you a chunk of capital to use to finance your ultimate dream.

The following are the most common sources of financing:

1. Self
2. Secured Loans (Real Estate, Stocks, Retirement Funds)
3. Unsecured Loans (Credit Cards, Life Insurance Policies)
4. Government Small Business Loans
5. Friends and Relatives
6. Individual Investors
7. Investment Groups/Clubs
8. Venture Capital
9. Manufacturer/Supplier Financing
10. Seller Financing
11. Stock/Investment Offering

All types of money sources are out there but it comes down to a focused idea, an absolute belief in your vision, the skill to negotiate with others, and an absolute ability to sell your dreams.

Wright

If you could tell our readers one simple step that would start the drive to negotiating their own future, what would it be?

Haynes

I have spent some time with billionaires and millionaires when they were just starting. People like Michael Dell of Dell Computers left me with one great idea. This guy is focused, and boy, does he believe! From a young age Dell was focused and he knew what he wanted. He told me a story once that he fired his entire board of directors because they did not completely believe in him or his plan. It doesn't mean they were bad people, they just did not see his vision at that moment.

When I asked him his secret he just repeated one word and that was, "Focus, focus, focus." Michael Dell had many small failures along the way and he could have sold out, changed directions, or settled for a smaller company. But he didn't—he had a dream.

So I guess the answer to your question is another question: Do you really have focus? Do you really know what it is that you want? I would tell you the one essential step—it is not simple but it is most important—it is to completely believe in something. Once you know what that is and you focus, you will be the best negotiator in the world. It will no longer be a strategy it will be a way of life.

Wright

T. Max, I've really enjoyed the time we've spent together. That was terrific. Thank you for being with us today on *Masters of Impact Negotiating.*

About The Author

For almost twenty years, T. Max has trained, consulted and shared his expertise with banks, resorts, associations, technology companies, and real estate executives. He tackles such diverse topics as: simplifying sales strategies, creating corporate culture, financial management in tough times, and implementing outstanding customer service.

A graduate of the University of Southern California's Entrepreneurship Program, where he also studied International Relations, he led U.S. business delegations abroad to Russia, China and Japan. T. Max has produced entrepreneurship educational videos and national conferences with Michael Dell (Dell Computers), Steve Jobs (Apple Computer founder) and Ted Turner (CNN founder). He has been featured in more than 500 TV, radio, and print interviews. He served on national advisory boards of the U.S. Small Business Administration (SBA) and the U.S. Department of Commerce where he deliberated U.S. economic and competitiveness issues. His experience, interactive style, straightforward approach, and bottom-line business savvy are the qualities that make him so impactful. T. Max is a "no-hype" strategist who provides "basic" tools that withstand the test of time.

T. Max Haynes
Post Office Box 12
Tahoe City, CA 96145
Phone: 530.583.2299
E-mail: info@tmaxhaynes.com
www.Tmaxhaynes.com

Chapter 13

Eric Trogdon

THE INTERVIEW

David Wright (Wright)

Today we're with Eric Trogdon. He is founder of STEPS Canada, an organization that specializes in the conduct of negotiations, facilitation of mediations between third parties, and he offers customized training programs in conflict resolution. His affiliations with organizations in education, parks and recreation, law enforcement, and business have won him numerous awards in conservation programs, hostage negotiations, and professional presentations. Previous experience includes Zookeeper, Naturalist, University Recruiter, Park Ranger, Police Officer, DARE Instructor, Child Abuse/Neglect Investigator, and SWAT Negotiator. Eric holds a Master's of Public Administration, Certifications in Mediation and Conflict Management, and Crisis Negotiation. He is a member of the Canadian Association of Professional Speakers, International Speakers Association, and Toastmasters International.

Eric, welcome to *The Masters of Impact Negotiating*.

Eric Trogdon (Trogdon)
Thank you, David.

Wright
You had the opportunity to serve as a successful Special Weapons and Tactics (SWAT) Negotiator during your eleven years in Law Enforcement. Will you give us advice on how someone becomes a SWAT Hostage Negotiator?

Trogdon
Well, David, through lots of negotiating and positioning I put myself in the right place at the right time, with the right people, and the decision-makers. I believe it has a lot to do with what you know, whom you know, and most importantly who knows you.

I was afforded opportunity to be in a law enforcement position after being a park ranger for a number of years. As a police officer, I had the option of working in different specialized services. If a person with the right qualifications has interest in working as a SWAT Negotiator, they must first become a law enforcement officer with that specific department. The person must also meet the requirements of service. Most departments require that the officer have at least three to five years of experience on patrol before being considered for such specialize services. An officer must have the practical experience in the community that he or she will be serving. In my case, I held the position of Senior Police Officer with Charlotte-Mecklenburg Police Department in Charlotte, North Carolina. The department was the second largest police department in the Southeastern United States. I managed to attain a law enforcement position where I could impress the SWAT decision-makers. They soon came to appreciate my work ethics, demeanor, enthusiasm, and attitude about police work, as well as my service to the community. They realized that I could be a major contributor to the team. I was therefore encouraged to apply. I went through the interview process and was successful in passing various character checks.

Anyone wishing to be a member of a SWAT Team must be willing to be a "team player." I believe that is probably one of the greatest skills a SWAT negotiator must possess—the ability to be part of a team of dedicated professionals who train together and are willing to trust each other with their lives. A person cannot be a successful Negotiator without the help of other team members. It is important that the Negotiator be able to appear empathic with the person who is being negotiated with, and be willing to recognize when he or she should step away and let someone else take over. It can be a very long and arduous process.

For people considering becoming SWAT Negotiators I would strongly suggest that they make sure their family supports them in their decision to go into a law enforcement career. Not only will the stress affect Negotiators, it will have a strong influence on their private life and family relationships. Negotiators look at the world in a different light, which can be very dark and unpleasant.

Wright

What exactly is involved in a crisis negotiation? Give us some ideas of the process from the initial call-out to the scene to the debriefing.

Trogdon

The job of a Negotiator is very exciting and very rewarding. It has probably been the most exciting part of my career to date. From the moment the Negotiator's pager goes off in the middle of the night, the excitement and adrenalin starts. I never knew what I was about to face. Each situation is different and to me it was always an exciting "Game." That is how I look at it—it is just a game, albeit a very serious game of skill and patience with human lives at risk. The pager goes off and the uniform and mindset goes on; I am out the door, and then en route to the scene in minutes.

As Negotiators, we have a lot of control over the scene. Until the Negotiators arrive, the scene is usually secured, locked down, and at a standstill. Upon arrival at the scene, the first action is information gathering. The Negotiators must meet with other team members, develop a flexible plan, and be willing to explore creative options. I use the term "Negotiators" because we usually never work as a single Negotiator. It is all about teamwork.

The goal is to have everyone come out of the situation uninjured, and with minimal property loss. There is seldom a perfect negotiation but the team works hard to meet that goal. Everybody needs to come out uninjured. When the suspect is under control, the public is safe, and SWAT administration is satisfied with the outcome, I consider it a successful negotiation. Usually debriefings are held immediately following the end of the incident. This is the opportunity to review our successes and look for areas to be improved. All persons involved are part of the debriefing with the exception of the person negotiated with of course!

Wright

After having experience with over forty-two negotiations and hundreds of investigations, you must have developed specialized skills that made you very good at resolving crisis situations. What are some of the skills that you learned over the years?

Trogdon

I believe that a Negotiator must be willing to interact with people whom he or she would not necessarily care to interact with in his or her own social sphere. In other words, negotiating put me in front of people or talking with people I had never come across and certainly never associated with before. Negotiators must have the ability to disengage from their biases and feelings toward that individual, and to not see the suspect as the problem. The incident or situation that led up to the incident is the problem. As I mentioned before, I tend to look at the situation as a "game." Some of my colleagues may disagree with that attitude, but that is how I have been able to work through very serious situations. Sometimes a situation involves a loss of life or has the potential that there will be a loss of life. It is easy to get so caught up in what is happening that you focus on the seriousness of the situation and fail to see all possible solutions.

I distance myself when I need to, recognizing that from time to time there are situations I cannot handle without being biased. If I have a conflict of interest or the suspect just doesn't like me for any reason, I must be willing to disengage and let my secondary Negotiator take the lead. The ability of seeing each situation as a game is a skill that has helped me be successful in negotiating during crises.

Wright

At the end of the day, how do you know if a negotiation was really successful?

Trogdon

During the debriefing, each team member has the opportunity to expresses his or her evaluation of the process and outcome. The team has to bring all the evaluations together and come up with a review of the incident and the process. If everyone comes out alive, that is a major consideration in determining if it was a successful negotiation.

If a negotiation did not result in a conclusion that the team and administrators had intended but were able to learn from it and could apply our findings to future situations, then this also may be considered a successful negotiation. Our goal is to have the minimal loss of property, ensure the public is safe, and to have all persons, including the suspect(s) we are negotiating with, leave the scene alive and unharmed. Processes and policies are sometimes developed from the debriefing and some of these ideas can save lives in the future. There is not always a perfect, successful negotiation but the team works hard to meet that goal. When the public is kept safe and our administration and team feels satisfied about the outcome, that is what I consider a successful negotiation.

Wright

You have served as a SWAT Negotiator and you work with many others. With your experience, do you now believe that someone is born with the ability to be a great negotiator or is it a learned skill?

Trogdon

I believe that the ability to be a successful SWAT Negotiator is a skill learned through knowledge and experience. It is part of a comprehensive individual growth process. The successful Negotiator has to be a person who is willing to help other individuals to succeed. I really do not believe that a great Negotiator is born.

I have seen people who try to be Negotiators but they do not realize the importance of being patient in crisis situations. During most crisis negotiations, time is on the side of law enforcement. Some people would be to quick to react and would have difficulty in slowing down to be able to complete the process and allow quality communication.

Wright

Eric, you have had experience with hundreds of crisis situations and investigations. Is there any hostage negotiation incident that stands out in your memory from all the others?

Trogdon

There are two incidents I remember very well. They occurred back-to-back over a two-day time span.

On the first night, I received the pager call-out at about one-thirty in the morning. It was September 28, 1998, and the team had been called out regarding an individual with a gun who had killed a young woman after he had followed her home that night. Police had followed the armed individual to the front of a convenience store where he was surrounded and asked to surrender. Negotiations and talks with him continued all through that morning, the afternoon, and into the following evening. We negotiated with the suspect for fourteen hours.

The suspect was actually locked outside the front of the convenience store. Luckily, the store clerk had been stocking the coolers in the back of the store at the time and had locked the door minutes before the gunman had driven up to the store. He had probably intended to take the clerk hostage. The suspect held us at bay while brandishing a 9mm handgun. We did not want to escalate the situation because we were in a neighborhood and beside a four-lane highway. I remember I was pretty tired when the other negotiator took over as lead. At about the fourteen-hour mark, the gunman decided he'd had enough and ended it by taking his own life. What makes this case so interesting is the twenty-seven-year-old gunman was very controlling of the entire incident.

At about four hours into the negotiation, we subsequently learned that he had been a perpetrator in a negotiation incident ten years previously when he was seventeen and a student in high school in South Dakota. He had taken his high school class hostage with a shotgun. When negotiating with him during the second situation, it was clear that he did not want to have the same outcome as in the first, ten years previously. We contacted the Negotiator who had been involved in the first situation. He advised us that the first hostage situation ended when a classmate took the opportunity to tackle the perpetrator during a diversion created when pizzas were being delivered. We were faced now with a gunman who was not going to make the same mistake. We also were able to make contact with the individual's father in Colorado.

I remember the words his father said when he found out what his son was doing. His first statement was, "Why haven't you shot him yet?" So we knew we had someone who had some serious issues and that he knew a lot about the negotiation process.

This incident helped us test our process in background gathering, locating people with the pertinent information and how to work hard on controlling the situation. The gunman ended the incident by shooting himself when he was sure that all the SWAT tactical team was watching him. He attempted to have full control of the incident until the end, but we had to remain in control for the safety of everyone involved. We also had to contend with the media. The local television stations and newspaper were flying their helicopters and planes near the area. The department had to get some control over the air space for the safety of the media. The tactical team also intercepted the father of the woman the suspect killed, as he attempted to work his way through the woods to get close to the scene.

The outcome was unfortunate but still considered a success. Suicidal urges cannot be controlled, but nobody else got hurt. I do remember going home that evening and finally getting to sleep at around 11:00 PM.

The second call came at around 3:30 AM. the following morning. Captain Stancill of the Mecklenburg County Sheriff Department was shot in the face while working off-duty at a Harris Teeter Grocery Store. The suspect had run from the scene and was still in the area armed. Captain Stancill died while trying to confront the suspect after the suspect had stolen a package of crab legs from the store. The SWAT team had been called out to find the suspect. This was a very unusual task for the team—no hostages and no negotiations, just teamwork in going into the community and finding someone who had killed a member of our law enforcement family. If he would kill a law enforcement officer, he would kill anyone who got in his way. The team had to gather information and develop a plan to search the area while relying on others in the community. The team worked through the night and into the morning and finally located the suspect walking along a roadway unarmed. Information from people interviewed and some old fashioned detective work gave us the information to identify the suspect, who had been hiding and thought that he had gotten away with the murder. The handgun was discovered a few hours later in a neighbor's mailbox.

Those two incidents seem to stick out over the others. They were very demanding, required great skill and attention to detail. It was a precise game of timing and teamwork.

Wright

You worked most of your career in the United States and now you operate your own Professional Speaking, Training, and Mediation business in Canada. Have the skills you learned as a Hostage Negotiator prepared you for the work you do today?

Trogdon

They have. The training and experiences I acquired while negotiating have caused me to realize that people are going to do things that will surprise you. When they do, I know not to get too focused on the situation. I have learned to distance myself and understand that I may not agree with how this person got to that point, but I have to understand what his or her reasoning may be that created the situation.

Another skill I have found to be a great asset is to work on slowing things down. When I work with people who are in conflict or in disputes, I can get them to just calm down and cool off which allows them to slow down and think a bit more. I am amazed at how this process gets people to start interacting and communicating more positively. The fear of communication is the most common problem in disputes. People just do not know or are not willing to just slowly talk and listen. I use my negotiation skills almost every day. It may be the skill of powerful listening, or how to ask the right questions, or just the ability to put people at ease while slowing the process down. My experience in Law Enforcement and Negotiations has given me great insight in many types of cultures, beliefs, and how people deal with stressful situations. This kind of education not taught in school or learned in a training program.

Wright

What part of being a hostage negotiator did you like the least and on the other side of the table, what part did you like the most?

Trogdon

I always resented an early morning call-out, driving half way to the scene, and then receiving a call from the dispatcher to cancel our response due the situation being resolved. I always got so psyched up for the unknown, and then I had to lose that momentum. That was very tough. The excitement begins the moment you get the call. That is part of the thrill of the game. When I was out of town, I never liked to miss a call-out because I may miss a very unusual incident. It was also frustrating to be tied up on a case as a patrol officer on the street, and not able to respond to a call-out. One of my fellow Park Rangers called it the "Wolf-Syndrome." The group hears or sees something happening and all want to go with the rest of the pack and be part of the excitement. Another negative is the affect that prolonged negotiations has on family. There's a lot of stress placed on the other family members as they see the danger and the possibility of your not coming home one day. As a law enforcement officer I was very good at handling the stress due to great training and practice. Training for the other family members of law enforcement officers should be offered.

What I liked most is the excitement, the unknown you are about to experience, and the chance to see a part of life you would never have had the opportunity to see anywhere else. I had the opportunity to work with people I highly respected and I was given the opportunity to train with the tactical team and their equipment. I was doing something that I never thought I would have an opportunity to do. I learned a lot about people and how my conflicts and problems were minor compared to what some people must deal with. I also learned a lot about myself and it made me appreciate the way my parents brought me up.

Wright

Is there any crisis situation or incident that should not be negotiated?

Trogdon

I think you can negotiate just about any situation under the right conditions with the right people. I don't think any one person has the ability to negotiate *all* situations. For instance, I would never negotiate in a situation if it involved someone I knew personally such as a family member or friend. I would have great difficulty in being truly objective in these situations and would not be able to distance myself from my emotions. I could not treat that incident as a game. If the situation is a case where time passing may cause a person to be killed or injured, then Negotiators must be part of the decision to allow the tactical team take control and use calculated force immediately.

I believe that you must even negotiate with terrorists. While negotiating, terrorists are being given the opportunity to be heard. Allowing them to feel that they can have some respect and be allowed some dignity, may dissuade them from escalating the situation to the next level. In my opinion, it is always worth trying as long as you can distance yourself emotionally, you have a well-trained team, and the team is willing to take whatever time is necessary to resolve the situation.

Wright

What advice would you give our readers or to anyone in the event they find themselves taken hostage?

Trogdon

When most people are taken hostage there is a feeling of, "this is not happening." There is the initial shock—they are stunned and they cannot react—which may not be a bad thing. Sometimes the person who reacts to the situation causes the hostage-taker to do something he or she did not plan on doing. Hostage-takers can get very confused and scared. A hostage has to understand that sometimes some things just happen and you just cannot prevent some things from happening. Hostages are in the situation just by being at the wrong place at the wrong time or because the suspect reacted to something another person did or did not do.

If I were taken hostage, I would try to become the person who is not noticed as much as the other hostages. I would plan not to be the hostage who is crying and being hysterical (I hope), and I would not be a hostage who is going to open his mouth and challenge the hostage-taker. A hostage needs to be the quiet person who just tries to be in the middle of the emotional road. About two hours into the incident, if it lasts that long, I would ask politely about being allowed to go to the restroom. That shows I am human and I have some needs. Hostage-takers are more likely than not to know those needs and are probably going to start feeling those same needs about the same time. If they can engage with me as a human being over a period of time, the likelihood of them hurting me or any other hostage diminishes. The longer you are a hostage, the more likely you will come out of the situation a live and unhurt.

Then there's the "Stockholm Syndrome." The syndrome is named after a bank robbery in Stockholm, Sweden. The term was coined by criminologist/psychologist Nils Bejerot who assisted the police during the robbery and referred to the syndrome in a news broadcast.

In 1973 robbers held bank employees hostage from August 23 to 28. The hostages became emotionally attached to their captors and even defended them after they were freed from their ordeal. There were situations during the incident where they had close interactions, even sexual interactions with their captors. They became so in tune with their captors that they didn't want to be rescued. That helped save their lives because the robbers became emotionally attached to their captors too. I would never recommend going to that extent, but our readers must understand that people will develop some attachment or understanding why the hostage-taker is doing what he or she is doing. That can be a good thing because everybody starts seeing everyone else as human beings.

I also suggest that if the hostage-taker is talking, yelling, or verbally abusing the hostages, it is a good idea to allow it and not interrupt. If hostage-takers are talking, that is a good sign. They are releasing their frustration and anger. Let them talk and just be quiet and listen. They will eventually work themselves down and become calmer and start thinking more clearly. Maybe at this point it is possible to engage in slow conversation. Do not ask too many questions and remember to allow them to answer even if they take a minute or so to respond.

Wright

Eric, you've held many different kinds of jobs. You've been a Zookeeper, a Naturalist, a University Recruiter, a Park Ranger, a Child Abuse Investigator, a DARE Officer, and a SWAT Negotiator. Why did you have so many jobs and do you feel that having a variety of jobs helped or hurt you in your career?

Trogdon

Well, I guess I am still trying to find out what I want to do when I grow up! There is so much in the world to discover and do. One thing I have learned is that if I enjoy something, I give it my all. If I get to the point where I would like to try something new, I go for it. I have been fortunate in the careers I have had and the dynamic people with whom I have had the privilege to work. I have lived in different parts of North America and have been able to find fun and enjoyment in the work. I strive to maintain a great attitude, even when things were not so good. It has not all been "guts and glory"—like being a highly skilled police officer working a traffic beat in the pouring rain, and being cursed out by ungrateful drivers. I have always tried to see the positive side of a situation. Life can be very miserable at times, but you only make it worse if you allow a negative attitude to take over.

I have been very fortunate to have worked with some very good people. All of these different jobs have helped open the world up to me. I have been given the opportunity to experience interactions with different individuals, cultures, and different ideas. Now, while training, or handling negotiation, during mediation cases, speaking engagments, or in training sessions, I have a wealth of experience to draw on. All of those experiences help me relate to more people and develop new connections. I have found that no one can be truly successful without the help of other successful people and quality relationships with the right people. I find everything I have done has been a great opportunity for me. I am very fortunate.

People ask if I will ever make up my mind about a single career path. Probably not! I am having too much fun learning new things and taking on new adventures.

Wright

As I take a look at the span of your experience I can see real interest and what you call excitement. I can also see helping.

There's one aspect where I would find it impossible to stay detached and that would be your stint as a Child Abuse/Neglect Investigator. Even when I read about child molestation in the newspaper it angers me. It's one of the few things I cannot understand.

Trogdon

I did not understand it until I actually sat in the room with an individual who had followed through on something that I too find totally inhuman and deplorable. I became detached and had to look at the investigation as a game. The individual had done something that I just could not comprehend. I had to ask myself, "Can I go into this game, keep my feelings back, and get this individual to tell me his story?" If the answer is, "yes," then I can do my job to the best of my abilities.

It is also important to ask the right questions until the suspect finally opens up.

I was amazed at the stories I would hear. I would persist in the questioning, but in a respectful manner, always giving them the opportunity to answer. If you don't ask the question, you will never get the answer you are looking for. You must never be afraid to ask.

Wright

And they were forthcoming?

Trogdon

Most of the time they were. I was sometimes very surprised. They seemed to want to open up and get rid of the weight of guilt. Some investigators were just amazed at the information I was able to obtain by simply asking a direct question. I would sometimes notice my fellow investigator looking at me in away that said, "I cannot believe you asked that!" I have to give them the opportunity, let them know I see them as a person, and just want to talk with them while respecting them. During the process, I know the information I am getting is going to help put the individual where they need to be. It is all a game, but at the end of the day I get to go home and the suspects usually do not.

Wright

Well, as the title of our book would imply, you've had a tremendous impact with your negotiating skills. This has been an interesting conversation, I've learned a lot and it gives me a lot to think about too. I know it has given our readers a lot to think about.

I really appreciate your spending this much time with me, Eric, to answer these questions and be as honest and forthcoming as you have been. It's been enjoyable for me.

Trogdon

David, it's been a pleasure. I hope that our readers find some things that will help them. Remember to let people talk, try to slow the situation down, ask questions, and listen some more. Also remember that you have to get the support of other successful people to be successful yourself.

For anyone who is interested in more information or if you would like to talk with me personally, you are welcome to contact me at STEPS Canada.

Wright

Today we've been talking with Eric Trogdon who is the founder of STEPS Canada, an organization that specializes in the conduct of negotiations, the facilitation of mediations between third parties, and customized training programs in communication and conflict resolution. And, as we have found out today, not only are his experiences varied but he knows a lot about the subject of negotiation.

Thank you so much, Eric, for being with us today on *The Masters of Impact Negotiating*.

About The Author

With over twenty-seven years of experience in conducting mediations, facilitating negotiations, and presenting customized programs, Eric Trogdon has built a reputation for being inspiring, entertaining, and memorable. He has worked with groups in education, parks and recreation, law enforcement, and small and large corporations. Eric has held the positions of University Recruiter, Zoo Keeper, Naturalist, Park Ranger, Police Officer, SWAT Negotiator, and Mediator, just to name some; all of which help him to bring a unique perspective to his message.

Eric holds a Master's of Public Administration, Certifications in Mediation and Conflict Management, and Crisis Negotiation. He has won numerous honors in conservation programs, hostage negotiations, and for professional presentations. Eric has appeared on television and radio programs and thoroughly enjoys giving live presentations.

Eric is a Professional member of the Canadian Association of Professional Speakers, Toastmasters International "ATM," and the International Federation for Professional Speakers. Eric believes that citizens should be active volunteers in their community.

Eric Trogdon
STEPS Canada
737 Brock Road, Suite 100
Dundas, Ontario L9H 5E4
Phone: 905-628-1112
Fax: 905-628-6271
E-mail: eric@stepscanada.ca
www.stepscanada.ca

"Being successful is mostly about allowing very bright and talented people to help you. A person who has given me tremendous support and guidance is Robin Scott with the Abel Thomas House Bed & Breakfast in Niagara-On-The-Lake in Ontario, Canada. (www.abelthomashouse.com). Robin, thank you for making sure that I do my best and for giving me encouragement when I needed it most. I can only wish that others may find a friend like you."

Chapter 14

RON KARR

THE INTERVIEW

David Wright (Wright)

Today we're talking with Ron Karr. Ron is an expert on negotiations and has over thirty years of experience in negotiating business deals. In one case he helped reposition a client, a transaction that ultimately led to a negotiated ten-year supply agreement valued at over $200 million.

Mr. Karr has conducted negotiation seminars and keynote addresses on three continents for clients including Morgan Stanley, Marriott, UPS, and Hertz.

He is author of *The Titan Principle®: The Number One Secret to Sales Success,* and articles written by Mr. Karr appear frequently in national publications. Media appearances include the CBS Morning Show, Bloomberg TV, The BBC, and hundreds of radio interviews.

Ron is an active member of the National Speakers Association.

Ron, welcome to *The Masters of Impact Negotiating.*

Ron Karr (Karr)

Thank you.

Wright

Would you describe for our readers a little bit about your background as an expert on negotiations in the commercial markets?

Karr

First of all, I grew up negotiating since the day I was born. I always found ways to get around certain situations—it was a trait I had. As I started my sales career I began to notice that I always got to my sales positions after the "heyday" of the company. What I mean is that the companies I went to work for had just made all their money and I had to sell in very difficult situations. Either the products I had to sell were not necessarily the products the market needed at the time or they were overpriced. I still had to produce my numbers for my manager and more importantly, I had to produce them for my earnings. I had to find some ways that I could still go in there and determine how best could I do a deal with companies when I didn't have the best fit. That is what really honed my negotiation skills and helped me write the book *The Titan Principle®*.

Wright

In your experience you claim there are four fundamental components of a negotiation. What are they?

Karr

The four fundamental components of a negotiation include:

Positioning: I think where a lot of people go wrong is that they separate the concept of a negotiation from getting the deal. What I mean by that is negotiation doesn't begin when you start discussing terms. Negotiation really begins the moment you start talking with the customer and you start framing your value proposition. It begins with how well you position yourself in the eyes of your customer. If you do a good enough job at positioning yourself at the highest level in the mind of the customer, when it comes time for the actual negotiation of terms and conditions you're automatically starting from a higher level of strength.

I urge my clients that when they get into deals with their customers to start from day one and ask themselves how best they can position themselves with being perceived as having a higher value proposition than they may have had before. Ultimately that is what's going to help them negotiate a better deal.

Strategy: Many people go into negotiations or meetings with the customer without figuring out how they're going to carry out the actual process. There are different strategies involved. For instance, in some situations you may be asked to go into a deal with the strategy of "all or nothing." You know that if you were able to elevate this deal where you wanted to get the entire package for the customer, there's a greater chance you can sell a greater value proposition than if you just divide and conquer and went after the individual pieces.

On the other hand, there are times when you have a greater strength going after the individual pieces because there may be some obstacles such as people who don't want you in the enterprise-wide solution; but if you can just get in there and start showing your value with the people who want you, then you may be able to spread out the relationship as time goes on.

What you really have to do is to sit back and ask yourself, "Based on this situation I'm dealing with—the people I know, the strengths and weaknesses I bring to the situation—what's the best strategy from which to operate?"

What I've found, working with a lot of sales minded executives, is we don't give the right amount of attention toward developing the proper strategy. We would have served ourselves better if we had thought about it a little bit more.

Wright

So you could use the words "strategy" and "planning" interchangeably?

Karr

Absolutely. It really is the same. A strategy is a qualitative measure of how you're going to go about an actual negotiation. Obviously you can't think about strategy if you don't plan and planning is a big component. Most of us don't plan enough—we go in by the seat of our pants and go after the sale and many times we're unprepared for certain situations so we can't respond from strength.

Karr

The third component of a negotiation is:

Tactics: Tactics are the tools you're going to use to get better terms and conditions. There are thirteen common tactics that everybody uses and we'll go through those later. Tactics are methods used to scope out your position and to get you to agree to terms you may not otherwise agree to. They are the gambits—the negotiating ploys people use.

There are some tactics that are very powerful and there are other tactics that could possibly have a reverse effect and negatively impact your overall positioning. What I mean by that is you have to be careful about what tactics you use because we do train buyers on how to buy from us in the future.

Here's an example: One of the most common tactics is "aim high and then compromise." That's fine, however, you have to remember that once you aim high and compromise you've now educated that customer that they can expect you to give things up in future negotiations. For every action you take there's going to be a reaction down the road and you have to make sure that what you do in the negotiation not only helps you in the current deal but sets you up probably for the relationship you want long-term.

Alignment of goals: I'm really about win-win negotiations. There are four options you can get in a negotiation. The first is where both parties lose. If that happens, they don't need you; they need to go see a shrink.

There's another scenario that can happen where you, the seller, could lose in a negotiation and the customer wins. For example, a customer could say to me, "Why don't you just give me this lower price today? It's coming up to December and give me the lower price and ease my budget this year and I promise to give you all my business next year." In a sense you're losing because you're not getting the value you think you should be getting and you're giving it up in hope of new business. That customer gave you that promise out of good intentions but things change and all of a sudden he may not be able to keep his promise next year. You start feeling you've been wronged and start putting pressure on this individual. Before you know it the relationship goes south. That's not a good situation to be in. You both have to win.

A third scenario is where I win and the customer loses. I've put something over on the customer and I've got the deal but the customer realizes he probably won't do another deal with me down the road.

The best negotiation is where both parties win. Both parties have terms and conditions they hold valuable to their cause and both parties align with each other to move forward together where without moving forward together, they would not be able to do as good a job.

Wright

You have written and spoken about classic mistakes salespeople make during their negotiations. What are some of those?

Karr

The most critical mistake starts with the actual negotiation and it's not dealing from a position of strength. When you don't deal from a position of strength and someone uses a horrible tactic on you, you can't walk away.

An example is I was doing a public program on negotiations in Brazil in Sao Paulo. During one of the breaks a gentleman came up to talk with me. He owned a small automobile parts manufacturing business. He said, "Lopez is killing me." (Lopez was the famed purchasing agent for one of the automakers. He was this notorious buyer who just beat up mercilessly on his vendors.) The man said, "When I sell to this company it's probably 30 percent of the overall demand that they need from the whole market. But what they buy from me is 70 percent of what I make. They're squeezing me down on my prices—I'm not making any more profit and I'm going to go out of business.

I told him his problem wasn't Lopez. He gave me a quizzical look and said, "What do you mean?"

"Your problem," I said, "is you don't have any other alternative sources to sell your products or you have not found any other products you can make with your machinery so that if this business doesn't make sense you can go someplace else. As long as you're in this position you are at the mercy of that buyer and you can't deal from strength."

If we don't have enough deals in our pipeline and need that deal so badly, we can't afford to react to certain tactics in a way we would normally respond and are forced to deal from a position of weakness. Automatically we set ourselves up for probably doing a deal with terms and conditions that don't meet our expectations.

The second big mistake is the salesperson doesn't own the offer. How many times have you been in a situation where you may have been buying something and you ask the person what it costs and they tell you hesitantly because they know it has a big price tag?

If you don't own the offer and there's hesitation on how you're presenting it and there's a quizzical look on your face, you're basically conveying a message that tells them there's room to negotiate the price.

The way you own your offer is, in a sense, if you're asking for a price higher than you've asked for before, practice it. Practice saying it with conviction; but at the end of the day, when someone hears it from you, that person has to believe that you really feel the value is what you're asking for.

You also have to know what your Points of Power are. Points of Power could be anything. It could mean demand outweighs supply. Obviously, if that's the case, then you know you're in the driver's seat because people need your product and they can't get it elsewhere. A time element may be a source of power. This is something that most salespeople don't do. They don't put a time element to their deals—they don't put a perceived sense of loss. Look at every negotiation like a transit union strike, etc. Whenever there's a potential strike there's always a time deadline—if the demands aren't met by a certain time there's a strike. In 90 percent or more of the time, miraculously you get a deal at the eleventh hour. You don't get that if you don't have a time element giving you that point of power.

If you have a good knowledge of the industry, that is a point of power because you know what's real and what isn't, so people can't put things over on you.

Obviously, if you have the best price, that's a point of power. If you have the best value you may have a point of power because even if your product is more expensive but will cost less over time, that's a point of power. If you have the best service, that's a point of power.

Where most people fall short is they immediately go into a negotiation without grounding themselves within those points of power. And then they're at a table negotiating with somebody and the other person uses a tactic to try to get a compromise. If they're not grounded in their points of power and because the tactic being used gives a perceived sense the deal is going to be lost, they will start to capitulate. If you're grounded in your point(s) of power and really understand that the other person has more to lose than you do, you're less likely to give in and compromise on things you didn't have to.

What we really urge people to do is before they go into that meeting, sit down and really ground themselves in their points of power. Understand what it is you're bringing to the table. Understand what the potential losses are for the customer if they don't deal with you and then use that to help give yourself the confidence to go and negotiate a deal that's proper for the value offered and for what they need.

Wright

You have written and talked about linear thinking versus all around thinking. Is the difference some sort of problem solving?

Karr

Yes. We've all grown up and gone through the school system to think in a linear way—start here and go straight out there. Linear thinking is great if it's on a line but the greatest solutions to any problem or negotiation is sometimes not on a straight line. Sometimes you have to think upward. Sometimes you have to think downward, sideways, or to the back, or around in circles.

What we have found to be the best negotiations was finding ways to help people think differently. What happens in a negotiation, for instance, is that people are negotiating on a certain thing and they get so stuck on that one thing that they don't look at it from a different point of view, therefore they can't come to a conclusion and they reach an impasse.

I'll give you an example. I was helping this company renegotiate a five million dollar deal with one of their biggest suppliers. The supplier was in the red and they decided that to get in the black the only way to do it was to reduce every existing contract they had by 18 percent. They hired a professional negotiator whose only job was to take apart all these contracts. My client is a big company we've all heard about and they went into that negotiation trying to talk about all the value added they had to offer.

The negotiator stopped them and said, "Listen, that's nice but here's the deal. Give us the 18 percent decrease now, then we'll talk about your value." Obviously the conversation didn't go anywhere and my customer flew back home. They decided to do a very intense proposal. One of the things they were trying to tell their customer about was the concept of renting versus leasing. They were the only ones who had a computer system that could track whether they should rent or lease and they could literally save them hundreds of thousands of dollars. They went back with this proposal and these numbers and they got stuck with the same problem—the negotiator refused to sign the deal unless the contract was 18 percent less.

Again, they left the negotiation without a contract. They then contacted me and asked what they were doing wrong.

I told them that first of all they were negotiating on the wrong thing. "You're negotiating on the 18 percent price decrease that you can't give so why are you negotiating this point? There's nowhere to go but to have this conversation turn out badly. What is that company really after? What they're really after is to go from being in the red to being in the black. Their perceived solution is to cut all contracts by 18 percent and they'll get there. What you need to do when you get into that meeting is ask them what they're really after. Ask them, 'Are you after an 18 percent price decrease, which in our case will give you X or are you looking to save as much money as possible?' " What do you think their answer was? It was to save as much money as possible.

They had the proof to tell the other company that they're going to get four times the return on the investment by resigning with them and using their technology to drive costs out of the other company's system.

That is an example of linear thinking. They kept going down one road that wasn't leading anywhere. It only takes one person to change the thinking of everybody in the room. You can do that with a different question, with a different viewpoint, and many times it's on the person who's trying to negotiate the deal. We took that responsibility. We got stuck on a road that wasn't going anywhere and we decided to change the path and say, "You're so ingrained on an 18 percent price decrease but is that all you want? Or are you going to look better when you get a lot more in return?"

Wright

Would that be letting assumptions drive your negotiating strategy?

Karr

Obviously assumptions were a big part of this and I can't tell you how many times I hear clients talk about their assumptions. I tell them they have to go in without the assumptions.

I once had a client who did a due diligence. They were going after a big supply agreement. They developed this incredible PowerPoint slide show with all the bells and whistles. A week later they presented their deal and after the hour presentation they asked how they did. The buyers and executives looked at them and said, "That was great but didn't you hear? We've reorganized since we talked with you last week. Everything you've just presented is null and void."

Our clients' environment is changing rapidly just as ours is. Things we knew to be real yesterday that we're basing assumptions on are probably not going to be real the day we're going to negotiate.

I see the world differently than the way you see it. This is why you can have two people on the corner of 42nd Street and Broadway witnessing a car accident and giving two distinct descriptions of what happened. That's why, when they had the Washington, D.C., sniper situation, the FBI kept saying they didn't have any reliable witnesses. They weren't saying the witnesses were lying, they were saying they couldn't get two or more people to give the same picture. When we know that we're different as to how we see the world, why are we using our assumptions as to how *we* think this is going to play out? You have to make sure the person on the opposite side of the table sees your assumptions the same way you see them. If you don't do that, you're having a one-sided conversation that very rarely closes a deal that makes sense for both sides.

Wright

How important is it, as far as communication is concerned, to empathize with the other party and really listen to them?

Karr

It's huge. One of the things we talk about is conflict resolution. One of the first steps in conflict resolution negotiating is you've got to acknowledge the issue. I'm not saying you take responsibility because we're in a very litigative society and I would never tell anyone to take responsibility. But there's a difference in taking responsibility and saying you did something wrong versus saying, "I understand you've been inconvenienced by what happened to you." If you say that, then the other party knows you've heard him or her. Anything you say after that will be listened to. If you don't acknowledge what the other person has said, and go straight to the solution, your customers have stopped listening. All they're thinking in their mind is, "Why is this person not acknowledging my pain? He has no clue about what I'm feeling." Whatever they're told after that, even if it's on point, is not going to be heard.

You have to have that empathy and you've got to be able to somehow prove that you've heard them. If you acknowledge what they're feeling, your solution and how you can help them will be heard.

Wright

You talked briefly about the Points of Power. Will you tell our readers a little more about this and why they are so important?

Karr

There are inherent Points of Power and then there are creative Points of Power. What I mean by this is that in your products, your service, and what you offer as an organization there are some inherent strengths. It could be that no one else makes your product and demand is just outstripping supply—that's inherent. You have to realize it exists so you can take advantage of it.

A time element, for instance, could be a point of power. You could say you could do something for the customer for two weeks but if they don't decide to do it within that timeframe, the deal is not on the table anymore. Forcing people to make a decision is a creative point of power. Most of the time we don't push people to make a decision but often you have to because if you don't, they could drag the process on forever.

What we've found is that often, time could be the enemy of a person. I'm right now involved in two negotiations with two clients. They're after these two deals. I keep telling them, "You've got the person interested, he wants to switch vendors, he's not pulling the hook yet and I'm telling you, if let this drag for the next month and you don't close this by the holidays you will lose momentum."

You've got to find some way to put a time element on the deal and encourage the individual to want to sit down, make a decision, and move forward.

Your knowledge of the situation is a point of power. If you understand what's happening more than your competitors do, certain tactics will not mislead you and you'll be able to stand up for what's rightfully yours.

Risk-taking ability is a point of power. If you have a full pipeline and you're only going to go after the deals that make sense for you, that's a point of power. So, understand you don't have to take the first deal that comes your way; you can take the deals that make sense.

Strategic relationships are a point of power. In the early 1980s when I was in sales I was selling disk drives. I worked for Control Data; at that time they were number eighty-four on a Fortune 100 list. They owned the disk drive manufacturing business and they were the best in the world.

What happened is that my little division took, on an OEM basis, disk drives and then we packaged them for end-user sales. We'd sell them to companies like Goldman Sachs. Every time these companies bought a PC they would take one of these external drives and add it on to the computer. The problem was that I was 40 percent higher than my competition. They were selling the same drives I was selling, manufactured by my company; but by the time we took it and added the mark-ups for overhead, for the talent at Minneapolis, and all this good stuff, I was 40 percent higher. I couldn't compete with the computer factories in the world and I had to find a way to find a reseller that needed me as much as I needed him.

I eventually found a start-up business in Princeton, Clancy/Paul. The president and co-founder, Glen Paul, was a graduate from Princeton University. I saw him advertising in the *New York Times* and I got an appointment with him. I asked what his challenges were. He said, "I'm a start-up. We want to be the best integrator for Fortune 100 companies but I don't have a lot of time. I have to get this done within six months because I only have so much money to use."

I said, "Then you need credibility." He agreed and I said, "We're number eighty-four on the Fortune 100 list. We have all the inroads to the *Wall Street Journal, New York Times,* etc. What if you sign on board and use our drives for every system you put out there and we will put out a press release that we have just signed a strategic partnership with you? He jumped at that in a second. Understand, we were very high in price; but what he needed most was credibility and I understood that was a point of power for me. We signed the deal and we did a half a million dollars worth of business with him that year.

Wright

If you were giving our readers some advice, what is the one thing someone could do to always insure he or she is negotiating from the very strongest position possible?

Karr

People first have to realize that it's not always about price. Price is important but many times people just beat you up in price when they feel that everything else is equal. You have to concentrate on the value you are providing and many times that has to go beyond product features. We get caught up with all the features we have to offer and they think they can get the same thing someplace else.

At the end of the day, the question that has to be answered is: How is this organization or individual going to be better off by doing business with me, with the mix I have to offer, my products and services, my own personal service, and my company's service? What are the outcomes they will achieve that they will probably not get elsewhere? This is where you have to look at all the points of power you have to offer and the value proposition.

You also have to do a good job of finding out from the customers what it is they're missing. Many times we go into a negotiation trying to negotiate a deal and we don't know much about our customers. Find out where they're trying to go and what's missing for them. Even though they're dealing with a vendor they like currently, there's probably something they wish they could have that they still don't have. Find out what that is and then find out what the consequences—what's at stake for them—if they don't get it. This is what's going to set you up for whatever it is you're asking for.

To put it in a nutshell: Understand your points of power, position yourself in the highest possible light with your customer (by finding out where they're trying to go, what's missing, and what's at stake if they don't get it) and then position your offering in a way that speaks directly to your customers' desired outcomes. At the end of the day, how is your customer going to be better off with you versus some other scenario?

Wright

What an enlightening conversation. Ron, I really appreciate your spending all this time with me answering these questions. I know I've learned a lot and I'm positive our readers will.

Karr

My pleasure. As you can tell, I get jazzed talking about this. If we make some impact on lives, that makes us feel good.

Wright

Today we've been talking with Ron Karr who is an expert on negotiations and author of *The Titan Principle®*. He conducts negotiation seminars and keynote addresses all over the U.S. and in other continents as well.

About the Author

RON KARR is a business negotiation expert who has helped clients build their businesses exponentially through power negotiations. In one case he helped reposition his client, which ultimately led to a negotiated ten-year supply agreement valued at over $200 million. In another case he helped a multi-national corporation thwart a competitive threat and win a significant increase in sales revenues.

Mr. Karr has conducted negotiation seminars and keynote addresses on three continents for clients including the NFL, Morgan Stanley, Marriott Hotels, UPS, Hertz, Cognis Chemicals and Agfa.

He is author of *The Titan Principle®: The Number One Secret to Sales Success.* Articles written by Mr. Karr are published monthly in national publications including *Entrepreneur* magazine and *Home Office* magazine. Media appearances include the CBS Morning Show, Bloomberg TV, The BBC and hundreds of radio stations throughout the world.

Ron is an active member of the National Speakers Association and is past president of its New York Tri-State Chapter.

Ron Karr
Karr Associates, Inc.
372 Kinderkamack Road
Westwood, NJ 07655
Phone: 201.666.7599 / 800.423.KARR (5277)
www.ronkarr.com

Chapter 15

ROBERT D. RUTHERFORD, PH.D.

THE INTERVIEW

David Wright (Wright)

Why do you think there is so much misunderstanding about what negotiating is and what it is not?

Robert D. Rutherford (Rutherford)

Negotiating has gotten a bad wrap. Ask virtually anyone—aside from those who professionally make their living negotiating—what they think of when they hear the word "negotiating" and you will get answers like: "Adversarial," "A battle—be careful," "Negotiating is only for the hardnosed, tough-minded person."

There is a belief among many that when one negotiates, one has to put his or her armor on and march off to battle to beat the other person and to give up as little as possible and gain as much as possible at the other party's expense.

As kids we were trained to share our toys, to be nice, not to be aggressive and confronting. For many the whole idea of demanding what you want, of asking for what you want, of give-and-take with another person is only for the pros.

I recall a time when I was selling my home in Pacific Palisades, California, because I had left the faculty at UCLA to join the faculty at Caltech in Pasadena. A young couple had come over to my home on three separate occasions to consider buying the property. The last time they called, I told them I had just reduced the price to $32,000, under the market value (you can imagine how many years ago that was!), for a quick sale if they wanted it. If not, I would rent it out.

The husband with his wife returned to see the house again. Then the husband, in a somewhat condescending tone (or at least that is the way I interpreted it), said to me, "Okay—I will give you $29,000 for the house." I remarked that he and I knew that $32,000 was a near steal. The house was his if he wanted it. If not, he was out of there and I would rent it.

He responded, "Okay, $29,500."

I said, "You are out of here."

Some years later after having rented the home, I decided to sell it. The market brought over $500,000. I can only imagine what the house might bring in today's market. I write this not to try to impress you but to impress upon you that you don't have to always get the "best buy" by continually trying to knock down the price and terms. If it is a good deal, take it.

I wish I had that couple's phone number so I could call them and share with the hardnosed negotiating husband that he could have purchased the house and several years later sold it for over half a million dollars—on an initial investment of $32,000!

Negotiating is not war; it is not about beating the other person. It is about crafting an exchange that benefits all parties to the transaction.

Key points:

- It is as important to know *when* and when *not* to negotiate, as it is to know *how* to negotiate.
- Just because you *can* negotiate doesn't mean that you necessarily *should* negotiate. Why? Because negotiating often takes significant time, energy, planning, and execution. Be selective.
- Reserve negotiating for those occasions where the possible payback in terms of money, satisfaction, and process is commensurate with the potential rewards of that negotiation.

Wright

If you were to give just one thing of power in negotiating, what would it be?

Rutherford

Many things give power in negotiating—skill, attitude, timing, leverage, other parties' needs and wants, expectations, and more. But if forced to give one item that above all else gives an individual power in negotiating opposite the other party, it is to have a strong B-O-O-N (Best Option Outside Negotiation). It is your walkout point; it is where you go when you say, "No deal. I am out of here."

It is almost a direct relationship that the stronger your BOON, the stronger you will be in the negotiation. The weaker your BOON, the weaker you will be.

Key points:

- An unrecognized BOON is the same as having no BOON at all. So, pay attention to what options are available outside negotiating with the party you are dealing with.
- Develop your options. The more viable options you have outside of any particular negotiation, the stronger you will be in the negotiation. Out of those several options there will be one that is the best: Your BOON.
- Know not only your own BOON, but know the other party's BOON as much as possible. Know that the other party is never going to GO for your offer unless they believe the offer you are giving them is better than their BOON.

Wright

What does win-win or mutual gain mean?

Rutherford

The term *win-win* has been so bandied about and means so many different things to different people. Therefore, it can serve one well in any negotiating arena to get an agreed-upon definition of win-win up front with your opposite party.

What does win-win mean? It depends on who is defining it. Win-win in general could be argued to mean that both parties get enough of what they want to feel that it was better to have negotiated than not. Put another way, the parties have to believe they received more value than they gave up.

Rather than referring to a negotiation as a win-win, I prefer the term "*mutual gain,*" where each party gains more from having negotiated with each other than if they hadn't. Win-win or mutual gain is especially important when the parties will have a working relationship after the negotiation is concluded, where the agreement needs to be implemented according to the letter and spirit of the agreement, and where there is a desire and/or opportunity for further dealings down the road.

Key points:

- Don't confuse win-win with a nice, soft feeling kind of negotiating. Win-win negotiators can negotiate hard and tough but fair and seeing mutual benefits from the deal.
- To effect a win-win agreement, all parties will seek fair dealings and mutual regard for each other's needs, wants, concerns, and goals in the negotiation.

Wright

When I get stuck in negotiating and neither party is willing to move from its position, what should be done to get unstuck?

Rutherford

Most of us, at one time or another, have gotten stuck in our attempt to get from NO to GO®; each side would not budge. Each side felt it had given all it could give and in some cases even more than it should have.

Being stuck can be likened to an iceberg: the tip of the iceberg represents the stuck position. It is a commonly known fact that the *Titanic* was not sunk by the tip of the iceberg; it was what was lurking below the surface that destroyed the ship.

In negotiating, to get unstuck, go behind the positions and see what is causing the parties to hold to their stuck positions.

Many years ago, when I was a young real estate broker starting out my career in Santa Barbara, California, I was attempting to get a listing and sell a six-unit apartment building owned by a Mr. Vickers. He wanted very much to sell his apartment building and I very much wanted to sell it for him. He had large equity in the building; in this case it was free and clear—no loans against it. He didn't like tenants and had gotten to the point where he was refusing to rent to anyone when the unit became empty. (Strange, I know, but that was the way it was.) There were now only three units rented, and he and Mrs. Vickers lived in one of them.

Mr. Vickers made it clear he would not take anything less than $600,000, although he recognized and admitted that the building was at best worth only $475,000. He hated the building, wanted to be free of it to travel, and yet wouldn't budge off his price. In fact, he told me he was going to die in that building before he would sell it for anything less than $600,000.

To solve this and get unstuck, we had to go behind the positions and discover Mr. Vickers' real motivations, fears, wants, desires, and hidden agendas. It turned out that Mr. Victor had paid $600,000 for the building four years before. He also indicated that he knew he'd paid too much for it and that there had been a recent downturn in property values in Santa Barbara. He remarked he loved his wife and children but that they wouldn't give him one day's rest if he sold the property for any less than what he paid for it. And Mr. Victor wasn't about to set himself up for that kind of ridicule.

In less than three weeks, I sold his building—yes, for $600,000 when it was worth only $475,000. (This involved a little creative exchanging—taking in a smaller overpriced duplex in trade and a creative owner carry-back financing with a moratorium on the interest and a heavy discount option at the end of five years.)

It was a good deal for the buyer and for the seller (and a good deal for me as the real estate broker with a growing family). Mr. and Mrs. Vickers could now do what they wanted to do—be free to travel in their twilight years.

Key points:

- In negotiations with colleagues, suppliers, and customers, there will be times when the NO to GO® process will get stuck. It may look hopeless. Maybe it is, but first check it out. Go behind the issues—negotiate the fears, wants, and personal agenda items. Ask—don't guess. Listen. Be creative.
- In Mr. Vickers' situation, he feared his family and friends and anyone else who was interested would ridicule him if he sold the building for one dollar less than what he had paid for it. He needed to save face and maintain his self-esteem by selling the building for what he had previously paid for it—$600.000.

Wright

Why is it important to know if you are in or out of the negotiating arena?

Rutherford

It is important to know whether you are negotiating or not, especially in the more serious areas of agreement making. If you don't think you are negotiating with the other party but you really are, you may be making all kinds of concessions and commitments that you did not intend to make.

There are certain things you do in the process of negotiating that you do not necessarily do outside the negotiation. Areas of concession include the way you plan or don't plan, the way you make your demands, the questions you ask, and the proposals you make. So know if you are in or out.

Let me give an example. At one time, one of my biggest clients was the University of South Carolina in Columbia. During football season, knowing that the U.S. Naval Academy played the University of South Carolina normally in Columbia, I would arrange to have my two-day NO to GO® negotiating programs scheduled the following Monday and Tuesday so I could see the game the previous Saturday.

In 1984 the game venue was changed from Columbia to Annapolis, Maryland, where in the college upset of the 1984 NCAA Division IA season, Navy beat second-ranked South Carolina, which ironically would most assuredly have been ranked number one had they not been defeated that Saturday.

I sat in the stands at the Naval Academy watching this Navy victory take place. After the game, I went down to the field and walked over to the co-captain of the Navy team who had been a one-man wrecking crew against South Carolina that day and was later named *Sports Illustrated* "Defensive Player of the Week." I invited him out to dinner that evening.

While we were having dinner I asked what I should say to the South Carolina executives I would be addressing the following Monday for a negotiation presentation. He thought for a moment and then said, "Well, Dad, why don't you tell them that we were not negotiating out there on the playing field today—we were there to beat them soundly."

My son, Eric Rutherford, defensive left guard, didn't say to the opposite offensive right guard, "Hey, fellow, nice to see you out here today. Why don't we negotiate a deal where you move slightly to the right and I will move slightly to my left and we won't be hitting each other and risk getting hurt?" Quite the contrary.

Key points:

- Know when to negotiate and when not to.
- If you are not sure that you are negotiating, ask the other party, "Do you see this as a negotiation?"

Wright

How can I defend myself against a hardnosed, unscrupulous, intimidating, and manipulative opponent—one who attempts to get concessions from me without giving anything back in return?

Rutherford

First, recognize manipulating dumpers for what they are—simply dumpers who wish you no joy and want to take advantage of you in any way they think best serves their own special interests. Second, they can only dump on you with your permission—when you allow them to dump and aggravate and upset you.

I am reminded of a story with a very real message about an incident in the Camarillo State Mental Hospital in California. A newly degreed M.D. intern was asked to observe patient behavior at noon in the exercise yard. On his first day, he noticed a patient pushing a wheelbarrow around the yard upside down. After several days of seeing the same routine, the doctor's curiosity was increased and he asked the patient why he was doing this (i.e., pushing the wheelbarrow upside down).

"Well, Doc," the patient explained, "I may be crazy but I am not stupid. I used to come out here every day as you have seen me, at noontime, and I pushed my wheelbarrow right side up around the yard. And Doc, do you know what happened to it by the end of the hour? So many people dumped so much garbage into my wheelbarrow that I couldn't push it anymore. So all I do now is turn it upside down and no one dumps into my wheelbarrow anymore." (The wheelbarrow story is adopted from an article I wrote in *Today's Manager,* March–April 1976, when I was four years old. [Just kidding about the four-years-old part.])

Note: The Camarillo State Hospital closed in July 1997. It is now the California State University–Channel Islands campus. No comment about the possible resemblance of the two.

While you cannot always stop people from trying to dump into your wheelbarrow, you can take powerful methods to protect yourself from these would-be dumpers. You and I control our reactions to what happens to us. We can choose to allow the dumpers to upset us or to not take personally their demeaning manner toward us.

Key points:

- Next time someone attempts to dump into your wheelbarrow, imagine in your mind turning your wheelbarrow upside down. Guard it against all the dumpers in your life.
- While we cannot always turn our "wheelbarrows of mind" upside down, we certainly can guard our "wheelbarrows" from people dumping all those negatives on us.

Wright

How can I know what the other party really wants in negotiating with me?

Rutherford

Truly asking the right questions and listening completely to the responses is key to learning what the other party needs and/or wants out of the negotiation.

Most of us probably don't ask the right questions in the way that encourages the other party to respond. Additionally, most of us don't listen attentively to others as we should. When this happens, everyone in the relationship loses.

One of my Hollywood High School classmates has become perhaps the world's most famous woman comedian. I'll never forget the remark she made about her friend Lucy Ball. She remarked that in real life Lucy was very different from her public persona on the *I Love Lucy Show*. She said, "Whenever I talked to Lucy, she became my best audience."

What do you think Carol Burnett was saying about her friend Lucy? That Lucy truly listened, cared, empathized, and actively was there for Carol.

To how many people are we their best audience?

What might happen in the next important negotiation if we were to truly become the other party's best audience? How much better would we understand their real concerns, issues, and rationales that support their positions? How much more creative could we be in putting the right and best deal together with suppliers, customers, project team members, partners, colleagues, and/or family?

It's highly unlikely that we can change others' opinion on anything and persuade them to do what we ask until they feel they have been listened to and understood.

Let's put a moratorium on deaf listening and blind looking. Let's work to become the other party's "best audience." We all may be totally amazed and pleased at what can be accomplished for all concerned.

I often ask myself, "Rob have you ever thought about how much you have lost in life by not asking?" Its twin question is, "Have you ever thought about how much you have lost in life by not listening?"

Key points:

- When understanding the other party, it is important strive to be their "best audience."
- Sometimes in negotiating, what the other party simply wants is to be listened to and understood.

Wright

What does "Never make a concession in negotiating without making it conditional" mean?

Rutherford

If there were an unwavering law in negotiating it would be: "Never make a concession while negotiating without making it conditional on getting something back in return."

Making all of your concessions conditional is critical to allowing you to get enough of what you want and need to make the deal. It works the same for your counterparty—they have to make their concessions conditional on getting enough of what they need and want.

A while back I had contracted to give a NO to GO® presentation to a group of twelve CEOs in Santa Clara, California. During the session, I asserted, "Never make a concession in the negotiating arena without making it conditional on getting something back in return."

One of the CEOs, in a gruff and arrogant tone said, in effect, that I didn't know what I was talking about. He said, "I put big deals together ranging in millions of dollars. I make concessions all the time on the small stuff without making them conditional." I interpreted his remarks to mean that I was an idiot, wasting his and others' time by talking such nonsense. He was adamant that he made concessions in negotiating without making them conditional.

What should I do? I thought for a moment and said, "Would you like to look at the principle in negotiating that says for every concession made, make it conditional on getting something back in return?"

He remarked that there was really nothing to look at, but if I wanted to go through it again, fine.

I asked him, "Is it possible that a deal you're working on might not go through?" He said, "Of course." As a matter of fact, he added, probably less than 50 percent of the potential deals go through.

"In those cases where the deal doesn't go through, what happens to all the little stuff that you gave away without making them conditional? Does the other party get to keep them? He said, "Of course not. The deal didn't go through."

I thanked him and went on with the presentation.

Were all the concessions of the little stuff made conditional? Of course—they were made conditional on the deal closing. The "conditional" part doesn't have to be spelled out in every case. It can be implied, understood.

Key points:

- Negotiating is not a unilateral concession. Don't think of making concessions—think of making trade-offs.
- Negotiating is a series of trade-offs and exchanges hopefully leading to mutual gains for all parties concerned.

Wright

Should I negotiate only with people who have authority to make the deal?

Rutherford

Common wisdom states that one should negotiate only with people who have authority to make concessions. Why talk to the monkey when you can talk to the organ grinder?

Authority is the ability or power to make a concession. So if you are in the negotiating arena and have authority but your counterpart has no authority, then who is the only party who can make a concession? You are, by definition, because the other party has no authority to make a concession.

Do not confuse "authority" with "influence." In organizations and in personal living, there are people who have authority but little or no influence; it is equally important to understand that there are people who have no authority (i.e., to make concessions in negotiating) but who have great influence over those who do have the authority to make deals.

It would be easy to argue not to negotiate with someone who does not have authority. Yet I personally have negotiated many times with a non-authority—in part, out of necessity—as the true decision-maker was not or did not want to be available. Sometimes I have negotiated out of choice, knowing it would be easier and more productive to negotiate with a non-authority.

In 1995 my eldest son, Ken Rutherford, decided he wanted to return to graduate school at Georgetown University to earn his Ph.D. and become a professor. He had asked me to help him find accommodations in the Washington, D.C.–Arlington, Virginia, area and help him negotiate the lease agreement.

We had some difficulty finding the right accommodations for Ken because the apartment unit needed to be on the GUTS (Georgetown University Transit System) line, which provides transportation to the university for the handicapped. (Two years earlier during the Black Hawk Down days in Somalia Ken had lost his legs to a landmine. He needed wheelchair access.)

We found just the place he wanted, located in River Towers, Arlington. The only problem was the unit would be available for rent in a week, after it had been cleaned. It was the end of June, and Ken wouldn't start school until August 15. That is when we wanted the rent to begin. How, then, to negotiate this agreement?

We had to determine what benefits and priorities this out-of-the-country owner had that would allow him to leave the apartment vacant for ninety days instead of renting it immediately. The owner wanted a reliable tenant to respect his property. Ken both owned property and had rented and respected real estate.

The owner wanted to be sure that he got paid on time, because a previous tenant had left without paying the last two months' rent. We were willing to pay first and last months' rents plus a security deposit of a month's rent—plus guarantee that the check would be in the owner's bank account two weeks before it was due.

It probably didn't hurt that Ken was going to be a Georgetown University student at the owner's alma mater, or that Ken had lost his legs while serving as an international rescue relief worker in Somalia, risking his life to help others. This gave the broker, Bill Groom, enough "bragging rights" that he could take to his owner to close the deal.

The challenge was to convince the broker, who had no authority but who had real influence with his owner, to recommend he take our offer.

After a lengthy discussion with us, Bill said he would fax our offer to the owner. I said, "Bill, you will recommend to your owner that he accept our offer, won't you?"

Bill thought for a moment and said, "Yes I will. I will recommend that my owner accept your offer."

And so it was that Ken began his tenancy August 15, 1995, in the River Towers Apartment. It was a great deal for Ken, a great deal for the owner, and a great deal for the broker—the owner gained peace of mind and care for his unit and on-time payments.

Key points:

- Do not confuse authority (the ability to make a concession and conclude a negotiated agreement) with influence (having clout—power to sway others to a desired action).
- The key in the negotiating example here was to gain the recommending power of the non-authority agent (the broker) to give him enough bragging rights that he could sell the deal to his client (the owner).

Wright

What should I do when I am not sure if I should say it's a Go or say it's a No and leave?

Rutherford

We don't always know—you can say you are at the fork in the road in this negotiating: which way should you go, No or Go?

You might recall the scene in the 1865 Lewis Carroll book, *Alice's Adventures in Wonderland,* where Alice comes to the fork in the road in the forest and doesn't know which way to go. She sees a Cheshire cat out on the limb of a tree.

"Which way should I go from here?" Alice asked.

"Well, that depends a great deal on where you would like to get to," the cat replied.

"Oh, I don't much care where I get to," said Alice.

"Well, then, it doesn't make much difference which path you take," the cat said.

Pretty smart cat, don't you think? It not only talked, but its words were wise.

You and I are constantly coming to the forks in the road of our work and lives: Should we accept our counterpart's offer or not? Should we go with this supplier over the other suppliers? Should I leave my current job to take advantage of a dot.com opportunity? Should I ask for a raise now or wait three months? It looks like a deal too good to be true; is it, and, if so, shouldn't I take it?

Yogi Berra, the famous Yankee baseball catcher from the late 1940s to the early 1960s (and who, incidentally, threw out the first ball in the 2000 World Series) had some advice on when one comes to the fork in the road. His advice was, "Take it." Not too helpful, is it?

The student asked the teacher, "Teacher, when I come to the fork in the road, how do I know which road to take?"

The teacher remarked, "You do not always know which road to take, but whatever road you take, travel it well, travel it wisely, and by all means enjoy."

Wow—but isn't that so true? We don't always know which road or path to take when we come to the forks in the road—in and out of the negotiating process; but we do know whatever road we take, while we are on it, to travel it well, wisely, and enjoy it as much as we can.

Key points:

- Keep in mind what your purpose and your intentions are as you negotiate and travel down the paths of your life.
- On your roads you can either see the road as too big to travel or too big to miss.
- Along your path, stop guessing and assuming and start asking and discovering.
- Stop and ask for directions, ask for help, ask for clarification. Don't assume others will understand what you ask them.
- Check it out. Don't look to others to do what you should be doing for yourself.
- Do your homework. Be prepared and be the responsible one.
- Stay focused and don't wobble, waffle, or dawdle. Stay the course; finish the race.
- All roads lead to somewhere. Are you on the right road? Until that's answered, travel it well, travel it wisely, and enjoy the journey.

Wright

I hear the expression, "If I am not willing to walk, I am not willing to talk." What does that mean?

Rutherford

This expression means that you recognize before you begin any negotiation that for any reason you choose, you have to be willing to say "No deal" and leave. It recognizes the power of having a BOON—a Best Option Outside Negotiation—with the other party.

Why is this important? Because if you are not willing to walk and the other party knows this, you have extended an open invitation to them to drive an exceedingly and unnecessarily hard and harsh bargain with you. They know that you are not willing to say "no" and leave.

In extreme cases it is nearly like taunting them to beat you up, knowing that you are not willing to draw the line anywhere and stand up and say, "I am out of here."

Is this real? You bet it is. We see people fall into this trap all the time. Salespeople are driven to make the sale and in the process cut profit margins so deeply that the sale can actually be lost. And we are not referring to a lost leader here—a come-on for a more profitable future sale. We see this in matters where the negotiator has become so emotionally involved in "making the deal" that they lose all sense of the cost and rewards in doing so. We see this when the party unwilling to walk sticks it out—stays with the game when the game is long over and any profit they may have gained is long gone.

In negotiating, each party has the veto power, unlike many other forms of contract making required by law. For example, if the other party will not negotiate with you they have, in effect vetoed, barred, and excluded negotiating as a way to gain agreement. No matter how good of a negotiator you may be, the negotiation will not take place without the other party's permission.

Key points:

- Confucius said, "When you walk, walk; when you sit, sit; when you talk, talk; but by all means do not wobble. So if the time comes to walk, walk and don't wobble."
- Stay focused on what you want and need to have from the deal—if you don't get that, get out and go to your BOON.

Wright

What is leverage and how can I get it and use it?

Rutherford

Archimedes (287–212 BC), the Greek mathematician, physicist, and inventor, remarked, "Give me a lever long enough and a place to stand and I will move the earth." That would truly be leverage.

When the power of leverage is understood and rightly applied, you will gain immense power in dealing with others.

Donald Trump, in his book *The Art of the Deal,* remarks, "Leverage is having something the other guy wants. Or better yet needs. Or best of all, simply cannot do without." Trump certainly seems to apply leverage to his advantage as he puts together awesome and, at times, seemingly impossible real estate transactions.

You and I don't need to be the Donald Trump of negotiating to use the concepts of leverage to one's advantage.

Unfortunately, leverage is often overlooked, underutilized, and too often misunderstood. Use your leverage to move your counterpart in your direction.

When do you have leverage? When the "balance of needs" in any particular negotiation falls in your favor. Ask yourself, "Who has the most to lose by not reaching an agreement?" He or she who has the most to lose has the least leverage, and he or she who has the least to lose has the most leverage.

I can vividly remember driving my fifteen-year-old Volkswagen Bug to a bank on State Street in Santa Barbara. I was applying for my first real estate loan in order to purchase a small duplex on the west side of town. At the time, my wife and I had two young children, ages one and two, and were living in a small two-room apartment above a garage nearby. I was a young college professor just out of the University of California, Berkeley. I had no money or savings in the bank; in fact, I was in debt, so that is why I needed a loan.

The loan officer looked at my loan application then looked and me and smiled. I thought, "Great!" Then he said something to me that I've always remembered. "Mr. Rutherford, we can't make the loan to you. I am sorry, but you see, you don't own any assets that we can loan against. You don't have a savings account, your checking account has only a few dollars in it, and you don't make much as a professor and you don't own anything that has any monetary value." (I guess he didn't think my Volkswagen was good collateral.)

Of course, I didn't have any assets. That's why I needed the loan. Where was my leverage? It must have been hiding where no one could find it.

Strange, isn't it? When you truly need the money as I did, the bank won't lend it to you. Now that I have acquired a few assets along the way, lenders of all sorts are constantly calling my office, sending me literature, seeking to give me loans I neither want nor need.

The next best thing to having leverage in dealing with others is to have them think you have leverage. Leverage is power and they will think you have power.

<u>*Key points:*</u>

- You have more leverage than you think and certainly more than you're using. Strengthen your BOON (Best Option Outside Negotiation) and demonstrate to the other party how much they have to lose by not reaching an agreement with you.
- Honor, respect, understand, and use your leverage wisely. You will surely profit when you do.

Wright

Will you explain what it means to say "the power of the written word"?

Rutherford

Never underestimate the power of the written word and work to let it be used for you and not against you.

When I was a young man and a college professor in Santa Barbara, California, I'd saved enough money to make a modest down payment on my first real estate investment property—a rather old but well-kept small duplex on the working man's west side of town. When the escrow closed, both tenants moved out. I then had my first experience renting to tenants. But I couldn't get anyone to rent my duplex.

I explained to prospective tenants that there were no four-legged animals allowed, no dogs and cats, as I didn't want animals messing up my newly acquired duplex. They might remark something like, "What do you want us to do with our dog, kid—shoot it?"

I also explained that there was a nonrefundable security deposit so that if they left before three months were up, they wouldn't get their money back because I didn't want someone coming in for just a few weeks and then moving, leaving me to clean and re-rent the unit. They might say something like, "Hey, you young whippersnapper—what are you trying to do, rip us off?"

Well, anyway, I couldn't get anyone to rent my duplex.

Then someone recommended that I call the local Board of Realtors. I called and told them my plight. They said, nicely, that they couldn't help me because I wasn't a broker and member of their organization. "All you have to do, though," the director said, "is go down to Banks Stationary Store on State Street and buy yourself some preprinted rental agreement forms and just fill in the blanks when a prospective tenant comes over.

I did. Then when a prospective tenant would come by, I'd show them the unit and explain to them that no four-legged animals were allowed, no dogs and cats, as I didn't want them messing up my newly acquired duplex. If they said something like, "What do you want us to do with our dog, kid—shoot it?" I'd reply, "Oh, no, sir. You see, it states right here in the lease, on page two, line twelve: 'No four-legged animals allowed.' " They'd look at the written statement, look at each other, shrug, and say, "Oh, well. Okay, then."

I'd also explain that there was a nonrefundable ninety-day security deposit, so that if they left before three months were up, they wouldn't get their money back because I didn't want someone coming in for a few weeks and then moving.

When they'd say something like, "Hey, you young whippersnapper—what are you trying to do, rip us off?" I'd reply, "Oh, no, sir. See, it says that right here in the lease on page three, line fourteen: 'Nonrefundable ninety-day deposit. If tenant leaves within ninety days from start of lease, tenant shall forfeit all security deposits monies.' " They'd look at it, look at each other, shrug, and say, "Oh, well. Okay."

Did it happen exactly this way? Pretty darn close to it.

Key points:

- Don't underestimate the power of the written word. The legitimacy of the written word can be awesome. Let it say some of your no's for you. "If it were up to me, we'd have a deal, but our company policy is . . ." and then show them the policy. It works.
- *Like any policy, procedure, custom, or way of doing things, don't let the written word be used against you, but let it be used for you to the extent that you can.*

Wright

Is there some kind of outline or checklist that I can have to help me in any negotiation I might be involved with?

Rutherford

Yes, there is. And the real pros use a checklist of some kind, even if it is simply embedded in their memory and attitude toward the negotiating. Regardless of how experienced a commercial pilot may be, they never fail to go through a checklist before lifting the plane off for its journey to its defined destination.

My checklist contains twenty-six steps in negotiating, divided into three general categories: I. Preparing for Negotiation, II. In the Negotiating Arena, and III. After the Negotiation.

THE MASTERPLAN FOR NO TO GO®
SUCCESSFUL NEGOTIATORS®

Preparing for Negotiation

Know the purpose
Understand issues thoroughly
For each party, list: needs, wants, concerns, strengths, and weaknesses
Best Option Outside Negotiation (BOON)
Assess ability to negotiate
Prioritize demands
Develop commitment to negotiate
Select appropriate strategies
Do a cost/benefit analysis

In the Negotiating Arena

Seek win-win results when possible
Expect to win
Manage both parties' expectations
Know what you want
Avoid "me vs. them" attitude
Watch body language
Be flexible
Develop viable options prior to and during negotiation
Give and take creatively
Use power sources
Focus on needs and wants
Keep score
Gain best agreement

After the Negotiation

Get a clear, signed agreement

Reaffirm value
Maintain good relationships
Reinforce the mutual benefits
Prepare for future negotiations

Key points:

- If asked which is the most important—preparing before or action during or afterward—there is no proven, set answer.
- If asked which one is most dangerously neglected, I used to say preparation but on further analysis and experience, I suspect equal if not greater neglect resides in afterward—not paying attention to the execution and application of the deal after terms have been agreed to and signed.

Wright

How can I more successfully handle giving and taking concessions?

Rutherford

There would be no negotiating without the giving and receiving of concessions. Listed below are strategies and tactics that can be used in the spirit of mutual gain negotiating.

Governing Principles of Successful NO to GO® Negotiating

1. Negotiating is an effort to resolve a conflict between two or more parties by reaching an agreement through the give-and-take process.
2. Each party works to satisfy its needs, wants, interests, and concerns through the giving and taking of concessions. There is no negotiating if there is no willingness to give and take.
3. Negotiation takes place in the minds of negotiators, each having their own perceptions of reality, their own frame of reference to what is right, fair, owing, needed, and wanted. Seek to understand both your frame of reference and theirs.
4. Manage expectations—yours as well as those of your counterpart. Be in the business of managing and making realistic the expectations of what your opponent can expect from you.
5. Sometimes it is more important how you give and take concessions than the concessions themselves.

6. The basic reason to give a concession is to gain a concession in return from the other party.
7. You can receive and processes a concession in many different ways, including:
    a. rejecting it
    b. rejecting part of it
    c. rejecting it for now
    d. conditionalizing it
    e. linking it with another concession
    f. accepting it
    g. accepting it for now
    h. putting it on hold
    i. negotiating the value of it
    j. ignoring it
8. You can give and receive concessions in many different ways, including:
    a. in the spirit of win-win, mutual gain
    b. in developing business for the future
    c. in ameliorating relationships
    d. in giving up something today to get something of importance tomorrow
    e. in laying the foundation for gain later
    f. for enlarging the negotiating pie

How to Avoid Making Unnecessary and Often Costly Concessions

1. Attempt to determine what concessions are truly essential to getting an agreement or resolving the exchange.
2. Determine your own negotiation settlement area by establishing your Highest Advanced Position (HAP) and Lowest Acceptable Position (LAP).
3. Don't be reluctant to ask for what you want and say no to what you don't want.
4. Confront your opponent's aspiration level. Move to lower it (make it more realistic in what they can expect to get from you).
5. Give concessions in such a way as to help block having to give another related or possible additional concession.
6. Before making a concession, confront the reasonableness, the legitimacy, and the rightness of the demand for a concession.

7. Ask yourself, is this concession really necessary? If so, what can I expect to get in return? (Remember, the only reason you would give a negotiating concession is to get the other party to give you a concession that you want in return.)

CAUTION! Why Some Concessions Are Dangerous to Give and to Take

1. Some concessions are misleading (you seem to be getting more than you are).
2. If you take a concession, your opponent might misconstrue that to mean that is all you expect.
3. Some concessions may be self-limiting in their nature. For example, you take this concession and that is all that you can expect.
4. Certain concessions may be booby traps. They may give you what you do not want: a boat when you wanted a house, or a dog when you wanted children.
5. Some concessions may be setting you up: "See how reasonable we have been? See, we give and give and give, and what do we get in return? We have given seven concessions. You have only given two in return."

Key points:

- In the art of getting and receiving concessions: think trade-offs.
- Recognize that it is only by the give-and-take process that you can negotiate.
- There are more potential win-win negotiating situations than most of us are willing to acknowledge.

About The Author

ROBERT D. RUTHERFORD, PH.D., is a highly respected and accomplished author, businessman, and teacher. From the faculties at UCLA and California Institute of Technology to real estate executive to the president of one of the nation's largest public management seminar companies to consultant and publisher, he speaks and writes with unusual power and authority.

Dr. Rutherford draws on three decades of experience teaching, negotiating professionally, writing, and speaking to thousands of men and women worldwide. He has taken the best of these experiences and has combined them with wisdom, humor, and his own insights to create excitingly presented, readily understandable advice on dealing successfully with anyone, anywhere, on any matter.

He has been called on to serve the negotiating and management development needs of executives and managers in a wide variety of small and large organizations. As president of the international management-training firm, RGI Inc., he has consulted with and trained tens of thousands of professionals. He consults to such organizations as California Institute of Technology (Caltech), Alcatel, Lucent Technologies, Honeywell, IBM, Chevron Oil, National Renewable Energy Laboratories, Sony, NASA, Motorola, Disney, Federal Laboratories Consortium, Seagate, Unisys, Southern California Edison, FBI, DEA, and the U.S. Departments of Navy, Army and Air Force.

Dr. Rutherford has hosted a weekly television show, served on the Board of Directors for several corporations. His work has been covered in such publications as *Business Week, Wall Street Journal,* and *Success* magazine and has been translated into foreign languages and syndicated by the *Los Angeles Times* and other major newspapers.

He is the author of such books as, *Just in Time: Immediate Help for the Time Pressured, Twenty-Five Most Common Mistakes Made in Negotiating* and *What You can do about them, How to Get From No to Go®: The Magic of Negotiating Winning Agreements,* and his latest forthcoming book, *The Price Trap-How to Make Value Trump Price When Buying/Selling/and Negotiating with Others.*

Rob Rutherford
1195 Fairfield Dr
Boulder, Colorado 80305
Phone: 303.494.9444
E-mail: rob.rutherford@no-to-go.com
www.No-TO-GO.com

Chapter 16

Linda Byars Swindling, JD, CSP

THE INTERVIEW

David Wright (Wright)

Today we're talking with Linda Byars Swindling, JD, CSP. *American Airways* magazine calls Linda Swindling "a bargaining expert" for her ability to help people get results through negotiation. After serving as partner in her own law firm and practicing employment, insurance, and corporate law for more than ten years, Linda calls herself a "recovering" attorney. The CEO of Passports to Success, a Dallas-based training and consulting firm, Linda is a recognized authority on negotiations, workplace issues, and influence. She is also an author, award-winning presenter, and the mother of two. Linda works with chief executives and key professionals to harness the power of positive influence, persuasion, and negotiation.

Linda, welcome to *The Masters of Impact Negotiating.*

Will you tell us some trends in negotiation, persuasion, and influence?

Linda Byars Swindling, JD, CSP (Swindling)

Sure. When I began consulting companies, the primary focus was negotiating with outside companies, eliminating workplace disputes, and providing negotiation techniques managers could use with their direct reports. The need to navigate through the hierarchy and reach the decision-maker was critical. Having confidence and knowing how to address power imbalances was very important. At that time, the need for leaders not to overexert their power or seem uncaring to employees was critical. There was a real fear in people who didn't feel empowered as they tried to gain that power through outside sources such as lawsuits and government complaints. Many organizations were trying to help people focus with changing workplaces experiencing layoffs, or rapid growth, and/or implementing new ways of doing business. They concentrated on persuading people to act differently.

When the economy became tight, the technology balloon burst and the threat of terrorism was looming. Concentration went to conquering or "winning" any remaining business and making sure to negotiate the best transaction possible with the deals you had in place. Employees were asked to do more with fewer people. Every area of business was examined to make sure that the return on investment was maximized. There was emphasis on negotiating time and resources and convincing others to use the least amount of materials. This type of persuasion reflected on scarcity and trying to work with what was already available.

Now it seems that the focus has changed once again. Companies are flatter. There are fewer traditional manager relationships. Teams and workgroups are constantly changing. One person may lead one project and that role might change depending on members who are added or the focus of the project. People are communicating electronically, outsourcing, and dealing with people all over the world. Now companies are looking for the ability to influence or impact decisions instead of negotiating. The focus is to enhance relations with everyone in the decision-making process, not just the "key decision-maker."

Wright

Start us off. What should we do to begin a negotiation?

Swindling

Persuading others isn't impossible but it does take effort and planning. Preparing to influence others and understanding the limits and strategies of others takes time. Every negotiation should start by asking these questions:

- What do I want?
- Why do I want it?

- Do I want to invest my time and effort to get it?

Being crystal clear about the outcome you want to reach with any negotiation is crucial. You need to know what constitutes a "win" or a stopping place for you. Once you achieve your goal or determine you will never reach it, you can feel comfortable with quitting. Unfortunately, many people don't do the simple act of writing out their desired outcome. Without clarity you can flounder and not realize whether you should quit or continue. If you don't know what your goal is in a negotiation, how do you know if you're getting close to reaching it?

If asked what you are trying to achieve, you should be able to list not only the desired end result but also the reasons to support that goal. You'll be surprised how many people are willing to help you reach your goals if you tell them your rationale for wanting them. For instance, a boss who is aware of your desire to make more presentations and train others could help scout out opportunities or shift those responsibilities from a coworker who doesn't like the performance aspect. If you are a good employee, it is in the boss's best interest to keep you happy, productive, and doing work for which you are best suited.

Some people just don't know what they want when they begin. These people may not understand the elements of a deal or risk being vulnerable to one who knows what is at stake. As a practicing mediator and a "recovering" attorney, it still amazes me how many people can be in a lawsuit for years and not know the result they really want. Many results cannot even be addressed by the court system. Litigants waste hours, weeks, even months of time pursuing a process that doesn't get them what they want. It is hard to evaluate how close you are to achieving a desired outcome if you haven't defined what constitutes a "win." Define where you are heading first.

Also, be clear that where you are spending your time and effort is a good investment. Most of us don't have the time to chase down paths that are not fruitful. We don't have the time to waste on solutions that don't produce the required results.

Wright

Many people report they are scared of negotiating. Why do you think that is?

Swindling

That's a good question. Many of us are afraid of the unknown. We are afraid of not being in control or being taken advantage of. One of the biggest problems is understanding that by negotiating you are not trying to cheat others; you are simply trying to get the best deal you can. You often see the same concerns or reluctance when people are having difficulty in sales. They don't want to appear greedy, or undesirable, or too manipulative.

The problem most people face is that they plan on one approach and are flustered when the other party takes a different stance than expected. Also, people are afraid of tricks and tactics. Very few tactics are effective. Most are amateurish and are structured to throw an opposing party off emotionally. You may see flinching, sighing, and yelling. However, if you stand your ground and know your position, you are going to be in much better shape than trying a counterattack. The secret to good negotiation is to remain cool, calm, and in control.

Wright

What are the biggest mistakes you see?

Swindling

There are three that seem to repeat:

1. Not preparing adequately,
2. Not taking calculated risks,
3. Not asking enough questions.

There is a lack of adequate preparation. It doesn't matter if you are a quick thinker and do well with little planning. Not preparing usually means you leave something on the table or forget one of the key aspects of the negotiation. It's dangerous if you don't distinguish between your wants and needs. If you don't differentiate, you give the signal that everything requested has equal value. This approach can confuse or even frustrate other parties. It is not unusual for another party to walk away from the appearance of too many demands that can't be fulfilled. Second, you can get confused. You may miss something critical to the negotiation because only some wants or unneeded requests were met. It is terrific to receive some items from your "wish" list but not at the expense of unmet essentials.

Some people prepare in great detail but forget to consider the interests of the other party. This is equally as dangerous. I conducted a mediation a few years ago with two doctors—former partners. While in a session with one of the partners, the other doctor had "decorated" my entire conference room with neatly written flip charts that showed "why he should win." When I asked the doctor about posters that reflected his former partner's interests or reasons the partner should agree to the position, there was silence. The doctor had methodically planned and thought about his position alone. I took a break and told the doctor that the mediation would continue after he prepared some posters representing his partner's side.

Fear and force are usually not good reasons to entice someone to negotiate with you. A good negotiator provides benefits that show the other side it makes sense to come to an agreement.

There is a fear of taking risks. Sometimes, you just have to chance looking stupid or hearing "No." If you are not hearing "No," you probably aren't asking for enough. It also helps to remember that you are taking *calculated* risks that you have thought through.

Luck does play a part in negotiating. However, negotiating rarely involves gambling your life savings on a roulette wheel or taking a chance that might endanger your life. The best outcomes come from minimizing the unknowns, structuring the elements you can control, and then taking risks by having the courage to act.

We don't ask enough questions. Asking questions is one of the only ways you will discover a party's true interest. Asking questions will garner not only what someone wants, but will also reveal what areas to avoid. Question every answer you receive; this will help you determine real needs and interests. When you doubt how you should act next, ask a question.

Wright

How do you know that you have made the best deal you could?

Swindling

There's an easy way to prevent second-guessing yourself—beat your BATNA. In the book, *Getting to Yes*, by Roger Fisher and William Ury, the term BATNA is an acronym for the Best Alternative to The Negotiated Agreement. It is a scholarly way of saying, examine your back-up plan—your Plan B. If the agreement you're facing isn't better than your BATNA or your Plan B, choose your Plan B. If your current deal is better than your BATNA, proceed knowing you've done a good job.

Another question you should be able to answer is, "Was this the best deal you could achieve at the time with the people present and the information you knew?" While it is true that you can always find out more information later that could enhance your results, there is a lost opportunity cost while you delay reaching an agreement. Also, that new information could work against you and in favor of the other party.

Wright

Win-win negotiation has been discussed for a long time. Is that concept still important?

Swindling

Not only is it important, the current business climate actually demands a win-win approach if you want a durable agreement. Offerings have expanded not retracted. You have more and more parties to choose to partner with. If one party doesn't worry about your interests, you usually have the ability to choose another who does. Choices have expanded on so many levels. Now, if an agreement doesn't meet the needs and wants of each of the parties, you just need to pick up a phone or surf the Internet for someone else to fill the requirement.

Look at sales training. Scripts are out. Formulaic procedures to show benefits and push standardized offerings have been replaced by consultative selling. Consultative selling focuses on customized requirements and meeting individual needs.

Remember what win-win stands for: it is an attempt for all the parties involved to get a better agreement for all involved by collaborating to meet each party's interests. If the other party believes its interests were not represented or they made a bad deal, they may try to sabotage it or look for your non-compliance.

While win-win is an easy concept to intellectualize, it is difficult to actually implement. So many people say they understand the need for win-win but then diligently fight against it. They don't share information. They compete instead of attempting to problem-solve. They don't make the first offer and they posture a position that is unrealistic. This attempt to conquer or a win-lose approach no longer works if you want to build long-term relationships. I am convinced that applying force, going to someone's superior, and attempting to only deal with decision-makers does not fit in the current professional environment.

Wright

What are some examples of influencing instead of traditional negotiating?

Swindling

Some people don't realize there are differences. Many professionals have to influence others internally to receive data, supporting materials, accounting information, and implementation help. These internal departments or teams have many people who are requesting the same type of information or support. For example, a benefits plan representative may rely on a partner outside the company such as a financial advisor or insurance broker to sell the plan to a client's human resources professional. This same benefits plan representative may need marketing materials from the marketing department to support the sales arm and then different information to inform the client's employees once the plan is selected. The representative may need to co-ordinate the efforts of the information technology department and the client company's technology department to ensure the technical requirements are met. There may be a training arm for implementing the plan, customer service functions, and (of course) billing to ensure payment. Most likely, that benefits representative is under a strict timeframe and can only apply past dealings, good graces, wit, and an ability to influence to get those resources aligned correctly.

Like the benefits representative, your success can depend on whether you can influence those people to process your requests first or at a high level of quality. You have no power over those people and do not want to go around them if possible because you must continue to work with them in the future.

Another common need for influencing is when your company has a partner or partners who are part of your supply chain. Perhaps they are distributors, or take your orders, or provide your customer support, or service the equipment you manufacture. Once again, you do not have control over these organizations' performance and they may have competing demands on their time. However, it is imperative that you persuade and partner effectively to do your job. Influencing effectively may be the only way to enhance performance with these partners.

Any time you're working together to promote each other or need to access shared resources you'll see a need to influence. With the amount of people who are outsourcing services to other companies, and locations (including other countries), the need to improve persuasion and influencing skills has never been greater.

Wright

What are some tough negotiations or persuasions you've seen and what actions do people take?

Swindling

There are a number of situations that come to mind. Here are some of them:

The unpopular position. Some negotiations have less to do with the products or services offered and more to do with overcoming a public perception. Consider selling an expensive, manufactured item like an aircraft or a piece of military equipment manufactured in an unpopular country. For example, at one time some Americans didn't hold warm feelings for France or Germany. The governments of these countries opposed the United States' military action. Many of the competitors of these French and German companies produced their equipment in America with American workers. Competing in the marketplace with a product manufactured in a country having political disagreements with another can be a challenge. Potential buyers don't want to be seen as supporting an unpopular cause or, in some cases, to be considered unpatriotic.

Whether it is public opinion, politics, or overcoming bad press, you must try to separate the emotional pulls from your offering. In this circumstance, you might acknowledge that governments may have opposing views but emphasize that the company is neutral in the affairs of politics. If selling to U.S. buyers, you should highlight that your product or service has a superior history and special attention has always been given to American clients. Many businesses will overlook politics if the offering is superior. Some won't. You must find the purchasers who will.

Increasing price or taking something away from a customer. Negotiating with clients can be very challenging. It isn't easy to offer your clients less services or fewer gratis items while increasing the cost of the base product. Yet this type of situation occurs all the time. The position becomes even more difficult if your competitors continue offering the same level of service or freebies. It's also hard to address customer needs that weren't met or explaining to a client why the order they placed will never be filled.

Laying an interest-based foundation for your relationship at the beginning is your best defense in this situation. Clients who believe you are honest and looking out for their best interest are more likely to work with you when things don't go as planned.

You've got bad feelings or bad history. Persuading others who have a history of mistrust or another agenda is another difficult situation. Union leaders and management issues usually come to mind. However, it might be military personnel working with civilian suppliers, volunteers working to persuade a government agency, or representatives from various civil groups competing for restricted funds. Anytime people feel that one side may not understand or respect their perspective or position, influence becomes more difficult.

To resolve these bad feelings, you must first find common ground. There are usually joint benefits to co-operating, even if the benefit is simply understanding a different viewpoint. Respect for another's point of view, even if you strongly disagree, is the start to a solution here. Disagree without being disagreeable and watch the relations improve.

It affects your wallet. Probably the toughest business decisions are ones that have a risk of personal economic impact for you or your team. For instance, influencing a team decision, especially an unpopular one that could lead to job reduction, is very difficult. So is negotiating with your boss for more authority, recognition, face time, less responsibility, and more communication because it deals directly with your earning ability. It is even difficult when you are negotiating for others such as requesting improved working conditions, or better recognition of peers, or more control over the use of resources.

In these instances, it helps to admit the truth or real condition. Yes, you understand that these changes could affect jobs in the future. Yes, you know your boss is extremely busy. Once awareness has been stated, present your request. Focus on why the change or request is merited and the ways you want to improve the relationship, condition, or outcome to the extent possible. Make sure you point out any benefits that the other party gains by adopting this course of action.

Wright

What do you do when you are surprised?

Swindling

Make sure you plan for surprises both pleasant and unpleasant. Below are some examples:

- *The Gift.* Occasionally you are thrown a *gift*—a very pleasant surprise. A gift occurs when the other party gives you a much better opening position than you anticipate. Before accepting, make sure that you have analyzed the bargain properly. For instance, if the initial offer of the other party is much higher or lower than you first anticipated, review your position before making your counter offer. An unexpected response may signal you have not realized exactly what the deal entails or even that you and the other party are talking about different expectations.
- *The Shock.* If someone throws out an unattractive offer, don't immediately dismiss it or get aggravated. Instead start asking questions in a *courteous* and *inquisitive* manner. You could ask questions such as, "Just so I understand, what were you including when you came up with that offer? How did you get to that number? What is that amount based on?" Good negotiators remember to discuss any offer that is made. They determine the reasoning behind an offer they didn't expect. Remember that it is rare to ask too many questions.
- *The Deadline.* Always remember to leave yourself an out or an escape. Some of the biggest negotiation nightmares occur when there isn't enough time to reflect or you are forced to make an uninformed decision. Negotiate the deadline before you negotiate a deal. Ask for a break. Get back to them when necessary but collect yourself first.

Wright

What are some behaviors to avoid in negotiations?

Swindling

Here are some behaviors you definitely want to avoid during negotiating:

Not putting your agreement in writing. People's memories fade. Disagreements occur regarding exact points of the negotiation. As soon as possible, preferably while all parties are still together, put the basics in writing. Clear up any misunderstandings before they become deal-breakers later.

Making assumptions about others' motivators, wants, or needs. Remember this: we don't know why people do what they do or exactly what they want. The same things that motivate us may not motivate other people. Their needs, wants, and desires will differ from yours. (Reflect on your personal relationships if you need proof.) Ask the people you are negotiating with what they want or need and ask about their motivation.

Accepting first offer. Rarely is the first offer the best. Accepting the first offer says two things about you: First, you are overeager to reach a conclusion. Second, you are not confident in your position. By not bartering, you also send a message to the other side that they have made a bad offer at the very beginning, which they may try to retract. If a first offer is better than you anticipated, one of two things has happened: Either you are missing something of value in your evaluation of your position, or the other party has not evaluated their position accurately. There are exceptions to this, but always pause and think before reacting.

Becoming emotionally involved. Emotions can register as excitement, anger, or even frustration. The saying "never let them see you sweat" is appropriate. Once any negotiation becomes personal instead of a business deal, you are in danger of receiving the poor end of the agreement. Instead, take a break. Get your emotions under control, or send in someone else to negotiate for you.

Not questioning. The more the other side talks the better your deal can be. Ask for explanations. Question the way values were established. You can only determine the other side's motivations and true interests through questions. Ask, ask, ask.

Not asking for more or less. Shoot for the moon. Know what is reasonable and ask for a little bit more. No, it isn't greedy to ask for more—you never know when you might get a little extra. Also, if you don't, you have nothing left to barter with to get you to what you consider is a reasonable position.

Not holding something back as a barter chip. Don't be surprised when the other party asks for "a little something extra" at the end. Know what you have that you can barter with and that is not essential to your position. If you don't have to play that card, you have a bonus. If you do, it is not unexpected.

Believing everything you are told. Yes, it is true. Not everything you hear in this world is the truth and not everyone's version of the truth is accurate. Just because information is written or produced in a graph does not make it valid. If what you are told "smells funny," is illogical, or does not follow what you have been told before, ask for independent support. Back to the basics: Ask, ask, ask.

Over-committing or over-attaching to the process. This attachment to the process is why some people make bad deals when purchasing a car. It takes a lot of emotional energy to trade in an existing car, pick the color and model of a new car, and determine an affordable price. Many buyers find themselves so entrenched in the purchase process that they will agree to pay more or purchase undesired options rather than starting the buying hassle all over again.

Not willing to walk away. This behavior relates to attachment and commitment. Once you lose your ability to walk away from a deal, you have greatly decreased your power in any negotiation. Always leave yourself an out and know what your options are if the current negotiation does not work out.

Wright

How do you know if you should pass or walk away?

Swindling

Some deals don't serve your purposes. It may be too time intensive or too costly to compete effectively. For instance, participating in a negotiation that offers a structured bid process may not suit your business needs. When government or large organizations ask for bids, there is usually a lower profit margin, a heightened expectation of service, tighter delivery deadlines, stricter quality issues, and required safety systems.

The benefits of these contracts are the possibility of large quantities over a long term—even years. However, the large investment in effort and time with no guarantee of business might not meet your business model. Choosing to lower your price might set a precedent you don't want to continue in the future.

Remember to trust your gut. If the deal doesn't feel right or you think it might be unethical, run don't walk. Your credibility and reputation is what will distinguish you over the long-term. Use your experience. Make sure the deal fits your needs.

Wright

You tell people that they should become students of negotiation. Can you speak more about that?

Swindling

In order to improve your ability to influence and persuade others, you should start examining what master negotiators do. Observe your co-workers, your vendors, your boss, your employees, your competitors, and your clients. Start asking yourself questions such as: Why did they begin with that comment? Why did they ask for that concession? How did they close or finish the discussion? How did they leave the other person feeling? What is it they do differently than you usually do?

After mediation training, but before we could actually perform any mediation, my classmates and I had to observe at least two master mediators. The rules were to be a "potted plant" which meant just observe and listen to what the mediator did. During breaks we were allowed to ask questions. As we observed these masters, we learned that each mediator had a distinctive style. Many of the techniques used in a real mediation were very different than techniques we learned in the training.

Being a potted plant goes beyond the business setting. Start watching people in restaurants or in the mall. How are they influencing outcomes? Your master negotiators may end up being the person in the grocery line ahead of you, the people sitting next to you in a restaurant, your spouse, or even your toddler.

Wright

What are some other tangible actions one can take to improve fast?

Swindling

There are actions we can take to improve. Here are some:

Go face to face. We communicate through technology that focuses on short, quick responses. So much of the rapport-building opportunities have been eliminated. You may deal with different people for each transaction and there isn't the time to really form long-lasting relationships. Look for opportunities to persuade on a personal level. Try to find ways to actually talk to human beings instead of pressing buttons and filling in forms. Invent ways for the other party to put a face with your voice or a voice with your e-mail message.

Watch your manners. Most people are starved for respect. Many will go the extra mile for people who are simply considerate of them.

Just showing common courtesy and listening to others will increase your results.

Start asking. Make outrageous requests. See what happens. So many of us stop ourselves by thinking, "This person will never do that," or "I'd never give someone that." This kind of self-monitoring keeps us from getting the deals we could. Ask and see what the response is.

Involve the other party. Ask the other party what is important to them. Stop trying to be a mind-reader and making decisions in a vacuum. Tell the other party your concerns and ask them for help solving them. Find out what other people have asked for or done. The old adage "people will support what they help build" works in negotiations as well. Let others help build or participate in the solution.

Stop looking in the rearview mirror. Stop limiting yourself because of a past mistake or a response you didn't like. Stop living in the past. If you made a mistake or someone didn't grant you a request, let it go. Today is a new day. This is a new negotiation with new people who don't know that you made a mistake five years ago.

Don't be lazy. As pressed as everyone is for time, it is tempting to stop once a solution is found. Don't. There are many options in most negotiations. Once you find a possible solution, document it, put it aside, and continue to brainstorm.

Determine the worst-case scenario. Figure out the worst result that can happen. If you can live with the outcome, go negotiate. If you can't, go back to the drawing board and create some options.

Have a sense of humor. We can turn a negotiation into something as fearful as a firing squad. Lighten up. Most of our negotiations are not rocket science, thank goodness.

Practice, practice, practice. Your first goal should be to practice on strangers. Go to flea markets, garage sales, and yard sales. Ask for an outrageous bargain or for something you stand no chance of getting and then see what happens. Ask for an upgraded hotel room, a dessert when dinner is late at a restaurant, and a discount for continued patronage of a service provider. Practice on your family. If you can persuade your own family to help you out or do something, you can persuade practically anyone.

Negotiations, like the people who are involved, are all different. Regardless of the opportunity, make sure you have a plan, map your strategy, and remember what your goal is. As long you get to your desired end result and you were ethical in the process, stop struggling with exactly how that result was achieved. Take some calculated risks. Ask questions. Know why everyone involved would benefit. When you get a deal that suits your need, stop negotiating and get ready for the next one.

You can harness the power of positive influence, persuasion, and negotiation. You can get what you want!

About the Author

LINDA BYARS SWINDLING, JD, CSP, brings a varied background to the field of negotiation and influence. From restaurant hostess to journalist to partner in her law firm, Linda's experience enabled her to build programs that provide practical techniques that work in today's professional environment. Linda works with CEOs and high performing professionals to enhance their ability to influence, persuade, and negotiate. Author of the popular *Passports to Success* series and co-author of seven other books, Linda's clients include Four Seasons Hotels and Resorts, Fidelity Investments, Menttium Corporation, American General Contractors Association, Pre-Paid Legal Services, and Promotional Products Association International. A Certified Speaking Professional and Platinum Speaker for Meeting Professionals International, Linda serves on the national board for the National Speakers Association.

Linda Byars Swindling, JD, CSP
Passports to Success
3509 Cimarron Drive
Carrollton, TX 75007
Phone: 972.416.3652
www.lindaswindling.com

Chapter 17

CHRISTINE MCMAHON

THE INTERVIEW

David Wright (Wright)

Today we're talking with Christine McMahon. Christine is a behavioral change expert who inspires, enlightens, and re-energizes sales professionals. She transforms limited beliefs and expectations into fully realized sales potential, recognizing that change doesn't happen from knowledge acquisition, but through real-world application. As a speaker, trainer, consultant, and columnist, Christine draws from her extensive background as a sales executive with Procter & Gamble, Slim-Fast Foods, and Nabisco as well as her own entrepreneurial experiences. She enriches every program with real-world, lessons-learned stories and she models every step.

Christine is a member of the National Register of *Who's Who for Executives and Professionals* and she has recently been nominated for the prestigious Ernst & Young Entrepreneur of the Year Award. She is a member of several professional associations including the National Speakers Association and ASTD.

Christine, welcome to *The Masters of Impact Negotiating.*

Is it possible to build trust during a negotiation?

Christine McMahon (McMahon)

Not only is it possible to build trust, it is *essential* to do so. Trust creates open communications and is the basis for developing mutually agreeable outcomes. Trust is built not by doing any one thing right, but by doing a number of things purposely and deliberately.

Here are some time-tested strategies I use for building trust:

- **Show respect**
  Practice effective listening and refrain from interrupting the other party when they speak. People want to be heard, and when you demonstrate a commitment to listening fully to what they have to say, it builds respect and trust. Let the other party know you understand his or her viewpoint. Use clever statements such as, *"I hear where you are coming from and wonder, have you considered . . ."* rather than, *"I hear what you are saying but I disagree with . . ."* The first statement builds alignment; the second creates conflict.

- **Be professional**
  Follow through with your commitments. If you cannot meet a deadline, renegotiate it. Forgetting to call at a prearranged time or showing up unprepared to a meeting compromises trust. People are naturally skeptical and cautious when confronted with new information, especially during negotiations. Give them every reason to doubt themselves, not you.

- **Demonstrate flexibility**
  When you encounter a roadblock, put on your creativity hat and explore new options for structuring the deal together. Resist the temptation to "dig in your heels;" you don't want to appear self-serving. To build trust with you, the other party must feel you are willing to identify a mutually agreeable solution.

- **Never make a concession without asking for something in return**
  By doing so, you not only invalidate your original position, you compromise your credibility as well. The other party may perceive that you are testing the waters to see what you can get away with rather than attempting to create the basis for a mutually respectful relationship. Too often, companies anxious to get their "foot in the door" use this strategy. They

reduce their prices—sometimes below cost—without thinking, just to get the opportunity to demonstrate their capabilities to a customer. This strategy works in the short-term, but quickly backfires when the customer decides he or she likes the product and uses the initial rock-bottom test price as his or her starting point for the negotiation.

- **Demonstrate emotional discipline**
  Remain calm, especially when talk gets tough or emotions run high. This can be more difficult than it sounds when the other party attempts to intimidate you. Intimidation is a deliberate strategy that prods you to become emotionally unglued. The other party knows that when you let emotions interfere with reason, you don't think clearly and ultimately you play into that person's hands, allowing him or her to gain the strategic advantage.

The bargaining table is fertile ground for triggering the best and worst in each of us. It's important to be proactive and position yourself for success, not failure.

Without exception, the most successful negotiators I know block time to prepare themselves. By developing strategies and viable options before engaging at the bargaining table, they minimize the risk of being caught off-guard and dramatically increase the opportunity for developing mutually agreeable solutions.

Wright

Christine, I've personally experienced situations where a prospective client loved my proposal and acknowledged that it was precisely what his organization needed. However, after presenting my proposal, he disclosed that he had a fixed $20,000 budget, which was significantly lower than my $38,000 fee. How would you resolve this situation without losing the deal?

McMahon

I'd like to fully answer your question. Before doing so, may I ask you a question?

Wright

Sure.

McMahon

Before developing your proposal, did you ask the client if he had allocated a budget for this project?

Wright

No.

McMahon

In sales, it's easy to get swept up in the excitement of scoping a project and strategizing how to win the deal. This is what many of us live for! However, handling this excitement is only part of what it means to be a sales professional.

Successful salespeople are greedy—with their time, energy, and resources. Early in the buying process, they ask *qualifying questions* to determine if the opportunity is worth pursuing or not. They know that not every prospect or project is the "right" fit for their product or service, and top performing sales professionals don't pursue low payoff projects or high maintenance clients. They're after the big win!

David, asking a budget question may feel invasive on the first or second meeting, however, you have every right to know if the prospective customer is in a position to move forward or not. To eliminate the risk of being blindsided and wasting valuable time and resources, consider using these budget related, qualifying questions during the first or second meeting:

- *"Mr. Prospect, what is your sense of urgency for completing this project?"*
- *"How will you know that we've been successful?"*
- *"Describe what will be better for . . . (you, your department(s), or the company) after we have completed the project."*
- *"Whose budget will support this initiative?"*
- *"Have you allocated a budget for this project?"*
- *"We can approach this project from different levels. We can take a basic approach where . . . or we could take a middle of the road approach where . . . or we could completely address all of these issues simultaneously which would involve . . . What level appeals to you and your budget?"*
- *"At that level, the investment would range from $10,000 to $30,000. Is that in line with your budget, or should we redefine what makes sense for your budget?"*

These questions will clarify the customer's desired outcomes, timelines, and budget for the potential project.

You will occasionally encounter customers who are in "discovery mode" and simply seek information. In these cases, submit estimates rather than comprehensive proposals. This will save a great deal of time for both parties without compromising the potential relationship.

Now, getting back to your original question: when the prospect says he or she doesn't have an adequate budget, use these strategies to explore potential options:

- **Unbundle the proposal**
  Review the proposal with the customer to identify the core aspects necessary to achieve their minimum desired outcomes, and then develop a revised budget that includes just those items. If the investment is equal to or less than $20,000, sign on the bottom line and move on to the implementation step. However, if the number is larger than $20,000, try one of the other strategies listed below.

- **Negotiate additional funding**
  Conduct research so you know who will be involved in the decision-making process, and if possible, learn what's important to each person and why. Then build a case that qualitatively shows how the project will advance the company's strategic plan, further its personal agenda, and/or generate a measurable ROI (return on investment).

- **Work the project in phases**
  Some projects can be phased in over time. For example, if you are upgrading the company's HVAC system, the client may need only one building completed this fiscal year and can wait until the next fiscal year to upgrade the remaining buildings. Flexibility like this would provide ample time to build the needed funds into the renegotiated budget.

- **Walk away**
  Sometimes it's in your best interest to simply pass on a particular project, especially if you feel that the customer is entirely price-driven. Companies that significantly reduce prices to "get their foot in the door" compromise credibility and undermine future bargaining power by setting unrealistic low price expectations up front.

Wright

How do you handle a situation where your newest "rising star" salesperson uncovers a sizable opportunity at a large prospective account that was, at one time, a customer. Discussions with key people were progressing nicely until the top decision-maker stepped in and told your rep, *"Based on a series of very bad experiences in the past, we will never do business with your company again."* Is a situation like this salvageable?

McMahon

Let's assume the salesperson researched the company and learned exactly what happened and why. It would only make sense that he or she would have developed a strategy for diffusing this situation before even making the initial contact. When working with salespeople to overcome customer resistance, I teach a simple two-step process called *Align and Redirect.*

To **Align**, you acknowledge the other party's emotional position. Put simply, you communicate to the other person that you understand his or her position or perspective (this doesn't mean you are agreeing *with* his or her position, but only with how he or she feels). By doing so, you release resistance.

In your example, to **Align** when the sales rep encountered Mr. Bigwig's resistance, the salesperson could have said, *"I understand and appreciate your position. If I were in your shoes, I'd be saying the very same thing. I would be resistant to the idea of even considering doing business with a supplier who jeopardized my credibility with my customers in the past."*

This is a powerful response because the salesperson acknowledged Mr. Bigwig's underlying concern and fear. Mr. Bigwig might continue to vent, but if the salesperson listens without becoming defensive, this might be the turning point in the relationship.

In this situation, the salesperson should do one more thing, and that's to **Redirect.** This is where the real magic happens. Redirecting is the process of shifting the antagonist's focus to a new point of understanding. In this case, the sales professional would say:

"Mr. Bigwig, I wouldn't be talking with your team unless I knew with absolute certainty that we have the capabilities to serve you with flawless execution. You see, the people and the equipment that were here three years ago have all been replaced—and for all the right reasons, I might add.

"I'm one of a four-member team that is dedicated to making sure your orders are fulfilled to your expectations.

"Mr. Bigwig, let's think about this. Do you think I would risk being here, knowing about our past failures, if I didn't have absolute confidence that we could deliver? Not a chance.

"And you have my word and the commitment of the three other managers that your orders will get top priority through the entire system. We are not *the same company we were three years ago.*

"I know our company is the best at . . . and we can help you . . .

"We've fixed our mistakes and now have the right infrastructure of people, systems, and equipment to serve you in a way that we were unable to carry out in the past.

"I don't expect you to trust me out of the box. I am asking if you would consider giving us a second chance. Cut us a small order to test our new capabilities; if you like the results, increase the volume whenever you want over the next six months.

"In six months' time, I would like for us to meet to review our performance. If you are pleased with the results, we can talk about how we move forward and under what conditions. If you don't, I'll quietly walk off into the sunset and you will never hear from our company again.

"Mr. Bigwig, I am so confident in our capability to please you that I have arranged to give you volume discount pricing over the next six months, in good faith, so that we will earn your trust back. I estimate this could mean over $10,000 in savings to you.

"Would you like time to talk this over with your team, or can we get your approval to move ahead?"

The objective in this situation is to diffuse Mr. Bigwig's resistance and establish an acceptable basis for building a relationship. By honoring Mr. Bigwig's feelings and taking ownership of past failures, the sales professional diffused a potentially volatile situation. And even though a response like this may not be enough to secure Mr. Bigwig's approval at the first meeting, it certainly sets a powerful foundation for future discussions.

Wright

A colleague who sells for a manufacturing company recently explained to me that he had been meeting with the top executive of a telecommunications company over the last several weeks. At their last meeting, they had worked through the final details of an agreement, only to receive a call the next morning from the executive saying there was one last condition: as the chairman of this year's United Way campaign, he would like a commitment that the rep's company would make a $1,000 donation to the campaign and *that* would "seal the deal." A $1,000 donation is equivalent to a 3 percent deduction. How would you handle a situation like this?

McMahon

The executive presented the sales person with an ultimatum—"take it or leave it." From my perspective, he crossed the line in doing what's good for the company to doing what's good for him, with a philanthropic spin. My response to his request would be simple and direct. I would inform him that the two situations are mutually exclusive. From my perspective, a business relationship is formed because it makes good business sense for both parties. The charitable donation situation is a separate issue.

I would confirm my interest in finalizing our agreement because we have the capability to help him achieve his business goals. Regarding the donation, I would let him know that I would be delighted to submit a letter from him requesting that a $1,000 donation be made to the United Way campaign. I would then explain that our community contributions are decided by our employees—by majority vote—so I couldn't guarantee the outcome.

My final comments would be, *"We've worked hard to develop a plan that works for both companies. I would like the opportunity to prove to you that we are everything we say on paper and more. I'm ready to sign the agreement and get started, how about you?"*

Wright

Can salespeople minimize or eliminate the need to negotiate?

McMahon

I find that inexperienced and sometimes even very tenured sales professionals spend a lot of time negotiating on the back end because they skipped qualifying the prospect on the front end.

To minimize the need to negotiate, sales professionals must dedicate time to understanding the benefit of taking action from the customer's point of view. The more compelling the benefits or ROI, the more anxious a customer will be to move into the implementation stage.

If a salesperson skips or rushes through this step and doesn't fully develop the value statement, any attempt to advance the sale may be interpreted as a desperate attempt to pitch a deal. And we all know people love to buy but hate to be sold.

Benjamin Franklin said, *"Men are best convinced by reasons they themselves discover."* Equate this to the buying/selling relationship and it's clear that the salesperson's role is to facilitate the buying process. This is accomplished by asking questions that help the customer think through the situation, reevaluate potential options, and come to his or her own conclusions about the value of making the investment.

While every buying situation is a bit different, here are a few questions to get the process started:

- *"Describe what would be better for your team (or company) after ___ is implemented."*
- *"How will you know when we've been successful?"*
- *"What metrics will you use to measure our success?"*

Timing is important. Questions of a strategic nature must be asked before you discuss budgets and prepare proposals. Any attempt to ask questions after you have reviewed options and budgets will be perceived as an opportunity to manipulate the situation in the salesperson's favor.

Wright

During a recent negotiation, the other party looked away from me several times when answering a simple "yes" or "no" question, and later leaned away from me, crossing his arms across his chest. I've read that when people look away they are being deceptive, and when they cross their arms, they're resistant. What are your thoughts?

McMahon

We've probably read some of the same books. I too have read where an author assigns a particular meaning to a movement or gesture. However, I contest that body language must be considered in its exact context. Some movements are habitual responses, others are deliberate, and others still are environmental. I believe that understanding the entire situation is necessary in order to accurately assess the meaning behind the move.

For example, during your negotiation, when the other person crossed his arms, most books would claim that person was resisting your idea, position, or statement. I believe this interpretation to be shortsighted, however. As a former leader of a multinational consumer products division, I bought a variety of products and services. I recall one negotiation where I crossed my arms because I was chilled—the ceiling air vent was blowing cold air down my neck. It was not at all about being resistant.

At another negotiation, not only did I cross my arms, but I leaned back in my chair and stared at the wall behind the other party's head for a period of time. Was I being ornery? Certainly not! I had simply received new information from the salesperson that caused me to reassess the situation. My movement helped me to process the implications of the various options. My brain is best at processing information visually, so I needed to "see" the change in my mind's eye. Was I being evasive or manipulative? Not at all! In fact, I was attempting to work through the options quickly so we could move on and make a decision.

Every movement, gesture, and comment must be considered within the context of the whole situation in order to assess their true meanings. From your description of the person who didn't look you in the eye when responding to your "yes" or "no" question, I too would be skeptical of his intentions. Looking away when answering a question is typically indicative of deceit, though again, I would prefer to know the specifics of the negotiation before passing judgment. Occasionally, I have encountered intensely shy people who had difficulty looking me in the eye. Their response was not one of deceit but rather one of respect for authority. It's what they were trained to do.

During a negotiation, everything matters; and how the other party interprets your intent will influence how he or she responds.

To build trust and rapport, use these strategies when negotiating:

- **Sit Forward**
  Gently lean forward toward the other party when sitting. This communicates that you are interested in him or her and what he or she has to say. This is a bridge builder.

- **Look people directly in their eyes**
  It's often easier to pick one eye to focus on rather than trying to look in both eyes (or switching between eyes, which can be distracting).

- **Take notes**
  Take notes when the other party is talking. Don't break eye contact for too long, but capture distinct words and phrases being said. People attach meaning and emotion to the words they use, and therefore capturing them and effectively using them at the right time builds rapport and credibility.

- **Use "the steeple"**
  People often ask, "What do I do with my hands?" My recommendation is to create a "steeple" when negotiating. This is when you connect the tips of all five fingers together to form a steeple or pyramid. It doesn't matter how wide apart your hands are, or the direction the tips of your fingers face; you can face them toward the ceiling and rest your chin slightly above the index fingers, position them in front of your chest by resting your elbows on the arms of the chair, or angle them toward the ceiling or wall in front of you. You can even simplify the position by connecting just your index fingers and thumbs, then rolling the remaining three sets of fingers toward the inside of your palms. Studies show that this movement communicates strength, confidence, and intelligence.

Wright

I have a team member who's been working with a prospective customer for months to close an important deal. It's the last week of the quarter, and the discussion stalls over what else—price! The customer calls and offers to split the difference so he can "just get the negotiation over with and move on to the implementation step." What is your reaction about agreeing to his offer?

McMahon

Depending upon the concessions the salesperson has already made, splitting the difference could result in a deeper loss for him and only a minor adjustment for the customer, otherwise why would he be offering it? As a general rule, I refuse to split the difference—unless, of course, the numbers work in my favor.

It's not uncommon to encounter customers whose strategy is to wear you down. By prolonging the process, making excessive demands, or making you work for every concession, their objective is to get what they want *on their terms.*

By offering to split the difference, the customer hopes to catch the salesperson at a vulnerable moment so he or she will respond with, *"Okay, let's just get this done and over with."* My recommendation would be to resist the temptation and not concede, and employ one or more of these counter-moves instead:

- **Refuse the offer**
  Be gracious and say, *"Thanks for the offer. I'm going to pass. I am confident that with our combined creativity, we can find a more viable solution."* Don't acquiesce to the other party; it will undermine your integrity and all future negotiating power. By giving in, you validate the other party's suspicion that initial bottom-line wasn't real to begin with. You were simply just trying to hold out to see if you could get more.

- **Reverse the concession to the other party**
  Remember: never make a concession without getting something in return. In this case, shift the liability to the other party by saying, "Jack, I will consider splitting the difference on price if you are willing to . . ."

- **Walk away**
  Tell the customer flat out, *"I would like the opportunity to do business with you, but making a price concession at this point would create a hardship for me. I had hoped we would find a viable solution, but it doesn't look like that's going to happen."* Continue by saying, *"We've invested a lot of time and effort into this project, and I'm disappointed that we couldn't find a way to make it work. Please know that while we couldn't make it work for our two companies, I would welcome the opportunity to be considered for future programs."* The other party might flat-out walk away from the deal, or may leave just for a period of time to explore other options. Don't be surprised if he or she calls back with a counter-offer within a short time.

- **Be bold and draw the line**
  Flat out ask the customer, *"How long are you willing to prolong this to get another price concession?"* You might hear some very funny responses, such as, *"I have allocated an hour a day for the next two months to see if we can get your price within reason,"* or *"Only until 2 PM today. We have your com-*

petitor in a holding pattern. We wanted to give you first right of refusal." You need to tell the customer in any situation, "This *is* my bottom line. Are you open to . . ."

Wright

What are the most common mistakes salespeople make when negotiating?

McMahon

Research indicates that 50 percent of mistakes happen prior to the negotiation, 35 percent happen during the negotiation, and 15 percent happen after the negotiation. And from my perspective, most are preventable.

Salespeople who are knowledgeable about how to negotiate, prepare their strategies, and know what is and is not acceptable consistently achieve better outcomes at the bargaining table. The majority of errors salespeople make are often the result of a lack of training and/or management support. Thousands of dollars are lost because salespeople don't know what to do or lack management's guidance and support.

The five most common errors I see salespeople make when negotiating are:

1. **Inadequate preparation.** Knowledge is power in a negotiation—not power over the other party, but power to *influence* the other party. Salespeople who fail to prepare surrender their initiative. They find themselves processing every move and counter-move from a place of instinct and emotion rather than of insight. Salespeople who prepare are confident and competent. They have digested the issues, compared the needs and wants of both parties, and have a variety of options for bridging the two positions. They know what is and is not acceptable, and have developed strategies for creating a mutually agreeable solution.

2. **Failure to negotiate internally first.** Salespeople who understand what is and is not acceptable to their company before walking into the negotiation have built the framework for making good decisions. Salespeople who *think* they can commit to a particular course of action, only to be denied approval when they return to the office, commit negotiation suicide.

They jeopardize their credibility, not only with their prospective client (bait and switch), but with their own company as well.

3. **Making a concession without knowing all demands.** Inexperienced salespeople often fall into this trap. They respond to each demand as a standalone request rather than learning the total scope of the other party's demands. After making a substantial concession to close the deal, the salesperson is taken aback when the customer initiates another request, and another, and yet another, each perceived to be the one that will clinch the deal. By asking, *"In addition to X, what else is important to you?"* after the first concession demand was presented, the salesperson would have understood some, and possibly all, of the concession demands up front.

4. **Making a concession without asking for something in return.** Salespeople who give in to concession pressures without asking for something in return aren't negotiating—in fact, they're not even selling. They are simply giving the customer what they want. And by default, they're setting a dangerous precedent: the customer learns the more pressure he/she exerts, the more concessions they receive. I don't believe for a moment that salespeople do this on purpose, but rather, they do it because they're intimidated or don't know what else to do.
   Here's the simplest and most effective way to handle this type of situation: *"Mr. Buyer, if the possibility to give you X exists, would you be able to provide us with Y?"*
   In the real world, this translates into: *"Mr. Buyer, if we are able to reduce the price to $10.00 per piece, would you agree to accept one shipment per week as opposed to two?"* This simple question shifts the ownership of the decision from the salesperson back to the customer, who must now reassess the situation.
   Time and time again, when salespeople learn this strategy and create a list of what they will ask for in return, they take back their power and admit to feeling more in control of the negotiation.

5. **Lack of follow-through.** Salespeople who hand projects over to the implementation team once contracts are signed make a fatal error. Post-negotiation is a time of heightened buyers' insecurity. It's "show time" for them, and all eyes are looking to see if they have made the right decision. Just because they said "yes" doesn't mean they're completely convinced that your company will deliver.

   When something goes astray, which usually does happen at some point in the engagement, the buyer wants the person he or she can trust the most to resolve the issue. The right salesperson can turn unforeseen circumstances into new streams of revenue if they are handled on a timely basis.

   An example that comes to mind is of a client who, during the implementation step, visited the customer once a week in person and then called the buyer a second time later in the week. During the third week's visit, the buyer complained about a component that wasn't working correctly. The salesperson took charge of the issue, fixed it with some engineering assistance, and delivered a better functioning product on time and at a higher margin due to the new specs.

   Salespeople who remain involved not only identify new opportunities, they resolve issues quickly and are better positioned to renegotiate new terms when project creep occurs.

Wright

Any last thoughts, Christine, as we wrap up our interview?

McMahon

It's important to keep in mind that a negotiation is a *process*, not an *event*. Achieving the best outcome requires quality information, gathered early in the buying process, and well-planned, adaptive strategies. Salespeople who understand what issues are most important to the customer and why, even before they discuss money and budgets, have real bargaining power.

People often say, *"This sounds like a lot of work. I just don't have that kind of time."* If something is a priority, you make time. And not every negotiation requires hours of preparation. I have developed successful game plans while sitting at a restaurant with a rep working through the pros and cons of different strategies on a placemat.

Great negotiators never risk setting themselves up to fail. They equate "winging it" to a surrendering of their initiative, and this is just not an option. They do whatever is needed to set themselves up to succeed in building the foundation for a respectful, long-lasting relationship.

About the Author

Christine McMahon inspires, enlightens, and re-energizes sales professionals, giving them the tools to overcome old habits and build successful careers. Graduates of her workshops leave with a greater understanding of, and excitement about, their personal potential. They experience measurable increases in confidence and productivity thanks to the laser-like focus Christine helps them develop.

As a speaker, trainer, coach, and columnist, Christine McMahon draws from her extensive background as a sales executive with Procter & Gamble, Slim-Fast Foods, and Nabisco. She taps into her own entrepreneurial experiences to enrich each workshop with real-world lessons and stories.

She is a member of the National Speakers Association and the Association for Training and Development, and she has been selected to the National Register of *Who's Who for Executives and Professionals.* She has been recently nominated for the prestigious Ernst & Young Entrepreneur of the Year award.

Christine McMahon
1563 S 101st Street
Milwaukee, WI 53214
Office Phone: 414.290.3344
E-mail: ccm@christinemcmahon.com
www.christinemcmahon.com

Chapter 18

JEFFREY HANSLER

THE INTERVIEW

David Wright (Wright)

Today we're talking with Jeffrey Hansler. Jeffrey Hansler had a breakthrough discovery in 1987 about communication. He discovered that he knew far less about persuasive communication than he thought he knew.

With his fast start and a great deal of success selling for Apple Computer and rising to the top management sales and marketing positions through the ranks of several organizations, he felt that his skills at communication were sound. And why should he think otherwise? He'd done well in school, received a congressional nomination to the Air Force Academy (only to be turned away because of mild color blindness), had experienced great success with each of the jobs he targeted to work his way through college. He even pulled his crew team to a Pacific Ten Western Sprints Conference Title in his senior year. To top all of this off, he was offered a spot in an exclusive accelerated PhD program in the area of psychology.

So how did it come about that in 1987 he was looking at financial crisis and career failure in a position that was entirely dependent upon his ability to generate support behind his ideas? It was this crisis and the discoveries he made in communication that have spurred him on with the desire to share with others. More importantly, he was able to identify specifically where his skills were lacking and how to learn the skills to quickly surmount the difficulties and propel himself and others to success.

He spent a great deal of his time during the next five years studying how people learn and he developed tools to create change in the abilities of others and further develop expertise in the area of persuasion. It was during this time when he chose a career in training and speaking about communication and began making a difference in the lives of others at a profound level.

We're here today to find out about this process and acquiring improved negotiation skills.

Jeffrey, where do we begin to learn negotiation skills?

Hansler

Young children are natural negotiators because they have a clear idea of what they want, a commitment to get it, and very little power in the decision. So in actuality everyone has the opportunity to become a talented negotiator.

Some people are fortunate enough to have been exposed to an environment where their learning of powerful negotiation and communication skills was encouraged. They were lucky enough to have mentors who understood the value of negotiation to guide and encourage them. They might have even gained their talents from parents, siblings, or as a result of their circumstances. The development of their skills was encouraged either openly or through the excitement of the rewards gained by use of their communication skills.

In these cases, their skills are so innately part of their daily communication, they may not even be aware that they are learned skills. Over the years, they have adapted tactics and strategies to their personality and style. To these few, the use of their skills is so innately a part of them, they may not even be aware of using them in every area of their communication with others. They know the value of negotiation because they experience the positive difference it makes in achieving what they desire without knowing how they acquired their skills.

Unfortunately, many were not in such a supportive environment and reached a far lower level of understanding of the power of effective negotiation and communication skills. In fact, many of us were exposed to negotiation as a negative concept. If your attempts at negotiation were cut off as a child with verbal reprimand or even physical punishment, it is easy to see negotiation situations as something to avoid. If your attempts at negotiation were met with dramatic failure, you might see it as something to fear.

Wright

So what is negotiation? How is it part of communication? How is it perceived?

Hansler

It is most often thought of as the process of coming to a compromised agreement through the use of tactics and strategy. It may or may not be part of your natural communication based on your awareness and experience with negotiation in your life. Although it would be hard to state that you *never* used negotiation, you might not be aware you were using it.

Your perception of negotiation might be positive or negative depending on your experience and the culture you grew up in. In some cultures, negotiation is seen as a demeaning activity done by those without proper means. It can be seen as manipulative, dishonest, and something without redeeming value. In other cultures, the opposite is true—negotiation is used with pride and mastery and is viewed as a sign of character and strength. In these cultures it is rude not to negotiate because it is seen as unsociable not to engage in the process of a negotiated exchange. To not negotiate would be as confusing to others as choosing not to breathe and it would be a demonstration of disrespect and ignorance.

Wright

So there are groups of individuals who view negotiation as a bad thing?

Hansler

In considering all possible experience and culture influences, there are three groups who view negotiation as a negative tool: the unaware, the uncomfortable, or the unconscionable.

The unaware group has either been protected by circumstance, the roles society has created for them, or have at some subconscious level grabbed onto the illusion that there is a pure and defining logic. They see the world as right or wrong, black or white, yes or no. They feel their decisions are solely based on logic and there is a measurable reason to justify their decision. Maybe they have a technical expertise that is so desired they have not had a reason to worry about position or finances or circumstances. The opportunity is either fair or not fair and if it is not fair then something is wrong. They do not question their communication skills and they look for simple answers and posted prices. If placed in an open-air market with negotiation going on at every stall with every vendor, they would exit with haste for fear of experiencing a new world.

What is important to realize is that even though they are unaware of their use of negotiation skills, and more importantly, the skills used by others in dealing with them, they are still affected by negotiation. Being unaware does not protect you nor prevent you from being impacted by negotiation. If they could become aware of the variables that impact communication, then they might be open to learning a few basics that would greatly enhance their life either through active negotiation or at least in protection. The irony of basing decisions on logic is that the two most common responses used without thought by those in this group are outrage at someone's position or whining, which are both emotional responses.

The uncomfortable group is conscious that negotiation opportunities exist. The uncomfortable group is the largest of the three groups. The participants in this group simply choose to avoid negotiation opportunities because they don't like them. They feel uncomfortable and unsafe when faced with negotiation. Maybe they had bad experiences growing up. Maybe parents in early negotiations shut them down. No matter the reason, the result is that they see negotiation as an opportunity for loss. Their focus is on the risk of the situation and not the possible success. They enjoy set prices and specific plans about roles and responsibilities. They find the greatest comfort in established patterns of interaction when dealing with issues that are important to them. If they do engage in negotiations, they are quick to be offended unless it's haggling over a price of something they don't need and it's just for fun. If they are ever faced with negotiations over an important issue, they resort to principles and rules of engagement to justify their position and even the other party's position.

The group that has done the most damage to the image of negotiation is the unconscionable group. This groups focuses on tactics and underlying needs in a heartless, self-centered, and savage manner to take advantage of those less skilled. They crawl out from under their rock to find people who don't even know that a negotiation is going on and take advantage of them. They leave a wake of destruction of everything from hurt feelings to financial ruin. They work the emotions of others to limit feelings, options, and desires. The only possible good this group can contribute to the world is that having experienced a transaction with them, you may finally realize the value of learning the art of negotiation, if only to protect yourself from the likes of these people who smile in your face and stab you in the back.

Wright

Can anyone learn the skills of negotiation?

Hansler

No matter what the circumstance, whether you grew up in an environment exposing you to effective communication and negotiation skills or in an environment that did not, the question becomes "Can you begin to acquire or take your skills to the next level?"

Wright

And the answer to that question is Yes?

Hansler

Thankfully, the answer is *yes!* And there are only five steps or levels of learning as part of the process of improving your communication and negotiation skills. These steps include awareness, tactics, needs, relationship, and transitional levels of understanding.

Wright

Obviously you have put a great deal of thought into this as a trainer. Will you outline the model for us?

Hansler

Sure. They are presented below as a model in a logical building order of skills (see Diagram).

As a model, the five levels are a guide to your learning. As such, each step will provide a focus point for you to work on to help you master that level.

We use models as guides to our learning all the time. Models help by providing a framework for learning elements at each level. They are general enough to allow flexibility and personal style to be developed that are critical to mastery. In fact, defining negotiation as being different from persuasion or influence or other communication skills is a model approach to learning. While persuasion can be defined as the ultimate objective of negotiation and influence defined as impacting an outcome through perspective, in application, there are no distinctions between negotiation, influence, and persuasion. They are all part of the communication process in creating change and bringing about decisions. Separating them out as distinctive disciplines is done as a model to contribute to the process of learning.

It is important on your road to mastery that you apply your knowledge without conscious use of the model, because the model is limiting by nature. It can be compared to learning a physical activity. While you may focus on your grip on the laces, the position of your arm, the motion forward, and the follow-through, as part of learning to throw a football, they all flow together without thought during the game.

You will discover that viewing the levels as distinctive and separate greatly contributes to your learning, while the reality is they are ever present in all of your communication. As you move forward in understanding negotiation, you will find you are about to enter a magical world of human interaction. It is a world I was introduced to through the contributions and sharing of some of those whose chapters you have just read in this book: Herb Cohen, Jim Hennig, Roger Dawson, John Patrick Dolan, and Robert Fisher. They have been mentors to me and have contributed greatly to the art of negotiation and the lives of countless millions. I thank them and you for continuing on the journey.

Diagram

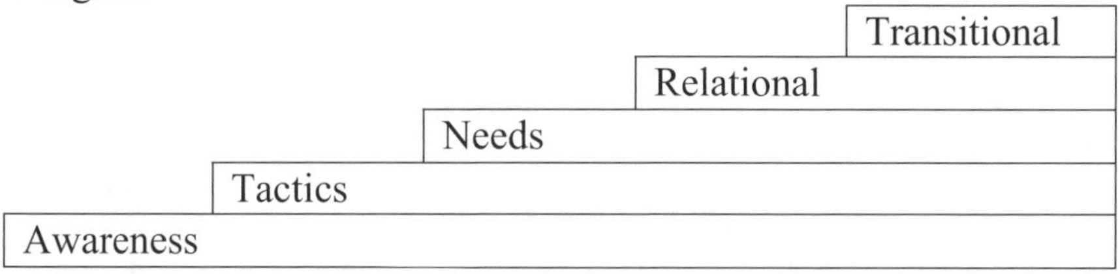

Transitional
Relational
Needs
Tactics
Awareness

Wright

Please go into more detail for us on each of the levels. The first one was "Awareness," right?

Hansler

Awareness begins the journey of learning. There are three parts to this step: awareness of self, awareness of others, and awareness of communication.

The greatest leap in this first step is awareness of self. Fear is a powerful roadblock to making this leap. As we grow, we find confidence and security in believing we are competent at life—and that includes our communication skills. It can be very frightening to admit that our communication is not as clear or powerful as we would like. It requires us to accept responsibility for our part of miscommunications in the past and our contribution to miscommunications in the future. It opens us up to the realization of the consequences of our miscommunication. It can be emotionally difficult to look at one's responsibility.

We have spent our whole life trying to separate ourselves from the images of having only the two communication skills we had in early childhood—crying and smiling. It is hard to consider that we have spent our entire life moving only slightly beyond these polar opposites of communication. Yet these are the two positions many people are limited to in negotiation. They are either smiling at what is presented to them or they are crying that it is unfair. They are unable to bring other communication skills to the table to create the result they desire.

So, for your very first step in this journey of improving your communication skills, take an inventory of your past few negotiation opportunities. Did you accept what they offered smiling or did you whine about it to get a change? Then ask yourself, "Am I willing to keep an honest eye on my negotiation skills from this point on?" Keeping an honest eye means acknowledging your strengths and weaknesses as they occur or as part of your analysis following interactions.

If you are willing to look at what you are good at and what you are not good at—a solid evaluation of areas where you didn't do so well—then you are in a position to learn and improve. If you are, then you have begun the commitment process to awareness of self. An honest eye is the ability to admit that you did well or not. If your only actions are accepting the deal at face value or whining about the options, then it is a fair bet that you could use some skill development.

The next part is a little easier because it can be a little less personal. It is awareness of others and their use of negotiation. One of the best ways to become aware of others and their communication and negotiation skills is to become an eavesdropper. That's right, start listening in to other people's conversations. By doing this, you are less involved emotionally in the conversation and have a greater chance of learning the nuances of communication. If you're part of the communication, then your emotions and your thought processes interfere because you begin to focus on yourself and not the other person. You begin to listen to your thoughts and consider the impact they're having on you. Self-focus is what limits our ability to effectively impact the outcome of the conversation. Once you have mastered listening as a non-participant to a conversation, then you can begin to hone your ability to be engaged in conversation and listen effectively to the other person. Listening is paramount to the next levels of negotiation development.

The final part is awareness of communication. Like the air we breathe, we have forgotten how critical words are to our survival. We go through most of the day without ever giving a thought to our need for oxygen. It is only when we tax our system that we realize how important each breath is to every organ in our body. Without enough oxygen our entire system begins to shut down. In the same way, we have taken for granted our speech patterns and the words we use. We have forgotten how important each word is to our survival—unless we are in the middle of a negotiation and unable to move it in the direction we desire. It is only then when we realize how important saying the right thing in the right way can be to turn the tide in our favor. Unfortunately, at that time, it's too late to learn the skills needed and we either walk away or risk failure with limited skills.

Awareness of communication and the importance of each word opens an entire universe of opportunity for improvement. Here are some examples of the impact of sentence structure and word choice:

When I say, "Don't think of a pink elephant." What do you think of? A pink elephant. Why? Because the mind works in pictures and to *not* think of a pink elephant you must first think of it. So when I say "Don't worry," what have I just set you up to do?

When I say, "I think you're great, but . . . " what are you waiting for? The criticism to follow, right? Why? Because we know from experience that the word "but" erases everything before it and sets up the context for the rest of the sentence. We've learned to protect ourselves from these comments by either tuning out what follows the word "but" or arguing with what is said.

Hear the difference as you say, "I think you're great, and . . ." The word "and" transitions you from the first part to the second part without creating the knee-jerk reaction that the word "but" does. This small three-letter word is the basis for learning about the power of *agreement* in language. It is a foundation negotiation premise that agreement is critical to all successful results. It is through agreement that two parties can cross the divide between them. Communicating that agreement begins or ends with the words you choose to use.

The greater your skill at analyzing the impact of conversation the better you will become at "detached involvement." It is a critical key to keeping your emotional involvement in the outcome at bay. It contributes to your ability to walk away from a deal and thus contributes to your power base. One of the easiest ways to increase your detached involvement is to develop an expression that works for you—an expression you can say in your mind as you enter a negotiation. It's one of the first tactics you can learn and put into use. For Herb Cohen, it's "I care, but not that much." For Roger Dawson, it's "What an interesting opening position to the negotiation." For me, it's "And then what happened . . ."

To become a master negotiator, in addition to your listening skills, you will want to develop your awareness and the impact of body language, tone, position in the room, position in relation to the group, use of objects, and the use of group size. These are the physical elements of communication that provide valuable insights and contributions to your verbal skills.

Learn from the best by studying and practicing and then develop your own style and personality as a negotiator. As you become aware of communication and the power of each word you use with the impact they have on the result, and as you are able to keep a detached involvement in the process, you can then transition to the next step in negotiation: tactics.

Wright

Will you describe for us the critical elements about tactics?

Hansler

Tactics are based on predicable responses to communication. It is predicable that when offered a choice between two decisions, a majority of people will choose between them. While such a choice may seem logical, it isn't. There are never only two choices. (And by the way, the term "never" is a generalization and a powerful tactic when used properly). In fact, there are usually an infinite number of choices.
For example, do you want to meet at two o'clock or three o'clock? Well, why don't we meet next week? Or why don't we not meet? Or why don't you meet someone else? Or why don't we not discuss this? Or why don't we talk about it now?

Why is it common that people choose between two different times of day or choose to meet versus not to meet? Because our entire system is designed to filter information and limit options! When they work as designed, your ears constantly pick up sound and your eyes constantly pick up objects, yet you aren't aware of most of the stimulus coming in. Why? Because you have learned to limit your field of sight or hearing, filter out most of the stimuli coming in, and focus on specific stimuli. The body's physiology is designed to feel pain; the brain then tells the body to secrete endorphins to relieve pain.

Thus we are very accustomed to limiting our field of choice to bring us to a decision. Tactics work by tapping into this filtering system. The tactic above is commonly called "alternate choice," and it is designed to limit the field of choice to two options within a larger option of one. In the example, meeting is the desired result and it doesn't matter if it's two or three o'clock.

The following word patterns are training tools for learning other negotiation tactics: "Let's set that aside . . ." "We're close . . ." and "What if . . ." All three of these work off the principle of agreement.

The negotiation tactic "Let's set that aside . . ." is used to move a difficult discussion point to a better time in the negotiation. It means, "I agree with you. This is important and I'm only asking that we deal with it at a later time." You will discover, as you improve your ability to use negotiation tactics, that once you establish agreement in other areas, you may not even need to address the point you set aside. If someone challenges you on your price as being too high, you can respond by saying, "True, and *let's set that aside* for a moment while you tell me a little more about what you want."

The negotiation tactic "We're close . . ." is used to establish hope and focus on what you agree upon versus the differences. As you become more confident with your use of tactics, you may begin to use this tactic more aggressively such as, "You want a 50 percent discount and we're willing to give you 0 percent—*we're close.*"

The negotiation tactic "What if . . ." creates new pictures and thus new possibilities. It allows something to be considered without the conscious fear that considering it relates to accepting it. The reality is that as soon as people begin to picture the possibilities, they begin to create acceptance in their mind with their own thoughts. If, for example, you asked, *"What if* you had to work with Julie on this project? How would you make that happen?"

One of the best features of tactics is that you don't have to know how they work to use them. It's like driving a car: you don't have to understand about engines or drive trains or electrical systems to use them. Tactics can be memorized and practiced without understanding how or why they work.

Commit to memorizing them and practicing them and becoming aware of when they are being used by others throughout the day. As you practice, you will develop greater understanding about them and greater awareness of their use by others in communicating with you. You will also discover that many people are content to remain at this level of understanding in negotiations. If you choose to go further in your study, then you will find the work you do in using and understanding tactics will greatly assist you in developing your negotiation and communication skills further.

As you practice these tactics and become proficient at them, you will discover that the words themselves are only a model for learning and you can create the same impact with other verbiage and word choices. In fact, this is one of the first areas where you can develop your uniqueness and personal style in negotiating—a very important part of creating credibility in your communication to others and building a powerful psychological base to operate from in your own mind.

You will also come to learn that there are eight foundational negotiation tactics. These eight are the building blocks of all negotiation tactics, and you have already been shown three of them. For example, the use of limited authority is a situational version of *set aside*. Because you have limited authority, you cannot supply a decision at that moment. If used properly, limited authority allows you to gather critical information while setting aside all of the decisions.

The tactic of playing dumb is a physical demonstration of *we're close*. It provides great hope to the other party that if they can only get you to see their point, you will be able to strike a deal. It contributes to full-disclosure because why should there be a fear of hiding something from someone so incompetent?

As you are probably beginning to see, while the tactics themselves are easy to learn the effective application of them can become a lifelong process of developing your art. To the amateur painter, paint is just paint. To the artist, it is something that can be changed in texture, color, application, and in combination with other materials to bring results that are as dramatic as they are pleasing.

The next step in improving your negotiation and communication skills comes with understanding the motives behind desires. It is by understanding the needs behind the requests that you take a major leap in your ability to negotiate effectively.

Wright

That makes it so clear. My biggest question is about the role needs play in the negotiation process. Can you give us some more detail on the needs level?

Hansler

There is a wonderful story about two sisters and an orange that has been shared for years as an example of effective negotiating. Two sisters are in the kitchen and they both reach for the only remaining orange. Each sister demands ownership of the orange for her meal preparation. And while both are skilled in agreement language and negotiation tactics, the best solution they come up with initially is to cut the orange in half—leaving each of them without enough orange for their projects. It is only when they share *why* they *need* the orange that they come up with the right solution. One sister explains she needs the peel for her pie and the other sister explains she needs the fruit for her salad. Once they see that their *needs* are actually different, then both can get the result that they want. (If you're learning to pay attention to language, you should be wondering why the story is about two sisters and not two brothers. What would be the impact of telling the story with two brothers as the characters?)

The first step in improving your communication and negotiation skills is awareness and one of the parts of this step is awareness of others. The needs step widens your attention from becoming aware of what others are doing and saying to include the motive behind those actions and the requests behind those needs. When you uncover what they are trying to achieve as a result and what that means to them, you begin to open up the world of possibilities for coming to agreement.

Behind every request is a motive to achieve a desired result. There are two levels of need awareness associated with a desired result: relative need and emotional need. To discover both of these needs requires only one skill: the ability to ask questions.

Specifically, there are two types of questions to ask: *Primary Questions* that seek facts and requests, followed by *Secondary Questions* that seek the needs (relative and emotional) behind the facts and requests.

In the story above, the primary question would be, "Do you need the orange?" The secondary question is, "What do you need the orange for?" In this case, we are seeking the relative (or physical) need behind the request for the orange, which is the peel for one sister and the fruit for the other. If you were going to apply statistics to the percentage of individuals who ask both primary and secondary questions in negotiation situations, you could approximate by stating that only 20 percent of the time do negotiations involve finding out the relative needs. Why? Because most of the time people do not practice asking secondary questions. They move from fact-finding (primary questions) to presenting options or supplying arguments without taking the time for discovery.

In statistical terms of finding the emotional needs, you could state with confidence that less than 20 percent of the 20 percent seek the emotional needs behind requests. While gathering this information could be critical to resolving a conflict, most of the time we operate on assumptive information, a real or perceived lack of time, a lack of curiosity, or a genuine self-centeredness.

In the story above, how could you resolve the conflict if each of the sisters needed the entire orange to complete their meal preparation? You'd have to discover the underlying emotional need driving the desire for the orange. The primary question could be the same, "Do you need the orange?" The secondary question might be, "What do you enjoy about making pies for our meal?"

The secondary question (or a series of secondary questions) might uncover the fact that making a pie is an expression of love. Once that is discovered, you might find another alternative to expressing love. Maybe the person would get the same feeling making a cake or making soup or decorating the table or singing a song. You get the idea.

Once you have mastered asking primary and secondary questions, you have mastered the skill to acquire the underlying emotional needs. The most difficult part is adjusting your mindset to take time to ask the secondary questions to uncover information.

Your biggest enemy to discovering needs is becoming emotionally involved in the process. The minute you lose your detached involvement status you begin to push your needs and stop listening to the other person's needs. It is at this juncture when things can begin to go awry. A very important step before entering a negotiation is learning to think through your own emotional triggers. By establishing a mental understanding of your emotional boundaries you can take steps to prevent an emotional outburst during negotiations.

Once you begin to uncover the underlying emotional needs, you are ready for the next level of negotiation and communication mastery: the relational level.

Wright

I've heard some comments about the relational level. You seem to believe there is a great responsibility for the more advanced negotiator to take extra efforts to enhance the relational level. Why is that?

Hansler

It has long been understood in a negotiation that the party with the most information usually comes out on top. Information helps in positioning, presenting options, and guiding the process to a negotiated agreement. Obviously, the ability to ask questions and listen is a key element to gathering that information. In the process of asking primary and secondary questions you will also gain insight into their relative and emotional needs. You are in the relational level of negotiation and communication mastery when you incorporate your knowledge, language, and approach to positively affect the relationship beyond the immediate desired result.

The relational level of negotiation is about establishing a foundation of trust—that you have an interest in helping them attain their emotional requirements beyond the immediate negotiation. To operate at this level requires heart, courage, confidence, and determination. Skills at this level will contribute to building strong, dependable relationships, even in situations where others do not have good communication skills. They can be useful in assisting others through difficult portions of a negotiation where they might be feeling uncomfortable about the process.

The foundation of trust begins with a full disclosure of sharing your desired outcome and the important elements about that outcome. Full disclosure is an important component to building a foundation of trust. It does so by showing commitment to the process and providing necessary information to consider options.

Full disclosure is sometimes misunderstood. Full disclosure is about being forthright about what is important as the result. It is not about tipping your hand or presenting an assumed final offer. In fact, full disclosure goes hand-in-hand with effective planning and involvement.

Making concessions is part of the process of negotiations. The tactic in making concessions is to make small concessions, make them slow, and make them progressively smaller. Jim Hennig is phenomenal at this skill. The reason for making concessions in this manner is that they signal an end to the negotiations and bring the communication full circle to your original full disclosure of the intended outcome. It solidifies the foundation of trust required for ongoing relationships by demonstrating great competence and providing the opportunity to find great satisfaction in the work involved in accomplishing the final result.

The foundation of trust continues by being assertive and upfront about key issues. Often, these issues or areas of information are the critical areas where people feel they are vulnerable or will have a disadvantage if they are disclosed. I refer to the questioning portion of dealing with these issues as having the ability to ask the "hard" questions in an effective manner. The hard questions are the ones people typically avoid because the foundation of trust can be eroded.

In a sales situation, a salesperson might be prospecting for interest in a product (or service). The person the salesperson is in contact with says, "We're not interested." While it would be easy to accept that answer, a salesperson who is working to engage at the relational level will ask, "Are you the decision-maker regarding these types of products?" This is a hard question because the contact could now be faced with the fact that his or her opinion is not important because he or she is not the decision-maker—a potentially embarrassing situation. Even though this situation could be embarrassing, it is a much better situation and of greater relational value than letting the conversation die at, "We're not interested."

Effective negotiators can adjust their questions to make it easier to engage at the relational level. They might soften the question by changing the tense and focus of the sentence to the past. They could ask a question like, "The last time your company looked at a product like this, who were the people involved?" They could follow the answer with, "Of those, who had the most say?" and follow that answer with, "Is that person still the key decision-maker on these products today?"

How do you get good at establishing relational level communication? Practice your ability to ask questions at every opportunity.

One other point about communication at the relational level is effective negotiators learn to admire the communication skills of their opponents in a negotiation. They understand that they are working to achieve an outcome and using every skill possible to achieve it. They look beyond the immediate issue and focus on building the relationship they desire. They see their communication skills as dedication to the art of communication and an artistic expression of self. They understand that with these skills the possibility of great contribution is expanded, which brings us to the transitional level of communication.

Wright

The relational level is not the end of the line though, is it? Will you tell us about the transitional level?

Hansler

At the point where you begin to release yourself from your perceptions as facts, you begin the final stage for effective negotiations and communication because you begin to rise above your emotional attachment to the outcome. It is your emotional involvement in the outcome that becomes the final limiting factor in your ability to be at your most effective negotiation level while in a negotiation.

The following story demonstrates the difference between someone who is in the transitional step and someone who is not.

A young warrior, victorious in many battles, wanted to know the difference between good and evil. He was told to seek out a wizard in the mountains who could teach him the difference. After a long and tiring journey filled with many perils and hardships he found himself standing before the wizard who had his eyes closed and was meditating. The warrior waited for the wizard to finish. After many hours, the warrior grew impatient.

"Wizard," he said. "I have come to learn the difference between good and evil." The wizard did not reply. The warrior waited for a response for many hours. The warrior grew impatient.

"Wizard! Please! I need to know the difference between good and evil!" the warrior begged. The wizard did not reply. The warrior grew angry.

"Wizard, if you do not tell me the answer, I will cut you down with my sword!" The wizard did not reply. The warrior lifted his sword.

"Wizard, this is your last chance! Tell me or die!" The wizard did not reply. The warrior swung his sword down to strike.

The wizard opened his eyes and said, "That is evil." And then returned to his meditation.

The stunned warrior fell to his knees. He thought of the greatness of the wizard who was willing to risk his life to teach him about evil. He thought of all the people he had killed in battle—those who had begged mercy and not received it. He grew despondent and fell in a dark depression in front of the wizard. After many days and near death from lack of food and water, the warrior asked forgiveness for his evil.

The wizard opened his eyes and said, "That is good."

The warrior thanked the wizard and left with joy and became a farmer.

The wizard shook his head with sadness that a warrior died that day.

The wizard was operating in the transitional level because he was aware that while both farmer and warrior were good and that the evil was thoughtlessness, the warrior had lost sight of his power and his value. The warrior had lost sight of his purpose to achieve his intended result. The wizard knew that the warrior could have shifted his intention without shifting his purpose.

The wizard was momentarily sad because the warrior had left thinking the wizard risked death, while the wizard knew that he had risked nothing because he had no fear of death, just as he had no fear of life. While the warrior was attached to the process, the wizard was not. The wizard was operating with *detached involvement* that allowed him to be in a state of greatest contribution to the process and to others.

When you can negotiate passionately for your desire while realizing that your perceptions are illusions about the possible outcomes for the future, you have entered the final stage of effective communication. No one can predict the future, and each step of your journey, whether it is the one you intended or the one you end up with, is just another step in life. This perception brings you back to detached involvement. It is the paradox of not caring about the outcome because you have separated yourself emotionally from it—you are in the most effective position to impact it the way you desire. When you begin to realize that the meaning you placed on the fact is only one perspective, you begin to realize that perspective is the key to effective negotiations and that the greater your ability to see things differently, the greater your impact on the outcome.

It is in the transitional level that you will begin to see the entire negotiation process in a new light. You will learn to read the physical clues people give off with their body language. You will be able to listen to the words they use, understand the importance of their sentence structure, and see the subtle shifts in their eye movements that show congruency or a lack of congruency about what they are presenting. It will no longer be only the words said, but the combination of words, body language, etc., where accurate analysis of the situation is not based on set patterns.

It is also at the transitional level that a certain amount of confusion will set in. Because you are able to take in so much information, you will see details that may not always match your instincts or gut feelings. It is at this stage when you will begin to see many mistakes in your actions. You will also discover that some people are not able to carry out what they fully intended from a negotiated agreement, and while the negotiation was perfect for both parties, the result is still disappointing. And you will also discover that some people have become very good at disguising their true intentions. Again, your detached involvement is a key to guiding you through these anomalies. Not caring so much about the outcome becomes a very powerful partner in enjoying the process.

In a way, operating in the transitional level is the logical outcome for someone with great awareness, command of tactics, and a deep understanding of needs and the impact they have on relationships. Once you reach this stage you realize that you have not only a right, you have a responsibility to use all your communication skills to achieve what you desire to provide your greatest contribution to the world. Your abilities will give you the choice of working to the best end for the long-term relationship or taking a short-term gain at the expense of another.

While everyone cares about the outcome, not everyone has the skills to influence the outcome. Your working through the five levels will assist you in defining your intention, operating with full disclosure, and succeeding in reaching the transitional level with nearly every negotiation you engage in.

Wright

Are you at the transitional level?

Hansler

I'd love to say, "Absolutely." I have my good days and bad days. I even have my whiney days. Knowing "what to do" and "doing it" under stress is very difficult. I realize this is a lifelong process that requires attention and effort each day.

Wright

You can certainly poke fun at yourself well. Any final comments?

Hansler

Yes. I wish everyone a never-ending desire for developing communication and negotiation skills. It makes the journey through life a wondrous experience.

Wright

Well, this has been a fabulous way to bring this project to a close. This five-level approach provides a methodology in which to apply all the great knowledge from the other experts in this book. Thank you for sharing.

About the Author

JEFFREY HANSLER'S understanding of negotiation has become transitional. He shares his skills through coaching, training, and speaking. The author of the best selling book, *Sell Little Red Hen! Sell!* he has created written, audio, and video tools to help others take their negotiation and communication skills to the next level. Jeffrey is president of Oxford Company, a Certified Speaking Professional with the National Speakers Association, and a member of the American Society of Training and Development. A specialist in sales, negotiation, influence, and persuasion, Jeffrey focuses on the dynamics and interaction in business to create alignment for individuals and organizations. He believes the impact of great communication is as important in one's personal life as it is in one's career.

Jeffrey Hansler, CSP
Oxford Company
213 2nd Street
Huntington Beach, CA 92648
Phone: 714.960.7461
Fax: 714.960.5107
E-mail: jhansler@oxfordco.com
www.oxfordco.com